SEALS AND MAN
A Study of Interactions

D0611725

SEALS AND MAN

A Study of Interactions

W. Nigel Bonner

A Washington Sea Grant Publication
Distributed by the University of Washington Press
Seattle and London

Publication of this book is supported in part by grant NA81AA-D-00030
from the National Oceanic and Atmospheric Administration to the
Washington Sea Grant Program, project E/F-4. The U.S. Government
is authorized to produce and distribute reprints for governmental
purposes notwithstanding any copyright notation that may appear hereon.

Library of Congress Cataloging in Publication Data

Bonner, W. Nigel (William Nigel)
  Seals and man.

  Includes bibliographical references and index.
  1. Seals (Animals) 2. Sealing. 3. Fishes—
Mortality. 4. Seals (Animals)—Control. 5. Man—
Influence on nature. I. Washington Sea Grant
Program. II. Title.
QL737.P6B68   333.95'9   81-69684
ISBN 0-295-95890-1 (University of Washington Press)
              AACR2

Contents

The Pinnipedia—An Overview   1
Pinniped Ancestors   1
Physical Adaptations to the Sea   4
Social Structure   9
References   16

Seals and Men—The First Contact   19
Early Hunting in Europe   20
Eskimos and Seals   22
Seals and the European Seal Hunter   28
Seals as Trophy   32
References   34

Seal Furs from the North—Harp Seals and Pribilof Fur Seals   35
The Harp Seal   35
Sealing at Jan Mayen   38
Sealing in the White Sea   39
Harp Seals in the Northwest Atlantic   41
The Northern Fur Seal   46
References   54

The Fur Seals of the Southern Hemisphere   57
References   70

The Southern Elephant Seal and the Elephant Oilers   73
References   88

The Antarctic Seals—An Unexploited Resource   89
Weddell Seal   90
Crabeater Seal   93
Leopard Seal   95
Ross Seal   97
Distribution and Food   98
Conservation   101
References   104

Seals and Fisheries   107
Direct Damage   108
Depletion of Fish Stocks by Seals   112
Population   112
Diet   114
Food Consumption   116
Seals as Parasite Hosts   118
Control Measures   120
Bounties   121
Harvesting   122
References   123

The Grey Seal in the United Kingdom—Abundance as a Conservation Problem   126
References   142

Indirect Human Impacts on Seals   143
Fishing Nets   143
Competition for Food   145
Pollution   147
Manmade Disturbance   153
Manmade Benefits   156
References   159

Illustrations

Figure 1.1   The three groups of modern pinnipeds—Phocidae, Otariidae, and Odobeniidae.

Figure 1.2   Evolutionary history of the Pinnipedia. 2

Figure 1.3   Composition of the diet of leopard and crabeater seals. 3

Figure 1.4   Diets of the northern fur seal, Steller sea lion, and harbor seal on the coast of British Columbia. 3

Figure 1.5   The surface/volume relationships. 5

Figure 1.6   Pilosebaceous units of a hair seal and a fur seal. 7

Figure 1.7   Pelt section of antarctic fur seal. 7

Figure 1.8   Moulting southern elephant seals haul out on land and congregate in large numbers, with extensive body contact. 8

Figure 1.9   The pups of harbor seals are born between tidemarks. 9

Figure 1.10   A breeding colony of harbor seals on a sandbank. 9

Figure 1.11   *Allodesmus*, a large otariid of the middle to late Miocene, had the specific anatomical characters found in modern polygynous pinnipeds. 11

Figure 1.12   A schematic model for the evolution of pinniped polygyny. 13

Figure 2.1   Upper paleolithic engravings of seals from the Dordogne district of France. 20

Figure 2.2   Map of the Kattegat region showing the location of the islands of Hesselø and Anholt. 20

Figure 2.3   Sub-Neolithic bone harpoon points from around the Baltic. 21

Figure 2.4   Stone Age rock engravings from Roddøy, Nordland, Norway. 23

Figure 2.5   Angiut, a Greenlandic seal spirit. 23

Figure 2.6   Inuit carvings. 23

Figure 2.7   A slate-pointed harpoon of the unang type. 24

Figure 2.8   Ringed seal breeding lair. 24

Figure 2.9   Killing seals from a kayak. 26

Figure 2.10   Inuit kayak harpoon. 26

Figure 2.11   Olaus Magnus's map of the Gulf of Bothnia, showing hunters armed with seal pikes menacing what are probably grey seals. 29

Figure 2.12   A floating trap for seals of the kind used in the Baltic. 30

Figure 3.1   Breeding grounds of the harp seal. 38

Figure 3.2   Catches of harp seals at Jan Mayen (West Ice), 1850-1969. 40

Figure 3.3   Catches of harp seals at the White Sea, 1897-1969. 40

Figure 3.4   Catches of harp seals at Newfoundland, 1893-1973. 40

Figure 3.5   Recent catches of capelin, *Mallotus villosus*, and shrimp, *Pandalus borealis*, in the North Atlantic. 45

Figure 3.6   Breeding localities and approximate range of the northern fur seal. 47

Figure 3.7   Distribution of northern fur seal harvests under the formula drawn up by the North Pacific Fur Seal Convention of 1911. 51

Figure 3.8   Average yearly kill of male northern fur seals on the Pribilof Islands, 1936-79 (five-year averages). 51

Figure 3.9   Harems of northern fur seals on the shore. 51

Figure 4.1   Distribution of *Arctocephalus* fur seals. 56

Figure 4.2   Pup production of fur seals at Bird Island, South Georgia. 65

Figure 4.3   Current breeding localities of antarctic fur seals at South Georgia and in the Scotia Sea region. 58

Figure 4.4   Juvenile male antarctic fur seal, showing white color variety. 68

Figure 5.1   Breeding grounds of southern elephant seals. 72

Figure 5.2   The build-up of an elephant seal breeding group. 72

Figure 5.3   A dominant bull elephant seal challenges a rival. 72

Figure 5.4   Annual cycle of the elephant seal in South Georgia. 76

Figure 5.5   A breeding beach of elephant seals in South Georgia. 76

Figure 5.6   The flensing cuts on a bull elephant seal. 81

Figure 5.7   Stages in flensing a bull elephant seal. 81

Figure 5.8   Sections of canine tooth of an elephant seal aged 10 years, showing the annual growth zones. 83

Figure 5.9   Variation of biomass with age in South Georgia elephant seals. 85

Figure 5.10   Average age of commercial catch of elephant seals at South Georgia. 85

Figure 6.1   Female Weddell seal and pup on fast ice in McMurdo Sound. 91

Figure 6.2   A female leopard seal and her pup on pack ice near the South Shetland Islands. Ross seal showing characteristic posture and patterning. Crabeater seal family group on pack ice near the South Shetland Islands. 91

Figure 6.3   Feeding ecology of antarctic seals. 99

Figure 6.4   Aerial survey technique used for censusing antarctic seals. 100

Figure 7.1   A common form of bag net used for taking salmon on their migrations along the coast. 109

Figure 7.2   Recoveries of harbor seals tagged in the Wash, East Anglia. 113

Figure 7.3   Occurrence of food items in the stomachs of harbor seals taken in Scottish waters. 115

Figure 7.4   Occurrence of food items in the stomachs of grey seals taken in Scottish waters. 115

Figure 7.5   Diagrammatic representation of the life cycle of a seal stomach worm. 119

Figure 8.1   The Hebrides, showing the location of North Rona, Gasker, Haskeir, and the Monach Isles. The Farne Islands, Northumbria. 130

Figure 8.2   Grey seal pup production for three major stocks in the U.K.   130

Figure 8.3   Increase of grey seal births at the Farne Islands.   133

Figure 8.4   Relation of pup mortality to extent of accessible shoreline for grey seals at the Farne Islands.   134

Figure 8.5   Starving pups of grey seals at the Farne Islands.   134

Figure 9.1   Juvenile male antarctic fur seal with collar of fish netting.   144

Figure 9.2   Landings of ground fish in the eastern Bering Sea by vessels from Japan, the USSR, and the Republic of Korea.   146

Figure 9.3   Age of sexual maturity of year classes of crabeater seals from the Bellingshausen Sea.   158

Tables

Table 1.1   Properties of air and water compared. 4

Table 3.1   Stock sizes of harp seals (thousands). 9

Table 3.2   Abundance and distribution of northern fur seals. 47

Table 5.1   Distribution of year of birth and age at first pup for 71 elephant seals aged 5 years and older. 86

Table 6.1   Crude estimates of antarctic seal populations, biomass, and food consumption. 101

Table 6.2   Catch limits for antarctic seals, as specified by the Convention for the Conservation of Antarctic Seals. 103

Table 8.1   Distribution of grey seal pups at the Farne Islands, 1969 and 1978.* 137

Table 9.1   Mean concentrations of organochlorines in blubber of adult seals. 148

Table 9.2   Organochlorine residues in tissues of grey seals. 149

Table 9.3   Levels of DDT and PCB (mg/kg) in extractable fat from ringed seals in Bothnian Bay. 151

Foreword

Since 1971, the School of Fisheries at the University of Washington annually has invited prominent scientists to lecture on the utilization and conservation of renewable marine resources. The general purpose has been to develop an understanding of the combined effects of man's harvests and of environmental changes on production within major ecosystems—especially on selected components within those ecosystems. These lectures and their publication have been possible with financial support from the Washington Sea Grant Program as part of its mission to extend useful information about the marine environment.

Nigel Bonner was the tenth speaker in this series. His nine lectures, presented here, supplement an earlier lecture series and resulting book by K. Radway Allen, *Conservation and Management of Whales*. Although both speakers have dealt with the topic of marine mammals, the similarities between their lectures end here.

Whales are marine mammals which spend their entire lives in the aquatic environment. Dominant members like the large rorquals could be harvested only after the development of powerful and fast catcher boats, harpoon grenades, and large shore-based or floating processing plants. Only the smaller species were sought consistently for subsistence purposes.

In contrast, seals reproduce and bear their young on land or solid ice and therefore lend themselves to subsistence hunting. The decline of many species came only when seal fur and blubber became saleable commodities.

The contrast does not end here. While K. Radway Allen discusses birth, mortality, growth, and harvesting rates in mathematical terms, Nigel Bonner approaches his subject with the keen eye of a naturalist who not only observes these phenomena in nature but also relates them to the underlying evolutionary strategy of the various species. It is this kind of intuitive understanding of vital processes, law, and order that historically has guided scientists of every discipline and shaped their formal descriptions of nature.

After finishing his degree in zoology at the University of London in 1953, Nigel Bonner went to South Georgia—initially to study elephant seals, but over the next eleven years extending his studies to other species as well, including antarctic fur seals. In 1962 he assumed a lecture-ship at Sir John Cass College in London where he remained for five years before returning to active seal studies in the United Kingdom as head of the Seal Research Division Unit.

Mr. Bonner closed the ring by his appointment to head the Life Science Division of the British Antarctic Survey—an assignment which once more took him back to South Georgia. It is the problems here that are closest to his heart and the mainspring of his scientific interest—especially the remarkable recovery of almost extinct populations of fur seals and southern sea elephants.

Ole A. Mathisen
January 1982

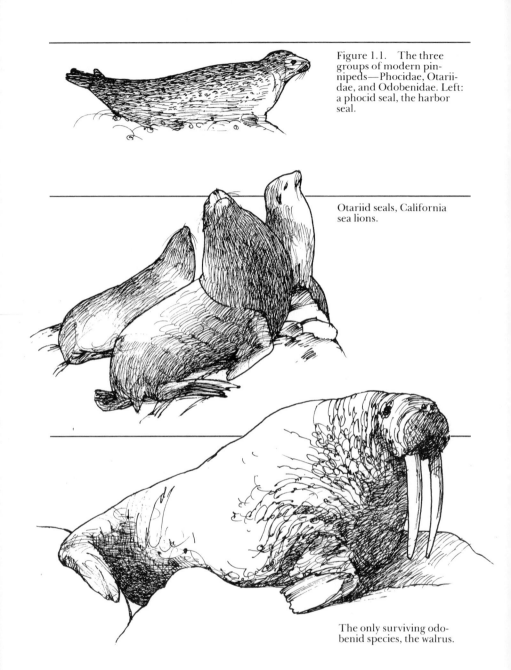

Figure 1.1.   The three
groups of modern pin-
nipeds—Phocidae, Otarii-
dae, and Odobenidae. Left:
a phocid seal, the harbor
seal.

Otariid seals, California
sea lions.

The only surviving odo-
benid species, the walrus.

CHAPTER ONE

The Pinnipedia
An Overview

The Pinnipedia, or seals in a broad sense, are a remarkably uniform group of mammals. They are familiar enough animals, and most people presented with a pinniped could correctly assign it to that group, though they might not be able to make the distinction between the true seals (Phocidae) and the eared seals (Otariidae). The third family, the walruses (Odobenidae), are so characteristic as to be instantly recognizable (Figure 1.1). The distinctiveness of the Pinnipedia from other mammals and the recognizable similarities among the three families that make up the group justify their being regarded as one of the orders of the class Mammalia, equal in rank to the Rodentia or the Artiodactyla, for example. The Pinnipedia form a small order (we can recognize about 34 species) and it is clearly one closely allied to the Carnivora. Indeed, many zoologists regard them as a suborder of the Carnivora, but the distinctions from the fissipede carnivores are so marked that it seems sensible to maintain separate ordinal rank for both groups (King, 1964).

Pinniped Ancestors

Whether the pinnipeds form a natural group derived from a single common ancestor or from two origins is still a matter for argument (Davies, 1958; McLaren, 1960; Mitchell, 1967). Most of the fossil evidence suggests a diphyletic origin, the true seals from an otterlike ancestor which took to the water in the North Atlantic and the eared seals and walruses from a doglike ancestor in the North Pacific (Repenning, 1980). Recognizable eared seals and true seals both appear in the fossil record in the Miocene, with the walruses appearing a little later (Lipps and Mitchell, 1976). However, since the origins of the pinnipeds have had no effect on their relations with man, which is the aspect of their biology that I wish to explore, I shall not pursue the matter further.

The similarity of the various pinniped species, which exceeds that of rodents or artiodactyls, is mostly to be explained by one factor: they are aquatic mammals. When a terrestrial animal returns to the water the selection pressures on it are great; profound changes take place and a high degree of convergence can be expected. This is indeed what we find in the pinnipeds (Mitchell, 1975) and what makes the question of mono-

Figure 1.2.   Evolutionary history of the Pinnipedia. From Lipps and Mitchell, 1976.

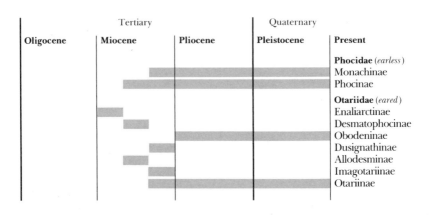

phyly or diphyly so difficult to answer. Of the three groups of mammals that have become secondarily aquatic—the Cetacea, the Sirenia, and the Pinnipedia—the pinnipeds alone have failed to make a total break with terra firma. All seals must return to land (or ice) to produce their young, and this restriction has meant that they have retained more of the typical mammalian organization than have either the Cetacea or the Sirenia. As I hope to make clear later, it is the adaptations of the pinnipeds to aquatic life, coupled with their reproductive need to inhabit coastlines, that have led to much of man's interaction with seals.

It is tempting to ask what led the pinniped ancestor (or ancestors) to abandon life on land and take to the sea, but the question is not really meaningful. As with all living creatures, small changes were constantly taking place in the anatomy and behavior of the protopinniped stock, which we may suppose lived a life already closely connected with water, perhaps by rivers or lakes, much as the otters do today. These changes would have led in all directions, but the ones that better equipped the ancestors for life in the sea were the ones that were successful, in the sense that it was the animals embodying these changes that left the pinniped descendants we see today.

Lipps and Mitchell (1976) have suggested that the radiation of pinnipeds in the Miocene, which included some groups now extinct (Figure 1.2), was a response to the appearance of increased available food stocks in the sea. These food stocks would have been closely related to an increase in the upwelling processes (caused by climatic or tectonic events) which bring nutrients to the surface. Upwelling is common along western coastlines, at high latitudes, and at current divergences, and it is in these places that we find major pinniped stocks today. Conditions of upwelling were similar, Lipps and Mitchell argue, in the Miocene and could have provided the trophic basis for the diversification of the ancestral seals.

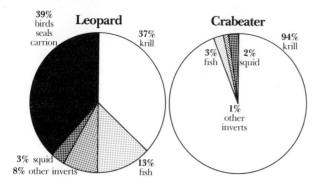

Figure 1.3. Composition of the diet of leopard and crabeater seals. The leopard seal feeds opportunistically at more than one trophic level; the crabeater seal is stenophagic and takes the great majority of its food at the primary consumer level.

We do not know what food these primitive pinnipeds ate. Modern seals feed at several levels in the ecosystem. The leopard seal, *Hydrurga leptonyx*, for example, feeds on planktonic crustaceans, fish, squid, penguins, and other seals. At the other end of the scale, the crabeater seal, *Lobodon carcinophagus*, feeds almost exclusively on a single planktonic species, *Euphausia superba*, or krill (Figure 1.3). The walrus, *Odobenus rosmarus*, feeds mainly on benthic invertebrates, but some individuals may actively hunt and kill ringed seals, *Phoca hispida* (Fay, 1960). More typically we find a wide variety of fish, mollusks, and crustacea forming the diet of seals. Figure 1.4 shows the composition of the diet of the northern fur seal, *Callorhinus ursinus*, the Steller sea lion, *Eumetopias stelleri*, and the harbor seal, *Phoca vitulina*, on the coast of British Columbia (Spalding, 1964). Of the 21 items listed, 10 contribute over 50 percent of the diet of each predator. There are ecological differences in the feeding patterns of these three pinnipeds, but they are not profound.

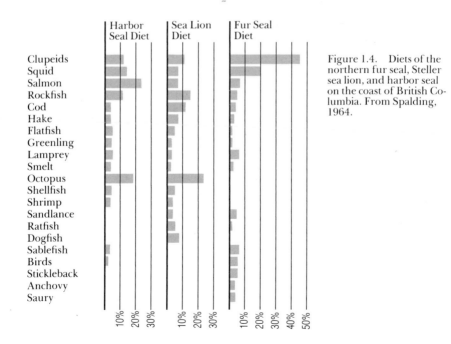

Figure 1.4. Diets of the northern fur seal, Steller sea lion, and harbor seal on the coast of British Columbia. From Spalding, 1964.

The ability to utilize a wide range of prey, which is characteristic of many seal species, was probably an important factor in this spread and perhaps explains also the relative lack of morphological radiation in the group. It is specialists like the walrus and bearded seal, *Erignathus barbatus*, which feed on benthic invertebrates, that stand out from the great generalist majority of phocid and otariid seal species. Breeding strategies, rather than feeding patterns, have created the differences that enable us to recognize the various pinniped species today.

Physical Adaptation to the Sea

To enable the pinniped ancestors to exploit the food available in the sea, the morphology that had served them in a more terrestrial environment had to be modified. Some of the modifications which were to fit them for a life in the water were also to pre-adapt them to the role of prey animals exploitable by man.

The most striking change that the ancestors of seals encountered when they abandoned the land and took to the sea was the nature of the medium surrounding them. Besides being denser and more viscous than air, water has a much higher thermal conductivity and a very much higher thermal capacity per unit volume (Table 1.1). Because of this, a warm-blooded animal in the sea—which is always colder, and often much colder, than the approximately 37°C at which mammals keep their blood—must somehow reduce its loss of heat to the water, which would otherwise represent an unsupportable drain on the animal's energy resources. This can be done in two main ways: by reducing the surface across which heat is lost, and by increasing the insulative properties of what surface there is.

Table 1.1.   Properties of air and water compared

Property	Units	Air	Water
1. Density	$kg \cdot m^{-1}$	1.22	1,025
2. Viscosity	$10^6 \cdot kg \cdot m^{-1} \cdot s^{-1}$	18	1,708
3. Thermal conductivity	$10^{-3} \cdot W \cdot m^{-1} \cdot L^{-1}$	1.3	16.4
4. Specific heat	$J \cdot K^{-1} \cdot kg^{-1}$	720	4,200
5. Heat capacity per unit volume	$J \cdot K^{-1} \cdot m^{-3}$	880	4,300,000

Surface area can be reduced by cutting down on projecting append-ages and adopting a sleeker, more rounded outline. Of all forms, a sphere has the minimum surface enclosing a given volume, and the nearer the shape of a marine mammal approaches a sphere, the less heat per unit weight it will lose to the sea. Of course, other considerations, largely those connected with locomotion, make a spherical seal impracti-cal; but seals have notably sleek outline, without such projecting append-ages as ear pinnae, and have the upper segments of the limbs, the hum-eri and femora, enclosed within the general body contour. These same modifications serve also to reduce drag in the water and thus increase the efficiency of locomotion in a viscous medium. Ultimately this prop-erty was to prove more important than thermoregulation in modifying body shape.

Another means of reducing effective surface area is a relative one. By increasing its bulk an animal, if its shape remains more or less the same, decreases the relative proportion of its surface. This is the familiar surface/volume relationship which has such a profound significance in so many fields of biology. The nature of the relationship can be under-stood most easily from a consideration of a simple geometrical shape. A cube of unit linear dimension has a surface/volume ratio of 6; on dou-bling its linear dimension, the ratio falls to 3; on trebling it, to 2; and so on (Figure 1.5). As the linear dimension increases, so the amount of sur-face compared with the volume decreases.

Marine mammals have exploited this principle to reduce their heat loss. Whales have carried this development to the greatest extent of any in the animal kingdom (though the extreme of this development in whales has been a response to pressures other than thermoregulation). Unrestricted by limitations of locomotion and support in a buoyant me-dium, whales have achieved a size greater than any other animal, living

Figure 1.5.
The surface/volume relationship
(After Bonner, 1980).

  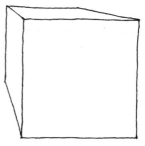

Side = 1   Side = 2   Side = 3
Surface = 6   Surface = $2^2 \times 6 = 24$ Surface = $3^2 \times 6 = 54$
Volume = 1   Volume = $2^3 = 8$ Volume = $3^3 = 27$
Surface/Volume = 6   **Surface/Volume = 3**   **Surface/Volume = 2**

or extinct. Seals, which still retain links with the land for breeding, cannot reach the size of the large whales; nevertheless, they are large mammals in the literal sense, and there are no small seals as there are small rodents, insectivores, or carnivores. The smallest pinniped, the ringed seal, averages about 65 kg, though fat adults may reach 90 kg. The crabeater seal, which makes up about half the number of pinnipeds alive today and two-thirds of the pinniped biomass, averages about 220–230 kg.

There are other selective advantages associated with large size besides that connected with heat conservation. The larger a marine mammal is, the faster it can swim. The resistance to movement in the water is, in general terms, the drag of the water against the surface of the moving body, which of course varies with the surface area, while the available motive force provided by the swimming muscles will vary with muscle volume. We have already seen how these are related. Another survival advantage of large size is that large animals are less likely to become the prey of other predators. Mostly because of their size (though of course other factors are also involved) adult seals have few predators and are at the apex of their food pyramid.

The body of the seal has two features which minimize heat loss by increasing the insulation of its surface. The first of these is that very characteristic mammalian feature, hair. With the exception of the very largest pinnipeds—the walrus and the elephant seals—all seals have an abundant layer of hair. Out of the water, hair forms an effective insulation by trapping a stationary layer of air which is soon warmed to its thermal capacity between the body surface and the exterior. In water, except in one group of pinnipeds, its insulative efficiency diminishes as the hair is wetted and the layer of air is driven out; nevertheless, even in the absence of a trapped air layer the hair retains a relatively stable water layer which, despite its higher conductivity and thermal capacity, reduces heat loss when the animal is moving through the water.

The pelage of a pinniped comprises a great number of pilosebaceous units, each consisting of a bundle of hairs and a pair of associated sebaceous glands emerging via a common pilosebaceous funnel and orifice (Figure 1.6). In each hair bundle, one long, stout, deeply rooted guard hair rises above the underfur of fine, short hair fibers. In the true seals and the sea lions, only a few (1–5) of these finer fibers grow in each bundle, but in the fur seals of the genera *Callorhinus* and *Arctocephalus* there may be more than 50 underfur fibers associated with each guard hair, giving fiber densities of about 57,000 cm^{-2} (Scheffer, 1962, 1964; Bonner, 1968). This dense mat of fine fur fibers is supported by the stout shafts of the guard hairs, which prevent the collapse of the underfur into a flattened felt (Figure 1.7). The water repellency of the underfur fibers and the angle at which their tips make contact with the water prevent the water from penetrating the fur to touch the skin of the seal.

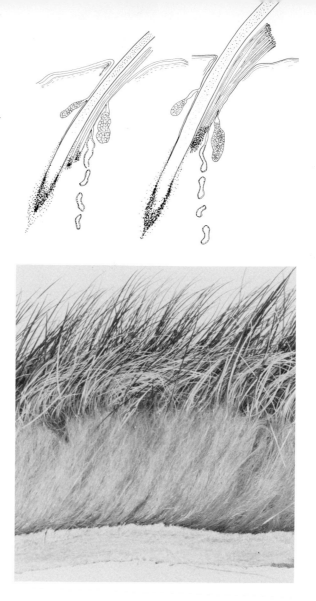

Figure 1.6. Pilosebaceous units of a hair seal (left) and a fur seal (right). Note how the primary hair (the guard hair of the fur seal pilosebaceous unit) is deeper rooted than the secondary hairs (underfur in the fur seal).

Figure 1.7. Pelt section of antarctic fur seal. The stout guard hairs support the dense mat of fine underfur fibers.

This system is of use only to relatively shallow divers, since the thickness of the trapped air layer is reduced by about half for every 10 m depth to which the seal dives. Because of this seals have developed a second insulative device—a thick layer of subcutaneous fat tissue, or blubber. Fat has a low thermal conductivity compared with ordinary connective tissue and is found as a heat-retentive device in many marine animals besides seals. A blubber layer is about half as effective an insulator in air as an equal thickness of fur, but in water the blubber insulation is reduced by about one-fourth of its value in air (Scholander et al., 1950), and this insulation is unaffected by the depth to which the seal dives.

Figure 1.8. Moulting southern elephant seals haul out on land and congregate in large numbers, with extensive body contact. This minimizes heat loss at a time when the blood flow to the skin must be increased. Signy Island, 1975.

Blubber is a vascular tissue, and by appropriate physiological responses heat can be lost more readily from a blubber-covered animal than from one invested in a thick coat of fur. This is done by increasing the blood supply to the superficial layers. The skin, of course, has an extensive system of blood capillaries, but normally little blood is circulated through these, most of the flow being diverted through special shunts between the arterioles and venules. These shunts are the arteriovenous anastomoses, or AVAs for short. When heat is to be lost the AVAs are constricted, thus directing the blood through the capillary bed, where it quickly loses heat to the exterior. AVAs are distributed widely over the whole body of a phocid seal (Molyneux and Bryden, 1978) and are much more numerous than in terrestrial mammals, such as the sheep. Fur seals have similar mechanisms, but in them they are concentrated in the naked skin of the flippers (Bryden and Molneux, 1978). The ability to lose heat is occasionally of high importance to large pinnipeds after strenuous activity on land, such as fights between males in the breeding season.

Conversely, when heat must be conserved, the blood supply to the skin has to be restricted, which results in low skin temperatures and consequently low metabolic activity in the skin. When seals moult they often become notably more terrestrial in their habits; some, such as the elephant seal, stay on land for many days. This allows them to increase the blood flow to the skin during moult without excessive heat loss. Moult in the elephant seal has been described as a catastrophic process, involving not only the hair, but also the superficial layer of the epidermis (Laws, 1956; Spearman, 1968). The need to restrict heat loss at this season is met by hauling out on land and congregating in large groups, with extensive body contact (Figure 1.8).

Another important function of fat is to act as a food reserve. Because of their extensive blubber layer, developed primarily as a means of heat conservation, pinnipeds are able to undergo prolonged periods of fasting. Their relatively large body size also helps in this, because of their low weight-relative metabolism. As we shall see, this has had profound effects on pinniped evolution.

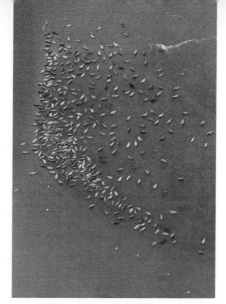

Figure 1.9.   The pups of harbor seals are born between tidemarks. This pup in Orkney is lying on a bed of wrack.

Figure 1.10.   A breeding colony of harbor seals on a sandbank. Photo Steven J. Jeffries.

Social Structure

In one respect, seals have not adapted perfectly to the aquatic environment. Unlike whales and Sirenia, seals must return to land (or to ice) to produce their young. Bartholomew (1970) has pointed out that the combination of offshore marine feeding and terrestrial breeding occurs together nowhere else in the mammalian series, though it is found in sea birds, marine turtles, and the strange marine iguana of the Galapagos.

Pinnipeds show a range of reproductive patterns varying from the simple association of a single male-female pair, through aggregations of approximately equal numbers of the sexes with no discernible social structure, to highly structured and intensely polygynous assemblies, where each year only a small percentage of the sexually mature males take part in breeding activities.

In solitary breeders the sexes tend to be much the same size, as in the harbor seal, *Phoca vitulina*, or the female may be slightly larger than the male, as in the leopard seal, *Hydrurga leptonyx*. The harbor seal may be considered a fairly typical example. It is a rather versatile pinniped, able to exploit different habitats over a wide geographic range. On very rocky coasts, harbor seals breed mostly as single family units or in small groups. No nest or den is made, and the single pup is born directly on the rocks or seaweed (Figure 1.9), usually between the tidemarks, and can swim almost as soon as it is born (Bonner, 1972; Hewer, 1974). In estuarine habitats the harbor seal population of the whole area may congregate on one or a few chosen sandbanks at low water to bring forth their young (Figure 1.10). This process is brief, as it is in all seals, and the young swim off with the rising tide. Although several tens or even hundreds of seals may be present, there is no obvious evidence of social organization. However, it can be noticed that some of the males during the breeding season bear scars around their necks which appear to be the result of fighting with other males. Such fighting seems to occur in the low-density rocky habitats as well as in the high-density estuarine ones.

The above remarks apply to harbor seals in the United Kingdom, but would apply equally well in many other parts of their wide range. However, conditions are not the same in all parts of the harbor seal's range. In the seals found in the Kuril Islands (sometimes termed *Phoca kurilensis*, but probably better regarded as the subspecies *P. vitulina kurilensis*), the males are conspicuously larger than the females (Naito and Nishiwaki, 1975). As I shall show later, this may be associated with a difference in the breeding behavior.

Harp seals, *Phoca groenlandica*, aggregate in huge herds or whelping patches on the sea ice in the spring. Despite the size and density of these aggregations there is no organized social structure; the seals behave as individual units of cow and pup, with the males mostly in the water between the floes. In such cases it is generally difficult to make observations which relate the direct sexual behavior of one seal to another. In the absence of firm evidence that each male serves only one female and that each female receives only one male, the animals are said to be "promiscuous," but it is likely that the association approaches monogyny more nearly.

Another grade of organization is presented by the grey seal, *Halichoerus grypus*. In some parts of its range the grey seal may breed as a family group on sea ice (Hook and Johnels, 1972), but the great majority form large breeding aggregations on land (Bonner, 1972; Mansfield and Beck, 1977). Bull grey seals are about half again as large as the cows, and there is a loose social organization. The males take up station ashore and remain there throughout the breeding season. They are highly intolerant of other males; threat behavior and, to a lesser extent, actual fights are frequent. Bulls dominate the area around them, but this changes from day to day, and there is no distinct "territory" with clearly definable boundaries. The number of breeding bulls ashore is much smaller than the number of cows, a ratio of 1:7.5 being recorded at the colony at North Rona, to the northwest of Scotland (Anderson et al., 1975). There are wide differences in copulation success among the bulls on the breeding grounds; the three most successful bulls of 31 observed at North Rona accounted for 35.6 percent of all copulations, so that a high degree of polygyny exists for some segment of the male populations, with consequent exclusion elsewhere.

Figure 1.11. *Allodesmus*, a large otariid of the middle to late Miocene, had the specific anatomical characters found in modern polygynous pinnipeds: sexual dimorphism, strong canines which could be used in fighting, and teeth with well-defined growth zones associated with periodic fasting. (After Dalzell, in Mitchell, 1978.)

In the elephant seals, *Mirounga*, this process has been carried even further. Breeding takes place in very large aggregations. I have seen an unbroken patch of nearly four thousand southern elephant seals on a beach in South Georgia. There is great sexual dimorphism, the bulls being about seven-and-a-half times as large as the cows (Laws, 1953; Bryden, 1972), and there is an even higher degree of polygyny.

The otariid seals all show a great development of social structure, polygyny, and sexual dimorphism. Northern fur seals gather at the breeding season in what have been described as the largest aggregations of mammals (apart from some cave-dwelling bats) in the world. The adult bulls hold rigidly defined territories throughout the season. They participate in highly ritualized boundary displays with their neighbors, and endeavor to accumulate cows in their territories and to prevent them from leaving once they have entered. The degree of polygyny is very high indeed. Bartholomew and Hoel (1953) calculated that a medium-large harem numbers forty cows.

Although I have presented these examples as a series, I do not intend to imply that they represent an evolutionary sequence. The harbor seal is not less highly evolved than the elephant seal. Rather the reverse, in fact, as it is a versatile seal, the precocity of whose young and length of active association between mother and young are unmatched elsewhere in the phocids. The characteristic of polygyny is a very ancient one in the pinniped line. Mitchell (1966) drew attention to the fact that *Allodesmus*, a large otariid of the Middle and Late Miocene, had the specific anatomical characters found in modern polygynous pinnipeds—sexual dimorphism, strong canines which could be used for fighting, and teeth with well-defined growth zones associated with periodic fasting (Figure 1.11).

Nevertheless, there is an evolutionary sequence involved in pinniped polygyny. (We are perhaps seeing this in action in the seals of the Kuril Islands.) The principles underlying this have been described and analyzed in a brilliant paper by the distinguished seal biologist George A. Bartholomew (1970).

Bartholomew was struck by the remarkable similarities of the pattern of social structure of breeding polygynous pinnipeds, whether they were otariids or phocids. Since these groups are not nearly related (or not related at all, if a diphyletic origin for the Pinnipedia is accepted), it is likely that the factors that led to the evolution of polygyny are few in number and are closely related to the main adaptive features that characterize the Pinnipedia. Starting from the two features that uniquely distinguish the group from the rest of the mammals—offshore marine feeding and terrestrial parturition—and incorporating a number of general mammalian attributes, Bartholomew devised a schematic model to describe the evolution of pinniped polygyny (Figure 1.12).

The model has to account for the extreme gregariousness shown by pinnipeds when ashore, for without this, polygyny on any scale would be impossible. Gregarious breeding permits large numbers of animals which are widely dispersed at sea during their feeding phase, and modified for maximum mobility during this phase, to utilize especially advantageous locations, such as oceanic islands or protected beaches, where suitable terrain and the absence of terrestrial predators allow them to breed successfully despite the aquatic modifications that render them less fitted for life on land. The limited terrestrial mobility of pinnipeds, combined with their tendency to aggregate ashore, results in breeding in exceedingly congested circumstances. Females may be in actual bodily contact with each other, and the males are often so closely spaced that aggressive interactions between adjacent males are almost continuous.

Males are more widely spaced than females because of their aggressive tendencies, mediated by sex hormones, toward each other. Aggressiveness between males is maximal during the breeding season, when testosterone levels in the blood are also highest. If the males are more widely spaced than the females, it follows that many of the males are excluded from a position among the breeding females and that in any year most of the breeding female population will be fertilized by a small number of males. Those males which are most vigorous and aggressive and can maintain their position on the breeding beaches for the longest time will pass on a disproportionate number of genes to the next generation. Bartholomew calculated that in the northern fur seal the fecundity of a territorial male, which might impregnate successfully about 80 percent of a harem of 40 cows in each of five breeding seasons, was about twenty-five times that of a breeding female, which would produce about six pups in her lifetime. Perhaps the discrepancy is not so great as this in most cases, since few males would be able to compete as dominant harem masters for five consecutive seasons, but there is certainly a great bias towards the genetic role of the male if only successful breeders are considered.

Figure 1.12. A schematic model for the evolution of pinniped polygyny. The large circles represent two key attributes of pinnipeds; the smaller circles are attributes common to most mammals; the rectangles show attributes and functions typical of polygynous pinnipeds. The broad arrows show positive feedback loops. For further explanation, see text. From Bartholomew, 1970.

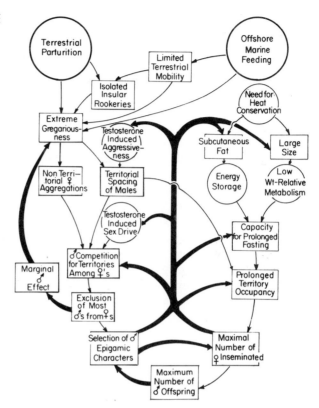

There will thus be a strong selection pressure toward the development of those characters which allow a male successfully to establish himself among the females and, once established, to maintain that position as long as there are estrous females, or those yet to come into estrus, in the vicinity. The relationship of some of these features is shown on the left side of Figure 1.12.

To establish a territory and defend it in the face of the testosterone-induced aggressiveness of neighboring males and newly arrived competitors, a male must be well equipped with a suite of epigamic characters such as aggressiveness, large size, large canines, a protective shield of hair or skin on the forequarters, and modified special structures used in threat displays and vocal challenges. Males which possess these characters (in combination with sexual vigor and fertility) will mate with the most females and produce the most offspring. To the extent that any of the epigamic characters are genetically determined, there will be a strong positive feedback to reinforce selection for these. Positive feedback loops are represented by broad arrows in the figure.

The length of time a position among the breeding females can be maintained is also critical to the genetic success of the individual bull. A bull fur seal or elephant seal in the breeding season will not feed for the whole of the period he remains on shore. To abandon his position on the beach to feed in the sea would mean running the risk of having his females come into estrus and mate with another male. Additionally, a returning bull would have to expend energy in re-establishing himself on the beach after an absence. By fasting for as much of the breeding season as possible, a bull improves his relative genetic efficiency. Prolonged fasting is more possible for a large mammal than for a small one because of the low weight-relative metabolic rate, and hence large size is a clear advantage here. Blubber, which in the water serves primarily as an insulative layer, functions on land as a major energy store to fuel the male machine during the extreme exertions of the breeding season. Because of the correlation between prolonged territorial maintenance (or staying ashore in contact with breeding females) and the number of females fertilized, there is a strong selection pressure in favor of large size and well-developed fat stores, with positive feedback loops connecting these energy relationships (right side of Figure 1.12). Because the same considerations do not apply to the females, such selection has led to the marked sexual dimorphism that is so characteristic of the polygynous pinnipeds.

The model, however, is not exclusively a male one. Three attributes of the female reproductive pattern which favor a brief, precisely timed annual breeding season are basic to it: a short postpartum estrus; a high level of sexual receptivity during estrus; and delayed implantation (or suspended development, as Hewer and Backhouse (1968) call it). Because estrus follows parturition promptly, it occurs on land, where the female is in close contact with the dominant male. With the female so receptive during estrus and estrus so brief, the bull need spend little time in courting and copulating with each cow and thus can devote more of his attention to guarding his territory from encroachment by other males. This enables a higher degree of polygyny to occur without the male risking losing his position or having one of his females fertilized by another male. Delayed implantation is the condition in which the fertilized egg divides to form a hollow fluid-filled blastocyst which then lies quiescent in the lumen of the uterus for a period until a change in the mother's hormonal level causes development to continue by the establishment of a placenta and the growth of the embryo. Delayed implantation allows the time of parturition of all females to be more nearly synchronized, irrespective of the time during the breeding season at which they were fertilized, thus allowing a compact breeding season. The mechanism that triggers the renewed development of the blastocyst has not yet been determined for seals, but it is likely to be photoperiod, as it is in mustelids.

The system described by Bartholomew is subject to various limits which, if exceeded, would result in the cessation of the directional changes postulated by the model; they would "open the feedback loops," in the language of cybernetics. These would be evolutionary processes happening on a timescale too great for human experimenters to observe, but we can see some local and temporary functions which have been documented in the most extremely polygynous of the pinnipeds— the northern fur seal and the elephant seals.

In both of these groups the males are completely oblivious of the welfare of the pups, especially during aggressive encounters with other males. The extent to which the bulls trample and kill their own progeny from the previous season obviously reduces their reproductive efficiency (though because of their high fecundity, this is of less importance than if a female were to show a behavioral trait that endangered one of her pups). Bull elephant seals are so large that they may be reaching the maximum size compatible with the locomotor activity on land that enables them to serve a large group of females; they rely largely on vocal threat to maintain their position on the beach and tolerate the presence of other (though subordinate) males in the group of females over which they have dominance. This contrasts strongly with bull otariids, which patrol their territorial boundaries in constant close contact with their neighbors.

Gregariousness itself can result in loss of pups. The mortality rate of pups on crowded beaches is notably higher than on less densely populated ones (Fogden, 1971; Bonner, 1975). Wynne-Edwards (1962) suggested that polygyny and gregariousness are the results of group selection that limits population size so as to prevent overutilization of the food resources on which the population depends. Group selection is not a popular concept nowadays. McClaren (1967) pointed out that any breeding female that moves away from the overcrowded areas is liable to be mated by a male that has been unsuccessful in establishing his status in competition with other males. To the extent that this "marginal male" lacks status because of genetic factors, his male progeny would be expected to show a similar tendency to a marginal position and hence impregnate a smaller portion of the females. In this way, the tendency of a female to move out of crowded areas would be self-limiting. The best reproductive strategy for a female to adopt is to position herself in an area where she will be mated by a dominant male. This marginal male effect is illustrated at the extreme left side of Figure 1.12. As long as some males are excluded from the breeding pool, gregariousness in females should be positively reinforced. Of course, all males were marginal males at an earlier stage of life; it is only the genetically inherited defects that determine the marginal status of *adult* males that contribute to the marginal male effect.

Too much weight has often been given to the effect of mortality of pups ashore, which is conspicuous to observers, compared with mortality at sea, which is never conspicuous and often known only for those species where age-specific mortality rates are available. Bartholomew calculated that for the 1961 year-class of northern fur seal pups, mortality on shore, some of which might be related to density-dependent factors, reduced the year-class by 14 percent, while mortality at sea reduced it by 50 percent. He concluded that pup mortality due to overcrowding is insufficient to open the feedback loop linking male territoriality and female gregariousness. My own observations on grey seals at the Farne Islands (Bonner, 1975) has led me to the same conclusion.

The characteristics of gregariousness, large size, well-developed blubber layer, and intense polygyny have been of prime importance in the evolution of the Otariidae and of the elephant seals and the grey seal amongst the Phocidae. They have also been highly significant in the relations between these groups and man, as I hope to show.

References

Anderson, S.S., Burton, R.W. and Summers, C.F. 1975. Behaviour of grey seals (*Halichoerus grypus*) during a breeding season at North Rona. J. Zool., Lond. 177:179–195.

Bartholomew, G.A. 1970. A model for the evolution of pinniped polygyny. Evolution 24:546–559.

Bartholomew, G.A. amd Hoel, P.G. 1953. Reproductive behavior of the Alaska fur seal, *Callorhinus ursinus*. J. Mammal. 34:417–436.

Bonner, W.N. 1968. The fur seal of South Georgia. Brit. Antarct. Surv. Sci. Rep. No. 56. 81pp.

Bonner, W.N. 1972. The grey seal and common seal in European waters. Oceanogr. Mar. Biol. Ann. Rev. 10:461–507.

Bonner, W.N. 1975. Population increase of grey seals at the Farne Islands. Rapp. P.-v. Réun. Cons. int. Explor. Mer, 169:366–370.

Bonner, W.N. 1980. Whale. Poole: Blondford Press.

Bryden, M.M. 1972. Growth and development in marine mammals. Pp. 1–79 in "Functional Anatomy of Marine Mammals" ed. R.J. Harrison. Vol. 2. Academic Press, London.

Bryden, M.M. and Molyneaux, G.S. 1978. Arteriovenous anastomoses in the skin of seals. ii. The California sea lion, *Zalophus californianus*, and the northern fur seal, *Callorhinus ursinus* (Pinnipedia: Otariidae). Anat. Rec. 191(2):253–260.

Davies, J.L. 1958. The Pinnipedia: an essay in zoogeography. Geog. Rev. 48:474–493.

Fay, F.H. 1960. Carnivorous walrus and some arctic zoonoses. Arctic 13:111–122.

Fogden, S.C.L. 1971. Mother-young behavior at grey seal breeding beaches. J. Zool., Lond. 164:61–92.

Hewer, H.R. 1974. British Seals. Collins New Naturalist, London.

Hewer, H.R. and Bachkhouse, K.M. 1968. Embryology and foetal growth of the grey seal, *Halichoerus grypus*. J. Zool., Lond. 155:507–533.

Hook, O. and Johnels, A.G. 1972. The breeding and distribution of the grey seal (*Halichoerus grypus* Fab.) in the Baltic Sea, with observations on other seals of the area. Proc. roy. Soc. Lond., B. 182:37–58.

King, J.E. 1964. Seals of the World. British Museum (Natural History), London.

Laws, R.M. 1953. The elephant seal (*Mirounga leonina* Linn.): 1. Growth and age. Sci. Rep. Falkland Is. Dependencies Surv. 8.

Laws, R.M. 1956. The elephant seal (*Mirounga leonina* Linn.): 2. General, social and reproductive behavior. Sci. Rep. Falkland Is. Dependencies Surv. 13.

Lipps, J.H. and Mitchell, E. 1976. Trophic model for the adaptive radiation and extinction of pelagic marine mammals. Paleobiol. 2(2):147–155.

Mansfield, A.W. and Beck, B. 1977. The grey seal in Eastern Canada. Dept. Fish. Envir. Fish. Mar. Serv., Technic. Rep. 704. 81pp.

McLaren, I.A. 1960. Are the Pinnipedia biphyletic? Syst. Zool. 9:18–28.

McLaren, I.A. 1967. Seals and group selection. Ecology 48:104–110.

Mitchell, E. 1966. The Miocene pinniped *Allodesmus*. Univ. Calif. Pub. Geol. Sci. 61:1–105.

Mitchell, E.D. 1967. Controversy over diphyly in pinnipeds. Syst. Zool. 16(4):350–351.

Mitchell, E.D. 1975. Paralellism and convergence in the evolution of Otariidae and Phocidae. Rapp. P.-v. Réun. Cons. int. Explor. Mer 169:12–26.

Molyneux, G.S. and Bryden, K.M. 1978. Arteriovenous anastomoses in the skin of seals: 1. The Weddell seal *Leptonychotes weddelli* and the elephant seal *Mirounga leonina* (Pinnipedia: Phocidae). Anat. Rec. 191:239–252.

Naito, Y. and Nishiwaki, M. 1975. Ecology and morphology of *Phoca vitulina largha* and *Phoca kurilensis* in the southern Sea of Okhotsk and northeast Hokkaido. Rapp. P.-v. Réun. Cons. int. Explor. Mer 169:379–386.

Repenning, C.A. 1980. Warm-blooded life in cold ocean currents: following the evolution of the seal. Oceans 13(3):18–24.

Scheffer, V.B. 1950. Probing the life secrets of the Alaska fur seal. Pacific Discovery 3:22–30.

Scheffer, V.B. 1962. Pelage and surface topography of the northern fur seal. North Amer. Fauna. No. 64. Fish Wildl. Serv. Washington.

Scheffer, V.B. 1964. Hair pattern in seals (Pinnipedia). J. Morphol. 115:291–304.

Scholander, P.F., Walters, V., Hock, R. and Irving, L. 1950. Body insulation of some arctic and tropical mammals and birds. Biol. Bull. Woods Hole 99:225–236.

Spalding, D.J. 1964. Comparative feeding habits of the fur seal, sea lion and harbour seal on the British Columbia coast. Fish. Res. Bd. Can., Bull. 146. 52pp.

Spearman, R.I.C. 1968. A histochemical examination of the epidermis of the southern elephant seal (*Mirounga leonina* L.) during the telogen stage of hair growth. Aust. J. Zool. 16:17–26.

Wynne-Edwards, V.C. 1962. Animal Dispersion in Relation to Social Behavior. Oliver and Boyd, Edinburgh.

CHAPTER TWO

Seals and Men
The First Contacts

When primitive man in the Northern Hemisphere first spread into those regions where seals were abundant—the northern coast of Europe, the coast of Asia from Japan northwards, and arctic North America and Greenland—he found waiting for him the pinnipeds, a group of mammals almost ideally suited to his needs.

The pinnipeds were sufficiently large that the pursuit and killing of a single animal provided an ample reward, yet not so large that there were major problems or serious risks involved in hunting them. Their furry skins made a tough and waterproof leather, besides having good thermoregulatory properties that could protect feeble, naked man from the elements. Beneath their skin was a thick layer of blubber which, besides its use as food with the rest of the carcass, could be burned in a primitive stone lamp to light the darkness of crude homes during the long winter nights and give out a little warmth. These convenient animals came ashore or onto floes to produce their relatively helpless young, which could be cropped each year without detriment to the breeding stock.

The other main character of the pinnipeds, their extreme gregariousness, was not fully exploited by primitive man. It was left to his more sophisticated successors from about the eighteenth century onwards to take full advantage of this.

The extent to which early man relied on seals can only be ascertained by inference, but it seems certain that to some coast-dwelling communities in northwest Europe during the Stone Age and after, seal hunting was an activity of vital interest. Our knowledge of these times is very incomplete. Cultures exploiting seals would naturally be located in coastal regions, but because of geographical changes since the Ice Age, only limited stretches of Stone Age coast are available for study above modern sea level. The coasts most depressed by the weight of the Pleistocene ice sheet, where we would hardly expect to find abundant traces of human colonization until a comparatively late stage (Clark, 1946), were the ones which isostatic displacement preserved; the others were inundated by the rising sea level as the ice melted, and potential sites of Stone Age seal hunting camps submerged. There are no known coastal settlements dating from late glacial times in northwest Europe in areas known

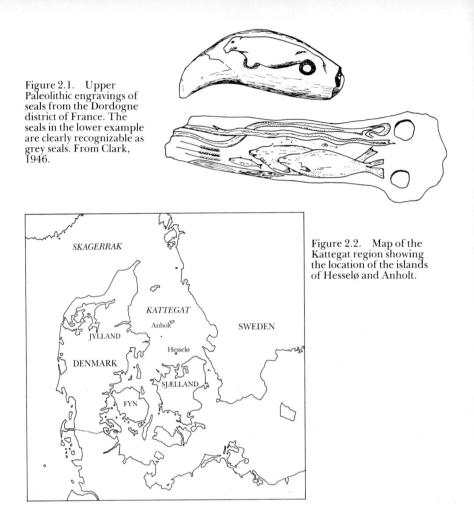

Figure 2.1. Upper Paleolithic engravings of seals from the Dordogne district of France. The seals in the lower example are clearly recognizable as grey seals. From Clark, 1946.

Figure 2.2. Map of the Kattegat region showing the location of the islands of Hesselø and Anholt.

to have been settled by Upper Paleolithic man, because even if they existed they would be below modern sea levels.

Early Hunting in Europe

The earliest evidence for seal hunting in Europe consists of some seal bones and engravings of seals from Upper Paleolithic deposits in the Dordogne Valley in France. Although these deposits are a considerable distance (some 200 km) from the sea, it is probable that they represent a local hunting industry which relied on the seals that swam up the river in pursuit of salmon. One of the engravings (Figure 2.1) is a remarkably lifelike representation of a pair of seals, clearly identifiable as grey seals, chasing a salmon (Capitan et al., 1906).

Clark calculated that about half the Stone Age sites in northwest Europe known to be associated with seal remains are concentrated on the

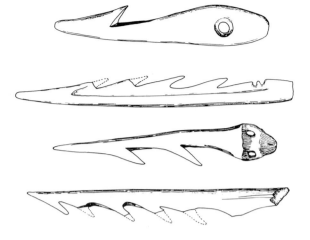

Figure 2.3. Sub-Neol-
ithic bone harpoon points
from around the Baltic.
Redrawn from Clark,
1946.

shores of the old Littorina Sea* in northern and eastern Jutland and on the Danish Islands. This does not mean, however, that this was the most active seal-hunting area, only that here the bone remains are best preserved. The tiny island of Hesselø in the Kattegat, about 25 km north of Zealand (Figure 2.2), was a sealing station in Stone Age times. More than 99 percent of the bone material there is derived from grey seals, including over four hundred canine teeth. No fewer than six wooden clubs, which might have been used to kill seals, were found in a bog at Hesselø. Because Hesselø is too small to support terrestrial game (it is about a mile long), it is reasonable to assume that the settlement was a seasonal one, the hunters visiting the island during the breeding season of the grey seals to provide themselves with skins, meat, and blubber (Møhl, 1970).

The clubs at Hesselø were a rare find; wood does not preserve well, except in bogs. The hard and durable harpoon point is more often unearthed as an artifact associated with seal hunting. Some of them have been found actually in association with seal bones. At Norrköping in 1907, for example, a bone harpoon head was discovered with the skeleton of a young ringed seal in a clay bed at approximately the present level of the Baltic Sea. Since the Littorina Sea surface is estimated to have been some 60 m higher, we can picture this harpooned seal sinking to the bottom of the Littorina Sea in a depth of water too great to permit its retrieval. Similarly, another harpoon head of elk bone was found in a harp seal skeleton at Närpes in 1935, in a deposit formed at the bottom of the Littorina Sea (Clark, 1946). I may note in passing that the harp seal no longer exists in the Baltic Sea.

Harpoon heads are more commonly found without the incriminating evidence of seal bones around them, of course, but it seems likely that they were used mostly, if not exclusively, for seal hunting. At Stora

*The Littorina Sea covered the site of what is now the Baltic Sea (in the wide sense) and a good deal of the surrounding coast.

21

Förvar, for example, a dozen simple harpoon points with a single barb and a single perforation through the swollen base (Figure 2.3) have been found. Since the only other mammal at all well represented at this site is the pig, which probably was not hunted in this way, it is reasonable to assume that the harpoons were used to catch seals (Clark, 1946).

Harpoons were probably used from boats. We know that primitive man at this period had considerable ability to navigate. Offshore islands with Stone Age remains, like Hesselø, testify to this. So, too, do some remarkable rock engravings at Rødøy in Nordland, Norway (Gjessing, 1936), which depict a hunter in a boat, a porpoise, and a seal (Figure 2.4). The juxtaposition of these marine mammals and a man in a boat is scarcely likely to be fortuitous, and we may interpret this as a hunting scene. It is not possible to identify a harpoon in the engraving, but we may suppose that a technique similar to that of the Eskimo kayak hunter was used, which I shall discuss later.

Probably the Stone Age hunters used many methods to take seals, varying them according to the season, the locality, and the species of seal hunted, just as the Eskimos did in more recent times. Nets and pitfall traps are possibilities, but neither is likely to have left surviving recognizable artifacts. Although the use of metal was lacking, the technology that did exist was remarkably sophisticated if we can draw an analogy with the Eskimos, who within recent times were living in a Stone Age culture, albeit a highly specialized one.

Eskimos and Seals

Coastal Eskimos, like most subsistence hunters, made use of all the game that came their way and they could catch, but their staple prey was the ringed seal. The importance of this species to their culture is illustrated by its identification with one of their more powerful spirits, known in Greenland as Angiut (Figure 2.5). Eskimo craftsmen have produced many beautiful ivory carvings of seals (Figure 2.6), and though these are today made for sale, they probably originally had a cult significance.

Men like Franz Boas, who made a notable field expedition on Baffin Island in 1883–84, were able to record an account of Eskimo hunting methods (Boas, 1888) that had changed little, if at all, since their first contacts with the arctic whalers at the beginning of the eighteenth century. The Eskimos owed their success—indeed, their survival—to their skill at hunting. Much of this was experience and a detailed knowledge of their hunting grounds and quarry, but the hardware of their hunting technology, their weapons and boats, were highly important and deserve description.

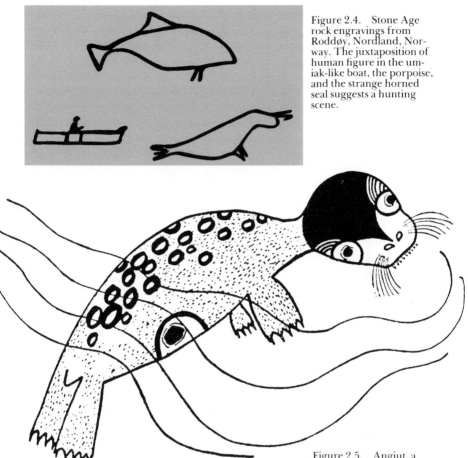

Figure 2.4. Stone Age rock engravings from Roddøy, Nordland, Norway. The juxtaposition of human figure in the umiak-like boat, the porpoise, and the strange horned seal suggests a hunting scene.

Figure 2.5. Angiut, a Greenlandic seal spirit.

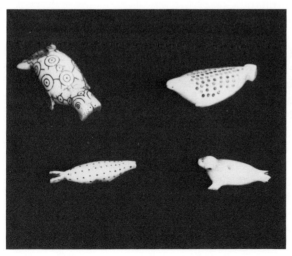

Figure 2.6. Inuit carvings. Top left, walrus; top right and bottom left, ringed seals; bottom right, harbor seal. Originals in Burke Memorial Washington State Museum, Seattle, Washington.

23

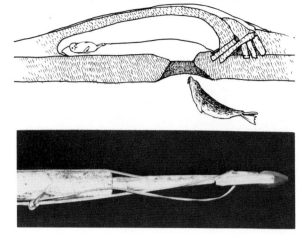

Figure 2.8. Ringed seal breeding lair. The lair is hollowed out in a snow-drift behind a ridge of pressure-ice. The breathing hole lies within the lair beneath the snow.

Figure 2.7. A slate-pointed harpoon of the unang type. Icy Cape, Alaska. Original in the Burke Memorial Washington State Museum, Seattle, Washington.

The harpoon was the weapon universally used by the Eskimos for taking seals. The basic type of harpoon was the *unang* (Figure 2.7). On Baffin Island in Boas's time, unangs always incorporated rod iron (traded from the whalers), but farther west in Alaska the old Stone Age pattern persisted. This consists of a wooden shaft whose ends are tipped with stout ivory points (made from walrus tusks) securely fastened to the shaft by strings of bowhead whale baleen. The upper ivory point holds the harpoon head, or *naulang,* which is 2½–5 cm long and usually also made of ivory. The base of the naulang is hollowed out or mortised so that it sits securely on the point of the unang; a piece of metal (if available) or stone set transversely in a groove across the top provides a cutting edge. The harpoon line, or *iparang,* made of sealskin, passes through a hole parallel to the blade of the point. Any strain coming on the line as the stricken seal darts away twists the harpoon point so that it comes away from its seating, turns at right angles to the line, and acts as a toggle. The iparang is several times as long as the harpoon, as it must allow for the struggles of the stricken seal. It terminates in a loop that the hunter can hold in his left hand.

This sort of harpoon was used to strike ringed seals at their breathing holes in the sea ice. The hunter waited, sometimes for hours at a stretch, at a breathing hole, or *allu.* When the seal returned to take a breath the hunter drove the harpoon down, striking the animal in the head or neck. While the hunter held the struggling seal on the line, he enlarged the allu so that the seal could be drawn up through it and killed with a kick or blow to the head.

Ringed seals could be taken also in their breeding lairs or dens in March and April. The seals produce their pups in dens scratched out of a snowdrift, often by a pressure ridge, above a breathing hole in the ice. It is interesting to note that the ringed seal, the smallest of the phocids and the most northern, is the only one to bring forth its young in any shelter (Figure 2.8). A detailed knowledge of the presence, structure, and location of these lairs allowed the Eskimos to exploit the abundant resource of ringed seals during this season (Smith and Stirling, 1975). The Eskimos used dogs to scent out occupied breeding dens. When one was located, the hunter broke through the roof as fast as possible, hoping to catch the mother seal before she could escape through the hole. Not surprisingly, this strategy was often unsuccessful, but the pup was usually secured. It could then be used as bait for the mother by attaching a line to one of its hind flippers and letting it down through the breathing hole. When the mother returned to her pup, the hunter harpooned her with his unang in the usual way.

There were many other methods that the Eskimos used for hunting seals from the ice—stalking sleeping seals, harpooning from the ice edge, and so forth—but they do not represent a basically different technology. The use of boats, however, added a new dimension to the hunt. Two forms of boat were used for hunting seals: the smaller *kayak*, a single-seater canoe of a pattern sufficiently familiar (and widely copied) to need no further description; and the larger *umiak*. The kayak could be used to attack all kinds of pinnipeds, but an umiak was necessary if large quantities of game had to be carried back. Umiaks are still in regular use as hunting boats, although today they are usually propelled by high-technology outboard engines. An umiak can comfortably seat six hunters and a considerable quantity of game. Both kayak and umiak were made of a wooden frame, over which was stretched sealskins, from ringed seals in the case of the kayak and from bearded seals (*Erignathus barbatus*) in the case of the heavier umiak.

A kayak is basically a weatherproof but very unstable craft. Were a hunter to harpoon a seal in the water from a kayak and retain hold of his harpoon line, he would invite an almost certain capsize. The Eskimos solved this problem by attaching a float to the end of the harpoon line (Figure 2.9). It could be cast over the side when a seal had been struck and then recovered when the animal was dead or exhausted. Equipped with this combination of harpoon and float (or floats), the Eskimos were able to tackle walruses and even whales.

The kayak harpoon is different from the unang. It consists of a stout pole 1.4–1.5 m long, with an ivory or bone support for the hand at its point of balance and, perpendicular to this, a small ivory knob for fastening the harpoon line. At the top of the shaft is a walrus tusk, held by a sinew binding to a mortised ivory socket, the *qatirn*. On the end of the tusk is the harpoon point itself, or *tokang*, made of ivory or hard bone. In Boas's time the tokang, like the naulang, was armed with a cutting point of iron; before metal was available, obsidian or slate was used (Figure 2.10). The harpoon line, made of seal hide, is fastened to the tokang, which is balanced on the walrus tusk by means of a mortised joint held tight by the tension of the line attached to the ivory knob near the hand rest.

Figure 2.9. Killing seals from a kayak. This Victorian engraving is wrong in many respects (for example, the attachment of the harpoon line), but it shows the essential float, made from an inflated ringed seal skin.

tokang

tusk

line

qatirn

peg

hand support

Figure 2.10. Inuit kayak harpoon. The harpoon below is shown ready to throw. The tokang is held in place on the tusk by the tension of the line hooked over the peg by the hand support. After the tokang is fast in the seal, the tusk swivels in the qatirn, allowing the line to slip free from the peg.

float (avautang)

When the harpoon was darted, the tokang penetrated the skin of the seal or walrus, followed by the smooth tusk. As soon as a strain came on the line the tusk bent in its ball-and-socket joint with the qatirn, thus shortening the distance between the tokang and the stud where the line was fastened and allowing the tokang to slip off the tusk and remain in the wound at right angles to the line, thus forming an effective toggle.

It can be seen that the harpoon was a sophisticated tool, carefully designed and expertly manufactured. Its essence is the detachable tokang. Had the line been attached to the shaft and the tokang rigidly mounted, the leverage once a strain came on the line would have torn the harpoon out of the wound. The Eskimo kayak harpoon, with its seven components, represents a far departure from the simple harpoon points found on the floor of the now vanished Littorina Sea. It demonstrates how highly developed was the hunting technique of the Eskimos, while still remaining totally within the compass of a Stone Age technology.

Once the harpoon had struck the prey, the hunter cast the line over the side, its end tied to an inflated sealskin (usually the skin of a ringed seal removed entire and inflated through a bone or ivory mouthpiece). This float, or *avautang*, created an impediment to the seal which prevented it from diving and hindered it in swimming. Extra floats could be attached if the quarry was large, such as a walrus, or a sea anchor made of a wooden frame covered with sealskin might be used. After the wounded animal tired a little, it was stabbed with an *anguvigang*, a lance with a pointed walrus tusk secured to the end.

Just as the Eskimo economy was based on seals, so their technology was heavily dependent on seal products. Apart from some wood (a very valuable material to dwellers in the high Arctic) and perhaps a little stone, all the many parts of the hunting weapons and boats were made from seal or walrus products. The ivory that figured so prominently as points, knobs, etc., was usually walrus ivory, though occasionally narwhal ivory was used. The hunter in the kayak might be clad in sealskin clothing, though generally furs from several kinds of animals were used.

All parts of the seal were utilized, but nothing was more important than the blubber. Blubber was eaten as it was, but its most important function was as fuel for lamps. Eskimos in their stone huts or snow houses might have survived without the heat from the blubber lamps, but they could scarcely have managed without their light through the long arctic night. Their fur clothing, weapons, and implements took many patient hours to fabricate and many more to maintain. This could never have been done in the dark, so it was essential to obtain blubber to keep the lamps lit through the winter.

The Eskimos made an abrupt and painful stride into the age of modern technology. Their hunting skills and knowledge of their environment began to deteriorate soon after their first contact with the whalers, later in the west than in the east. Although they still number many hunters in their society, the hard but stimulating concept of self-sufficiency is being replaced by a deculturization process which leaves an increasing number of these people without any clear role in life.

Technological changes have affected their relationship with seals very markedly. Firearms have almost completely replaced other methods of hunting seals. In 1965 each Eskimo household in Wainwright, Alaska owned an average of 2 high-powered rifles, 1.1 .22-caliber rifles, and 1.3 shotguns (Nelson, 1969; Nelson gives 1.7 .22-caliber rifles per household, but this appears to be a miscalculation). The use of rifles, with their ability to kill from a distance, has altered the balance between hunter and quarry. In particular, the loss rate of seals killed has increased greatly. At Wainwright during a summer hunt Nelson noted that, of 22 seals killed, only 12 were retrieved, and he thought that the average loss rate was even higher. During the winter, when the seals are fatter, nearly all of them float after they are dead and losses are thus lower.

Seals and the European Seal Hunter

Although civilization came quickly to the Eskimos, it was a more gradual process for the people of northwestern Europe, and we may return to see how the role of the seal hunter developed there. There is evidence that Norwegian seal hunters by the end of the Stone Age were basically farmers who supplemented their food supply by seasonal hunting and fishing (Clark, 1946). This was a pattern that was to continue almost to the present day in many parts. Within the last hundred years the crofters of the Outer Hebrides were living in exactly this manner. Martin Martin in 1703 recorded that the crofters of North Uist made a yearly expedition at the end of October to club the grey seals breeding on the islet of Causamul, a practice which had been going on beyond memory or history. It continued into this century, though in a sporadic manner, the human depopulation of the Hebrides perhaps having more to do with its decline than any shortage of seals.

A strong tradition of seal hunting persisted in the Baltic, and the methods used were varied. Olaus Magnus published a map (Figure 2.11) in 1539 which included a scene from the Gulf of Bothnia showing a pair of hunters armed with barbed pikes kneeling on floes and menacing a group of seals, one of which is shown accompanied by a pup. This could be a grey seal pup, since we have seen that grey seals breed in family groups on the ice in the Baltic. It is not clear whether these pikes have detachable heads, like an Eskimo harpoon (such gear was known to be in use in Sweden around 1700), or whether they were of solid construction after the fashion of a gaff. The latter type of instrument, called a *väckare*,

Figure 2.11.   Olaus Magnus's map of the Gulf of Bothnia, showing hunters armed with seal pikes menacing what are probably grey seals. Reproduced by courtesy of the British Museum.

was still in use until quite recently in Sweden and Finland on seal-hunting expeditions. Its main use was to prod the ice to test its strength (*väcker* means to stab the ice), but it was also an essential tool for killing badly shot seals or retrieving them from the water (Söderberg, 1972).

Seals were caught by netting in many areas including the Arctic and the Hebrides. The nets were placed in channels leading from sandbanks or around rocks. Linnaeus, in the diary of his journey to Öland and Gothland in 1741 (Linnaeus, 1745), describes the use of two types of nets for catching what appear from the account to be harbor seals. "Lying nets" were placed in a square around a stone on which seals were in the habit of hauling out to bask. The outer and inner ends were held open by transverse rods, and one end of a long rope was fastened to the innermost rod; the other end of the rope was carried ashore. The frame of netting was allowed to lie on the bottom until a seal had clambered onto the stone, whereupon the man ashore pulled the rope, causing the frame to rise so that the upper edge of the net was level with the surface of the water. The seal, alarmed by the movement around it, dove off the rock and became entangled in the net, where the hunter could kill it with a harpoon or some other instrument. "Standing nets" were simpler; they formed a half-circle on the seaward side of a seal-stone. The seals were said always to climb onto the stones from the landward side and so did not notice the nets, but when they were frightened they clambered down the rock on the seaward side and so got caught in the nets. If there was no hauling-out area by a farmer's land, he placed suitable stones in the

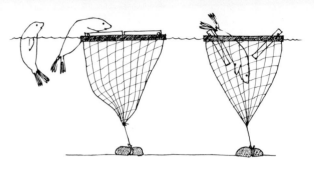

Figure 2.12. A floating trap for seals of the kind used in the Baltic. After Staffen Söderberg, 1972.

water to attract the seals. Söderberg (1972) says that the false rocks might be made from fire-blackened pieces of wood. He notes also that the nets, which had a mesh width of 30 cm, had spindle-shaped floats with sharpened ends which helped to entangle the seal in the net.

Seals were caught in traps as well as on nets. Their habit of hauling out on floating platforms made the construction of pitfall traps easy. A platform with hinged doors was prepared and floated in the sea. When a seal hauled out on the top of the platform, the doors gave way beneath it, dropping it into a netting bag suspended below (Figure 2.12). Gin traps, mounted in a wooden frame beneath the surface and baited with fish, were used in conjunction with salmon or herring nets which led the seal to the trap.

Snag hooks were also used. A seal rock, preferably covered with seaweed, was girdled at low-water level with a stout rope to which heavy three-pronged hooks were attached. The seals swam over the submerged rope and hauled out on the rock as the tide fell. At low water the hunter scared them off; when the seals slid into the water, the hooks, now exposed, impaled and held them until the hunter killed them.

No tradition of hunting can have a long history unless the hunters and their quarry reach some kind of balance. It is easy to see how such a balance would be achieved if seals were being caught casually with nets or traps. The effort of maintaining the catching gear and keeping a watch on it would be worthwhile only as long as there was a fair stock of seals in the vicinity. Should the stock decline, so would the catching effort, and the seals would get a chance to recover.

It is less easy to see how hunting directed toward large breeding aggregations of a species like the grey seal, whose young must spend from three to four weeks ashore before they can take to the water, can be limited so that colonies are not eradicated in the course of a few years. No doubt this was exactly what happened in a good many cases, but in others there is evidence that sealing had been going on over a great many years. Hesselø, the site where the Neolithic sealing had taken place, was still being used for sealing in the sixteenth century. Anholt, an even more remote though larger island in the Kattegat (Figure 2.2), was another Neolithic sealing site where hunting persisted even longer.

A vivid account of sealing at Anholt at the end of the eighteenth century is given by Bynch (quoted in Møhl, 1970). Bynch describes how on Christmas Day (grey seals in Denmark bred in January) the whole north coast of the island was declared a prohibited area and all loose dogs on the island had to be confined. On Candlemas Day (February 2) the three aldermen and the sheriff visited the seal rookery to see what the hunt might yield and whether the young were big enough to be killed. Hunters took only the weaned young, about three or four weeks old (Bynch says four or five weeks, but analogy with existing stocks of grey seals suggests that this is an overestimate), and hunting was carried out so as to disturb the adults as little as possible. Two or three men crept down to the beach and killed the selected pups with a blow to the head from a wooden club fitted with an iron spike. The dead pups were dragged back behind the beach and concealed. Killing took place every four or five days. Only the young were killed at this stage; the mothers were never disturbed.

Hunting continued through February and early March till it ended in the "Store Slag," the killing of some of the old bulls. In what Bynch describes as "a difficult, dangerous and blood-dripping spectacle," all the hunters set off down the beach, each armed with his pike, to try to kill as many of the old bull seals as possible before they escaped into the sea. However, only a few bulls could be caught in this way. At the end of the season the proceeds of the hunt were divided in a closely regulated manner among the landowners, the farmers, the men appointed to guard the seals, and the priest.

Without suggesting that the peasants of Anholt at the end of the eighteenth century had not advanced beyond a Neolithic culture stage, it seems to me quite likely that the hunting methods described by Bynch had survived virtually unchanged from the Neolithic exploitation of the seals. Indeed, the survival of the seals themselves, which could so easily have been exterminated by unrestrained hunting, implies the continuing existence of regulations of some sort.

The rules devised by the Anholters, and regarded by them as handed down from time immemorial, were those required for rational, sustained exploitation: absolute protection from Christmas to Candlemas, when the seals were assembling and the young were being born; no killing of adult females, the producers of the crop; exploitation of the young at the optimum yield stage, before natural mortality (apart from perinatal mortality) had taken its toll; spacing the hunting episodes to allow a reasonable escapement; and the cropping of part of the adult male stock, which in a highly polygynous species would have no effect on pup production.

There are no other accounts of hunting grey seals that go into such detail as the one left by Bynch, yet I expect that some such regime—developed empirically, no doubt—existed at other colonies of relatively accessible seals where the sealing persisted over a long period. Anholt sealing went on until the end of the nineteenth century, when the seals were quickly exterminated by shooting for bounty payments, introduced in 1889. In the first year of the bounty period, 304 grey seals were killed (Joensen et al., 1976).

The types of exploitation which I have described in this chapter may be termed "subsistence sealing." For the Eskimos it was a true subsistence economy; very little trading, if any, was done before the arrival of the whalers. However, this was not the case elsewhere. Clark (1946) has suggested that some trade in seal products already existed in the Neolithic, since the larger communities made possible by farming created a market for wild products and thus imposed greater demands on the hunting and catching economy than were involved in merely providing subsistence for the small and sparsely settled groups of food-gatherers themselves. Actual records of cash trading exist from the fourteenth century. In 1372–73, for example, the Master of Farne received six shillings and eight pence for four flagons of oil extracted from seals and porpoises, and in 1378–79 four shillings and six pence were paid for a "celys calfe." Seal calves from the Farne Islands were being sold to the Bishop of Durham and the Earl of Westmoreland in 1533–34, according to the "Durham Household Book" (Hickling, 1962). The attraction of high society to seal meat in those days may relate to the fact that seals were classed as fish and so could be eaten on fast-days, a significant advantage for those clerics and noblemen who liked their meat red!

Subsistence sealing has continued to the present day in many parts of the world, although on a much reduced scale. As we have seen, it had little impact on the seal stocks concerned. Stock depletion by hunting began only when full-scale commercial exploitation, as opposed to local use, entered the sealing scene. This new development forms the subject of the next three chapters.

Seals as Trophy

Before leaving the subject of subsistence sealing, I should like to consider a modern development, where the economic return of small-scale seal hunting operations greatly exceeds the conventional value of the seal products obtained. This concerns trophy hunting, wherein a local hunter or guide, with expertise in the nature of the terrain and the habits of the quarry, conducts a sportsman to a situation where he can be sure of obtaining a specimen of the animal he wishes to kill with little more skill and experience than that required to aim his weapon correctly. This kind of hunting dates from the nineteenth century. Seals were not high in the list of species sought after by sportsmen of that age, but there are a great many records of such hunting of grey seals in Scotland and Ireland (e.g., Bell, 1874).

In Europe, trophy hunting persisted longest perhaps in Germany. In Schleswig-Holstein and Nieder Sachsen, registered professional seal hunters were allowed to organize the hunting of harbor seals in the German Wattenmeer. Sportsmen wishing to secure trophy specimens had to engage the services of one of these professionals, who would charge a basic fee to which would be added payments for the hire of boats, license fee for the seal taken, skinning and preparation of the pelt, and accommodation at the guide's house. These charges together might amount to between DM 300 and DM 500 for each seal taken (H. Eberhard Drescher, Institut für Haustierkunde, Universität Kiel, personal communication).

Because of the high financial reward, there was a tendency to take the first seal seen, to ensure that a specimen of some sort was obtained, and consequently a large part of the total take consisted of young pups. The early start of the permitted hunting season meant that some 40 percent of the total catch was taken during the nursing period, with consequent damaging disturbance of the breeding groups. Eventually, on the evidence of declining stocks, this type of hunting was banned, first in Nieder Sachsen in 1969 and then in 1973 in Schleswig Holstein.

Although trophy hunting had a damaging effect on the Wattenmeer harbor seals, whose stocks were threatened by other influences as well (Drescher, 1979), the opposite may have been the case with walrus trophy hunting in Alaska. There, the regulations by which Eskimo guides provided services to trophy hunters actually reduced the number of walruses killed while still allowing an attractive monetary return to the Eskimos. Because guides (and their boat crews) were not permitted to take game while guiding, each guided hunt eliminated a day's traditional boat hunting in which many walruses might be killed.

When walrus trophy hunting was prohibited in Alaska under the terms of the Marine Mammal Protection Act of 1972, the Eskimos, to satisfy their economic needs, responded by increasing their take of walruses to provide ivory for carvings (Kenyon, 1978). To prohibit wasteful killing, the sale of raw or unworked walrus ivory was prohibited, so the tusks of the walruses killed (which today represent the main and by far the most valuable product of the hunt) are now converted into carvings, generally of a traditional style. Some of them are of great artistic merit, though others far less so; all, however, are sold at high or very high prices. As the price of world ivory stocks, from whatever source, continues to rise, the economic return from this type of walrus hunting is likely to increase, always provided the walrus stocks can continue to support the harvest involved.

References

Bell, T. 1874. A History of British Quadrupeds including the Cetacea. 2nd edition. John van Voorst, London.

Boas, F. 1888. The Central Eskimo. Sixth Annual Rep. Bureau of Ethnology, Smithsonian Inst., Washington.

Capitan, L., Breuil, H., Burrinet, D. and Peyrony, D. 1906. L'Abri Mège. Une station magdalénienne à Teyat (Dordogne). Rev. de l'école d'anthropologie de Paris 6:196–212.

Clark, J.G.D. 1946. Seal-hunting in the Stone Age of north-western Europe: a study in economic prehistory. Proc. Prehist. Soc. 12(2):12–48.

Drescher, H.E. 1979. Biologie, Ökologie und Schutz der Seehunde im schleswig-holsteinischen Wattenmeer. Beiträge zur Wildbiologie Heft 1. Deutschen Jagdschutzverband. Meldorf. 73pp.

Gjessing, G. 1936. Nordenfjelske Ristninger og Malinger av den artiske Gruppe. Oslo.

Hickling, G. 1962. Grey seals and the Farne Islands. London. Routledge and Kegan Paul.

Joensen, A.H., Søndergaard, N-O and Hansen, E.B. 1976. Occurrence of seals and seal hunting in Denmark. Danish Rev. Game Biol. 10(1):1–20.

Kenyon, K.W. 1978. Walrus. Pp. 178–183 *in* Marine Mammals of Eastern North Pacific and Arctic Waters, ed. Delphine Haley. Pacific Search Press, Seattle.

Linnaeus, C. 1745. Öländska och Gothländska Resa 1741. (Öland and Gotland Journey, 1741.) trs. M. Åsberg and W.T. Stearn. Biol. J. Linn. Soc. 5(2):109–220.

Martin, M. 1703. A Description of the Western Isles of Scotland. (reprinted 1934) Stirling.

Møhl, U. 1970. Fangstdyrene ved de Danske strande: den zoologiske baggrund for harpunerne. KUML (Årbog for Tysk Arkaeologiske Selskab) 1970:297–329.

Nelson, R.K. 1969. Hunters of the Northern Ice. University of Chicago Press, Chicago and London.

Smith, T.G. and Stirling, I. 1975. The breeding habitat of the ringed seal (*Phoca hispida*). The birth lair and associated structures. Can. J. Zool. 53(9):1297–1305.

Söderberg, S. 1972. Gears and methods used for seal hunting in Sweden. ICES C.M. 1972/N:8 (mimeo).

CHAPTER THREE

Seal Furs from the North
Harp Seals and Pribilof Fur Seals

The difference between subsistence sealing and commercial sealing is not a sharp one. Subsistence sealing may be regarded as the exploitation of seal stocks by the hunter for products which he uses himself or perhaps trades for other direct-use products. The concept of investing in hunting equipment and engaging crews with the object of securing the largest catch of seals possible, to be sold in the market on a cash basis, introduced a new dimension into the exploitation of seals. Commercial sealing in this sense hardly existed at all before the beginning of the eighteenth century.

In the Northern Hemisphere three species, drawn from the three divisions of the Pinnipedia, were to bear the brunt of commercial sealing. These were the northern fur seal, *Callorhinus ursinus*, the walrus, *Odobenus rosmarus*, and the harp seal, *Phoca groenlandica*.* Walruses were exploited mostly as a secondary catch of some other hunt, usually for whales. Initially, the same was true of the harp seals.

The Harp Seal

Even as early as the sixteenth century, hunters from the Basque country, Brittany, and Jersey were catching harp seals in the Strait of Belle Isle, between Quebec and Newfoundland (Colman, 1949), though this activity was incidental to cod-fishing and whaling. It took the form of setting nets in the path of the seals during their southward migration in November, but few details of the hunt are available.

The full development of the harp sealing industry depended on the great concentration of the seals at their breeding season. It is therefore appropriate here to give a brief description of the biology of the harp seal.

The harp seal reproduces on the pack ice as three widely separated populations. One is located at Jan Mayen in the Arctic Ocean northwest of Norway, and another in the White Sea in the northwest corner of the USSR. The third population breeds in the northwest Atlantic around

* This species is often referred to as *Pagophilus groenlandicus*, but as Burns and Fay (1970) have very properly pointed out, there is no justification for separating *Pagophilus* from *Phoca* at the generic level.

Newfoundland, and is divided into two subpopulations, one on the southward-drifting pack ice on the "Front" east of southern Labrador and the other in the southern part of the Gulf of St. Lawrence. In terms of skull and body dimensions, the two eastern populations resemble each other more closely than either resembles the northwest Atlantic seals (Yablokov and Sergeant, 1963). Indeed, tagging studies (Sergeant, 1973b), though their data are sparse, suggest that exchange is frequent between the Jan Mayen and the White Sea populations, but rare between either of them and the northwest Atlantic population.

The timing of the breeding season varies slightly among the three populations, the seals in the White Sea breeding in late February and early March, the northwest Atlantic population a few days later, and the Jan Mayen seals in late March. As Sergeant (1976) points out, the differences in breeding date can be related to the onset of spring in the three localities. In view of the genetic exchange that may occur between the Jan Mayen and the White Sea seals, this implies that the pregnant females themselves exert control over the time at which they give birth to their pups. This would seem unorthodox behavior for a mammal, whose duration of gestation is usually reckoned to be a highly determined character, but the selective advantages of such a control are obvious for a mammal that lives in water but comes to land (or, in the case of the harp seal, to ice) to produce its pup.

Pupping, or whelping as it is generally known in the harp seal, takes place in large aggregations, or whelping patches, on the ice. The pregnant females haul out on the ice for a few days before producing their pups, and it seems that the presence of the early whelping females in the patches attracts those that are to whelp later, a demonstration of female gregariousness. The pups are born in a white pup coat or lanugo (initially stained yellowish by the amniotic fluid) which is retained for about two and a half weeks. The birthweight of about 9–10 kg increases to around 35 kg during the 16–18 day lactation period. This rapid growth has been explained as an adaptive response in an animal living on pack ice which is susceptible to premature break-up or rafting when winds press the ice heavily against shoals.

At the end of lactation, the cow abandons her pup and mates in the water with a male or males that have been consorting with the groups of females, and then leaves the ice for some weeks of intensive feeding to replenish body stores depleted by the strenuous lactation. Mating, like the rest of the social structure, appears to be unorganized. Sexual dimorphism is negligible. Males and females are found in equal numbers throughout the breeding season, and it is assumed that the seals are promiscuous or monogynous.

The pups moult the white lanugo gradually from about ten days after birth, being known as "ragged jackets" until at about three weeks old they are fully moulted into their yearling coats of gray with black spots. They are then known as "beaters," a corruption of "bêtes de la mer."

These young seals feed at first mainly on planktonic crustacea and move northwards through May and June. They are solitary at this stage, though all other age groups are highly social (except for the cows with pups, which maintain a spacing between individuals, and presumably the breeding males).

During the summer the seal herd migrates north, following the pack ice and exploiting a wide range of food. For the younger seals the smaller species are the most important, with Euphausiid crustaceans being especially significant. Older seals in the west Atlantic herds eat mainly capelin, *Mallotus villosus*; and polar cod, *Boreogadus saida*, is important at high latitudes. Herring, cod, and some shrimp, *Pandalus borealis*, are taken from species important to man, but not in quantities approaching the commercial catches (Sergeant, 1973a). In the Barents Sea, polar cod is more important than capelin, while in the Greenland Sea the amphipod crustaceans that the seals find beneath the ice are an important food (Sergeant, 1976).

Following the feeding period there is a slow, well-defined southward migration in early winter just ahead of the new ice. This migration involves all the adults and some of the immatures, though some younger juveniles remain in northern waters throughout the year.

The modal age of the attainment of sexual maturity in the now heavily exploited populations is four years, with the cows producing their first pup at the age of five. Harp seals are long-lived animals and can reach at least thirty years in both sexes. Natural mortality has been estimated at about 10 percent per year for both male and female adults (Winter, 1978), but Beddington (1979), using new techniques (described later), finds the best estimate to be 13.75 percent, much higher than previously quoted values. Young adult females remain in the spotted juvenile coat for some years before moulting to a coat with a pale saddle on the back; males pass quickly to a black saddle pattern with a black snout within one or two years.

The characteristics of the harp seal which have facilitated the development of the sealing industry are the localized nature of the breeding aggregations, where millions of seals can be found at one time in a restricted area, and the rapid growth of the pup before it takes to the water, leading to the build-up of a thick layer of valuable blubber (the industry initially was based on oil, rather than fur). Currently, the principal products of the hunt are the skins of the pups, either as white coats or as beaters (though adult skins are also valuable for leather), as well as the blubber of all age groups. Because of the value of these products, all populations of harp seals have suffered severely from human

Figure 3.1. Breeding grounds of the harp seal.

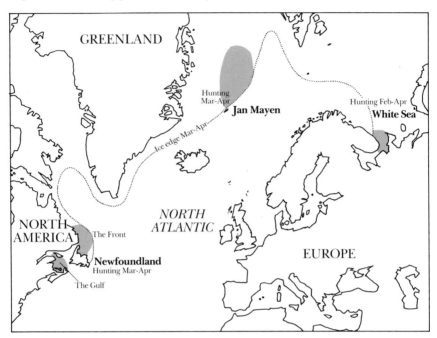

predation, and current populations represent only about 20 percent of what are believed to have been initial populations (Table 3.1).

Although commercial hunting probably has the longest history in the northwest Atlantic, it is convenient to deal with the White Sea and Jan Mayen stocks first. I will return later to the larger question of the Labrador harp seals.

Sealing at Jan Mayen

The Jan Mayen seals were first hunted by the arctic whalers. Pups, of course, were not available during the usual whaling season, which did not begin until about May, but as the Greenland right whales became less abundant, the whalers turned more and more to the seals. By the beginning of the eighteenth century the whalers were taking a large part of their cargoes in the form of seal skins and blubber. As early as 1720 ships set out from the Weser to visit the sealing grounds around Jan Mayen, and most of the northern European nations were engaged in the hunt.

By the middle of the nineteenth century, however, sealing at Jan Mayen had passed almost entirely to the Norwegians. It was from Os-

Table 3.1. Stock sizes of harp seals (thousands). The initial values are those assumed to have existed before the inception of large-scale hunting.

	Initial	Current
White Sea	3,000	500–700
Jan Mayen	3,000	100
Northwest Atlantic	3,000–4,000	1,000–1,500
Total	9,000–10,000	1,600–2,300

lofjord, especially from Tønsberg in Vestfold, that the Norwegian sealers sailed, and great fortunes were made in the nineteenth century. Svend Foyn, the pioneer of the techniques of modern whaling, was a Tønsberg sealer; with the profits he made from sealing voyages to Jan Mayen he financed the long years of his development of the first practical steam catcher and explosive harpoon. In the twentieth century, however, emphasis has shifted to ports in the west and north of Norway, Aalesund and Tromsø, which lie close to the sealing grounds.

At Jan Mayen the catch of harp seals fell from a maximum of around 120,000 in 1873 to around 20,000–40,000 in the present century. A Northeast Atlantic Sealing Commission, established in 1958, gradually brought in protection for females and immatures and in 1971 set a yearly total allowable catch (TAC) of 15,000. Adult protection was waived in 1974 and the TAC raised to 16,500. Catches over the period 1971–77 averaged 8,000 whitecoats, 3,300 beaters, and 1,200 older seals, or a total of only 12,500. The USSR briefly joined the hunting at Jan Mayen in 1956, but withdrew after 1966.

Sealing in the White Sea

Falling catches at Jan Mayen in the later nineteenth century (Figure 3.2) led the Norwegians to explore the sealing potential of the White Sea. Heavier vessels were required to penetrate the ice, but large stocks of seals were found. In the 1920s the USSR began using icebreakers to take seals in the White Sea. Their share of the catch overtook Norway's in about 1930 (Figure 3.3), and in 1946, following a great decline in catch that began in 1925, the USSR excluded Norway from the White Sea seal hunt.

Figure 3.2.   Catches of harp seals at Jan Mayen (West Ice), 1850–1969.
From Sergeant, 1976.

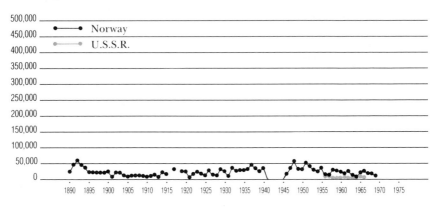

Figure 3.3.   Catches of harp seals at the White Sea, 1897–1969.
From Sergeant, 1976.

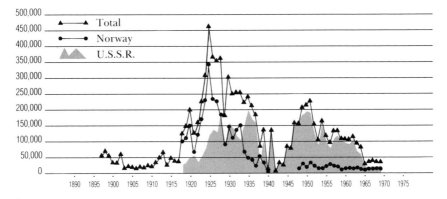

Figure 3.4.   Catches of harp seals at Newfoundland, 1893–1973.
From Sergeant, 1976.

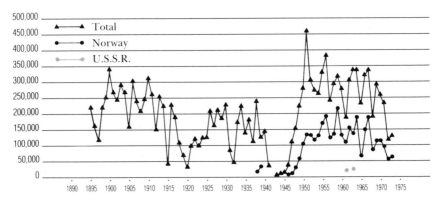

Most of the sealing in the White Sea is now carried out from Russian state farms around the coast. They have developed a technique in which they use helicopters to bring ashore ragged jackets to the farms, where they complete their moult (they do not require further food at this stage) before they are slaughtered. In this way better quality control can be exercised and humane killing and full use of the meat ensured (Sergeant, 1976).

Following evidence of a further decline in the 1960s, the White Sea herd was given fuller protection from 1965 to 1969, but thereafter limited quotas have been allowed, and the herd is said to be increasing. Current annual catches in the White Sea are of the order of 30,000 white coats, 4,500 beaters, and 5,500 older seals. Norway is allowed to take up to 14,000 seals as they move out of the White Sea.

Harp Seals in the Northwest Atlantic

Prior to the eighteenth century very few seals had been caught from Newfoundland as there were few settlers there and the crews that used the place as a summer fishing station did not arrive until after the seals had returned to the Arctic (Colman, 1937). Gradually, as the island was settled, the coastal net-fishery for seals developed, and towards the end of the eighteenth century the schooner was introduced as a means of getting out to the whelping patches. These vessels increased in size, up to 150–200 tons, and by the second quarter of the nineteenth century as many as three hundred schooners were sailing to the sealing grounds with 12,000 men, taking more than a half-million seals yearly. Catches of 680,000, 740,000 and 686,000 seals were reported in 1831, 1832, and 1844 respectively (these catches included some hood seals).

The schooners seriously reduced the numbers of seals, and profits fell so that the sealing fleet was halved in the 1860s, but in 1863 the introduction of steam ships breathed new life into the industry. The new ships were built in Dundee (and owed much to the experience there of whaling in the ice)—heavy vessels of 200–300 tons with steam auxiliary engines, whose wooden hulls were strong enough to withstand all but the worst ice pressure. Although steamers were more expensive to operate than sailing vessels, the steamers were better assured of penetrating the ice and getting a cargo of seals. Besides the steamers specially built for the job, many of the ships operating in Newfoundland waters in the late nineteenth century were properly arctic whalers on their way from Dundee or Peterhead to the Davis Straits in pursuit of Greenland right whales.

The wooden steamers were superseded early in this century by the introduction of larger steel ships with icebreaker bows which obviated the violent ice-ramming that had earlier been necessary. Just before the

1914–18 war there were nine steel ships and about a dozen of the old wooden steamers left (Colman, 1949).

Between the wars the Newfoundland sealing fleet, hurt by the Depression, was reduced to four vessels by 1932. The outbreak of war in 1939 further reduced sealing and actually brought it to a halt in 1943. Sealing recovered rapidly after the war, but this was largely due to the involvement of foreign-registry vessels. Superior technology in the late 1940s, when the old Newfoundland steamers were competing with Norwegian diesel-powered vessels, effectively killed the Newfoundland industry, though the Norwegians established companies in Canada to operate the sealing enterprises, employing mostly Newfoundlanders or Nova Scotians. The Russians made two trips to the Front ice in 1961 and 1963, but then withdrew.

Following the low pelagic catches of the war years and the introduction of more powerful sealing vessels, catches rose rapidly (Figure 3.4), reaching over 456,000 in 1951, and averaging 316,000 between 1951 and 1960 (Capstick et al., 1976). These were distributed between two major hunting categories: the large vessels (now only Canadian and Norwegian); and the landsmen, or shore-based hunters, who use small boats to reach the seals. The large vessel hunt operates in the whelping patches strictly within the limits of the officially appointed season, but the landsmen's hunt is more complex. Landsmen take seals opportunistically, and many take large numbers of adults and immatures.

Adult seals are shot by rifles whose ammunition must conform to strict standards, but the pups are killed by clubbing. In Canada a club shaped like a large baseball bat is used; the Norwegians use an instrument called a *hakapik* (pickaxe) or a *slagkrok* (a sort of heavy iron hook with a long handle). Several blows are usually struck, though the first usually renders the pup unconscious if it does not kill it outright. Both Canadian and Norwegian authorities issue stringent regulations about killing methods and the instruments to be employed. All are effective, but the hakapik is preferred. It has the advantage of inflicting wounds that are more readily recognizable to nonveterinarians as providing one clear criterion for humane killing—a smashed skull (Rowsell, 1975). After clubbing, the pup is turned on its back and cut down the midline to expose the major blood vessels to the flippers. These are cut and the pup allowed to bleed. Killed in this manner, the seal pup certainly suffers no more than an animal in a slaughterhouse, and probably far less, since prior stress is absent. However, to many people clubbing per se is inhumane, and there has been much public protest at the clubbing of baby seals (rather as though it would be more acceptable to shoot older ones!).

Frequent claims have been made that pups are skinned while they are still conscious or at least alive. While it is certainly possible that there are some psychotic sadists among the sealers (as there are in all walks of life), I believe that this sort of thing done deliberately, if it occurs at all, is vanishingly rare. Even if the sealers were completely uncaring of the suffering of the pups (which they are not), they must deal with large numbers of pups daily, and so their aim is to kill as quickly and as efficiently as possible. Anything else wastes valuable time. To attempt to skin a struggling pup on the ice would certainly put the sealer at risk of cutting himself with the skinning knife.

After killing and bleeding, the pups and adults are pelted and the skins brought back to the ship, where they are stored in chilled brine or treated with antioxidant before being taken to the processing plant at the end of the season for deblubbering and dressing. The landsmen make some use of the meat, particularly the flippers, but in general a large part of the potential product of the hunt is wasted.

In 1950 and 1951, when Canadian fishery scientists made their first attempts to assess the seal stocks, pup production was estimated at 645,000. This figure led to concern, since the catch in 1951 had been 456,000 seals, leaving only a small potential escapement (Fisher, 1952; Lavigne, 1979; Sergeant, 1973b). Despite warnings, hunting effort intensified. In 1962 helicopters and light aircraft were introduced to ferry sealers and skins between the shore and the ice; this was additional to the earlier practice of using spotter aircraft for locating the whelping patches.

In 1966 control of the sealing was placed in the hands of the International Commission on Northwest Atlantic Fisheries (ICNAF). The following year the Seals Assessment working group reported that the harp seal stock at the Front had sustained a marked decline in the previous fifteen years, though this could not be quantified accurately. In 1968 the duration of the hunt was shortened, killing of adults in the whelping patches was prohibited, and it was agreed to use planes for spotting only. In 1970 Canada closed the Gulf to airborne hunting.

Quota management was introduced in 1971 with a total allowable catch of 245,000 for both the Gulf and the Front, distributed as 100,000 each for the Canadians and the Norwegians and 45,000 for the landsmen. Despite the fact that the landsmen exceeded their allocation, the quota was not reached (Lavigne, 1979), perhaps indicating the scarcity of seals.

Meanwhile, the Canadian Department of the Environment set up a special committee, the Committee on Seals and Sealing (COSS), to report on seal stocks and their conservation. COSS recommended in 1972 that the harp seal hunt by the Canadians and Norwegians in the northwest Atlantic should be phased out by 1974 and followed by a six-year moratorium on sealing. These recommendations were not taken up, but in 1972 the TAC was reduced to 150,000 (a level which was maintained until 1976), and commercial sealing in the Gulf was banned altogether.

By this time several bodies were working on population assessments of the seals, and in 1975 their results were presented to the ICNAF meeting. No agreement could be reached as to what constituted the best estimate of pup production that year. A model by Benjaminsen and Øritsland (1975) suggested that population and sustainable yield had been greatly underestimated and that the TAC could safely be increased to 200,000. Other reports estimated the TAC to be in the range of from 90,000 to 127,000 (ICNAF, 1976). Eventually a quota for 1976 was set at 127,000, but the catch that year was 160,000, the overkill caused mainly by the landsmen exceeding their allocation.

The disagreement continued to prevail at the ICNAF meeting in 1976. A model based on cohort analysis and computer simulation of data from 1951 onwards indicated a stock that was slowly increasing and had been doing so since 1972. Pup production was estimated at from 310,000 to 340,000 and sustainable yield at 190,000 ± 22,000, assuming a harvesting pattern of 80 percent pups and 20 percent older animals (Lett and Benjaminsen, 1977). This assessment agreed broadly with two others (Winters, 1978; Benjaminsen and Øritsland, 1976) but differed widely from a model produced by the University of Guelph (Capstick et al., 1976), which indicated substantially lower sustainable yields of between 113,000 and 140,000, a difference caused by using higher natural mortality rates and a different starting value for the basis of the population projection.

In 1977 the quota was increased to 180,000, and in 1979 a best estimate of pup production of 352,000 was agreed with estimates of sustainable yield and replacement yield of 237,000 and 205,400 respectively (NAFO, 1979). The stated policy of those responsible for setting the quota is to set TACs at levels which will allow slow recovery to a target population of around 1.6 million seals. The TAC is explicitly intended to represent not a maximum sustainable yield (Mercer, 1977) but rather a sustainable yield at a level substantially below the maximum. It is assumed by quota setters that the northwest Atlantic harp seal population is continuing to increase after declining to a minimum level of about one million animals in 1972, but as Lavigne (1979) pointed out, this assumption was based only on indirect evidence of population abundance, and the conclusion awaits empirical corroboration.

Beddington and Williams (1979) examined the previously used modeling techniques, which all followed the same general sequence, though they differed in detail, and concluded that they tended to underestimate natural mortality rates and the degree of decline of the population. These authors designed a technique—the minimum chi-squared method—which they claim is free of biases. Their method depends on using the detailed catch-at-age data directly to form a cumulative chi-square for catch observed and catch expected according to a specified population model. Manipulating the parameters of the model varies the expected catch; the model is then made the basis of an algorithm to search for the minimum chi-squared and associated parameter values corresponding to the best fit. Once the values have been determined, estimates of annual pup production, etc., can be made.

Using their new model, Beddington and Williams found that adult mortality was 13.75 percent, a much higher value than most previous estimates, which clustered around 10–11 percent. The higher mortality indicated that the decline in both adult population size and pup production had been greater than hitherto thought. Clearly, the Beddington-Williams model needs to be carefully considered by those responsible for setting harp seal quotas if serious harm is not to be done to the population.

However, it is not only the size and mortality of the stock that are important in making useful predictions of the behavior of the herd. The concept of sustainable yields assumes a surplus of recruitment over mortality, and this will indeed be the case for most populations if the environment is suitable. A single-species model must assume stability (and adequacy) of the environment, yet a highly significant variable in the environment of the harp seal is the available food supply. Beddington and Williams (1979) have drawn attention to the importance of critical periods of food abundance to pregnancy rates and attainment of sexual maturity, both vital factors in calculating future recruitment.

With as euryphagous an animal as the harp seal, it is scarcely possible to consider the status of each potential food species separately. However, it is clear that fishery pressure in the northwest Atlantic has in-

Figure 3.5. Recent catches of capelin, *Mallotus villosus*, and shrimp, *Pandalus borealis*, in the North Atlantic. After Beddington and Williams, 1979.

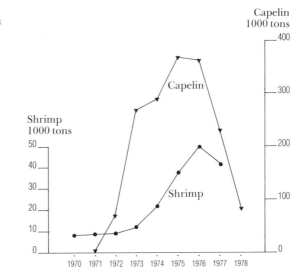

45

creased in recent years. Beddington and Williams have collected data relating to two commercial species, the shrimp *Pandalus borealis* and capelin, *Mallotus villosus*, both of which figure in the diet of harp seals (and many other higher predators) and both of which have suffered greatly increased fishing mortality in the past decade (Figure 3.5). The capelin fishery increased from about 6,000 tons in 1971 to around 360,000 tons in 1975 and 1976, before declining to less than 100,000 tons in 1978, with a predominance of immature fish in the catch (Fisheries and Environment Canada, 1978). Nursing female harp seals examined in 1978 were found to have lower energy stores than a similar sample obtained in 1976 (Innes et al., 1978). This may be only a coincidence; clearly harp seals can find other food resources besides capelin, but the general picture remains of increasing human predation on the food base of harp seal stocks. It is a subject I shall return to later.

Despite the uncertainties both in population modeling and in the general stability of the ecosystem of which the harp seal forms a part, the current (1980) quota for harp seals in the northwest Atlantic is set at 180,000, including an allowance of 10,000 for Greenland. The sealing season is fixed at from March 10 to April 24. In 1979 the catch was 158,319 harp seals. The value added to the Canadian economy in that year by the seal hunt was estimated at $9.5 million.

The Northern Fur Seal

While harp sealing was being established in the northwest Atlantic, the other of the world's two famous sealing industries was about to be established in the North Pacific. The northern fur seal, *Callorhinus ursinus*, was first known to science in 1742, when Georg Wilhelm Steller described it from Bering Island in the Commander Islands group. Although Steller found the seal was already an article of commerce in Kamchatka, the chief resource of the Russian fur traders was the skins of the sea otter, *Enhydra lutris*. As the sea otters became scarcer owing to heavy exploitation, the hunters began to search for the breeding place of the fur seals which they regularly observed on their migration paths in the spring and autumn. In 1786 St. George Island was discovered, and in the following year the other main island of the Pribilof group, St. Paul, was discovered. The Pribilofs and, to a lesser degree, the Commander Islands were the principal breeding grounds of the northern fur seal.

The northern fur seal ranges the cool waters of the North Pacific. Besides the breeding groups on the Pribilofs and the Commander Islands, there is a third group at Robben Island in the Sea of Okhotsk. A much smaller population, whose reappearance dates from the 1950s, is found on the central Kuril Islands, and a very small colony has been es-

Figure 3.6.   Breeding localities and approximate range of the northern fur seal.
From information supplied by C.H. Fiscus.

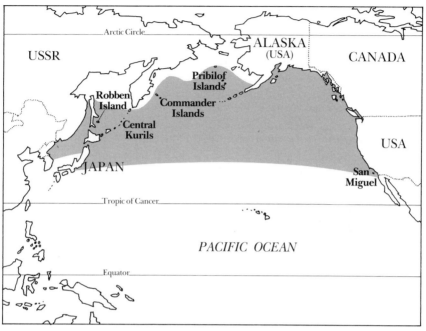

Table 3.2.   Abundance and distribution of northern fur seals
(Lander and Kajimura, 1976)

Locality	Population size (1000s)
Pribilof Islands, E. Bering Sea	1,300
Commander Islands, W. Bering Sea	265
Robben Island, Sea of Okhotsk	165
Kuril Islands, W. North Pacific	33
San Miguel Island, E. North Pacific	2

tablished since 1968 on San Miguel Island off California (Figure 3.6, Table 3.2). After breeding in the summer the seals leave the islands in October and November and migrate south (except for the San Miguel population). The Robben Island seals winter in the Sea of Japan; those from the Commander Islands move down the coast of Japan; the Pribilof Islands stock migrate down the North American coast. On both sides of the Pacific the southern limit of migration is about 32°N. The smaller seals, the females and younger males, make the longest migration, with the adult males probably staying in the vicinity of the breeding islands throughout the year (Lander and Kajimura, 1976).

The early history of sealing at the Pribilof Islands is imperfectly known. Perhaps 2.5 million seals were killed in the period 1786–1867 (Sims, 1906), and the killing at first was quite indiscriminate, with rival concerns vying for the greatest possible catches. The many early sealing firms were consolidated into the Russian-American Company in 1805 and some control established, including a closed season in 1806 and 1807. However, it was not until 1834 that the Russian overseers finally recognized the dangers of over-exploitation. From 1835 to 1867 the killing of females was forbidden and the killing of male seals on land restricted. These measures allowed the herd to recover, and by the time the United States purchased Alaska in 1867 the population numbered 2–2.5 million, within the range of the probable pre-exploitation population, and was sustaining an annual kill of several thousand males (Lander and Kajimura, 1976).

Although it was the intention of the U.S. government to maintain the policies of the Russians under which the seal herd had increased, sealing in the first years of the American administration was exceedingly heavy, perhaps reaching 329,000 in 1868 and 1869 (Osgood et al., 1915). In 1869 the Pribilofs were declared a special reservation for fur seals, and the Treasury sold the sealing rights to the Alaska Commercial Company. The company had to pay a rental and tax on each skin taken. Sealing was allowed only in June, July, September, and October, and the killing of females and seals younger than one year was forbidden. A total quota of 100,000 was set, and catches ranged from 71,884 to 99,408 between 1871 and 1889 (Roppel and Davey, 1965).

Most of those in charge of the Pribilof sealing operations evidently believed that a kill of 100,000 males each year was sustainable, though the basis for this reasoning is not clear. Elliott (1884) had estimated the total herd size at about three million seals, but this estimate was based on the calculation of the area occupied by the rookeries and the assumption that each seal required an average of 2 square feet. This assumption was, however, faulty, since it was shown in 1917 that the seals required something like an average of 6 square feet each (Hanna, 1918, in Roppel and Davey, 1965), thus cutting Elliott's population estimate by two-thirds, to a little over one million seals.

The expiration of the Alaska Commercial Company's lease in 1889 and the granting of a new lease to the North America Commercial Company gave an opportunity for more stringent conditions. The quota was reduced from year to year, varying from a high of 60,000 to a low of 7,500, though mostly in the range of 15,000–30,000. However, the kill on land was now a less significant drain on the resources of the herd than the kill of seals at sea. Shore-based sealing operations from 1890 to 1909 accounted for about 346,000 seals (70 percent of the permitted total quotas), while in the same period pelagic sealing took at least 659,875 seals (Riley, 1961), with an unknown number killed and lost.

Pelagic sealing had begun about 1886 and blossomed; by 1889 many specially equipped vessels were employed. Not only was the pelagic kill completely uncontrolled, it also most affected the seals the herd could least easily spare, the lactating females, thus directly affecting stock size. The United States seized a number of sealing vessels in the eastern Bering Sea in the late 1880s, and a controversy ensued with Great Britain (representing Canada, the flag state of many of the vessels concerned). This controversy was resolved when a treaty was concluded in 1892 by the Paris Tribunal of Arbitration, which banned sealing within 60 miles of the Pribilofs and forbade pelagic sealing from May 1 to July 31. These restrictions were ineffective since they covered neither the whole area of operation nor the whole season. The appearance of Japan as a major pelagic sealing nation exacerbated the situation.

Pelagic sealing continued until it expired for want of material. By 1911–12 the herd had been reduced to its lowest level, about 300,000 seals (Lander and Kajimura, 1976). At this point the governments of Great Britain (representing Canada), Japan, Russia, and the United States, meeting at the North Pacific Fur Seal Convention of 1911, agreed to prohibit pelagic sealing (except by aboriginal peoples using primitive equipment). They also devised a formula of compensation for relinquishing pelagic operations. Under this formula Japan and Canada were each to receive 15 percent of the sealskins taken on the Russian-owned Commander Islands and 15 percent of those taken on the American Pribilof Islands, while Canada, Russia and the United States each received 10 percent of the skins taken on Robben Island (which was then Japanese-owned) (Figure 3.7).

Under the North Pacific Fur Seal Convention the Pribilof herd had a chance to recover. Killing of seals (except to provide food for the Pribilof Aleuts) was banned from 1912 to 1917. Annual quotas of 35,000 were set from 1918 to 1920 and 30,000 thereafter until 1923, when it was set at 25,800. Since 1924 formal male quotas have not been set, the kill being limited by the availability of seals of a specified size (or age) in the permitted sealing season.

Kills rose steadily from 1923 to the 1940s, when a population plateau was reached. In 1940 Japan announced her intention to abrogate the Fur Seal Convention on the grounds that the increased number of seals were damaging her fisheries. Partly to appease Japan and partly to prevent further increase of the number of idle bulls, the harvest was increased in 1941. The war-time evacuation of the Pribilofs prevented a normal harvest in 1942, but this was made up in 1943 when 116,407 males were killed (together with 757 females), the largest controlled take of seals recorded.

Scientific research at the Pribilofs intensified from the 1940s on. Tagging schemes, photographic surveys, and other research provided data of a quality not before available. The method developed by Victor Scheffer (1950) to determine the age of seals accurately from a study of incremental layers in the cementum of the canine teeth allowed a great step forward in the scientific management of the fur seal herd. Pelagic and onshore collection of females enabled data to be assembled on age at sexual maturity, pregnancy rates, etc., while age-specific survival rates were successfully calculated for the first time. Much of this research was done by the United States in collaboration with the other members of the North Pacific Fur Seal Commission—Canada, Japan, and the USSR—who together with the United States had negotiated a new Interim Convention on Conservation of Fur Seals of the North Pacific Ocean in 1957 (amended by Protocol in 1963), whose object was to achieve the maximum sustainable productivity of the fur seals of the North Pacific so as to provide the greatest harvest year after year, with due regard to the productivity of other marine living resources. The reports of the Commission's researches (from 1962) are classics of biological investigation.

One of the earlier findings was that year-class survival of the seals was highly variable, and the variability was recognized as a by-product of a peak population (Roppel and Davey, 1965). This finding suggested that a reduction in the size of the herd would result in increased survival of the young so that total productivity could be maintained with a smaller breeding stock, a concept supported by findings in many other animal populations. Plans were made to reduce the number of breeding females (those aged 4 and older) by about one-third, from 1.2 million to 800,000. The reduction was expected to stabilize pup production at 500,000, a number which should have yielded annually a surplus of 60,000 males and 30,000 females (Roppel and Davey, 1965). Large kills of females were instituted in 1956 and continued until 1968, during which time 321,000 females were killed.

Critical examination by Chapman (1964, 1973) of the population estimations showed that the maximum sustainable yield values were about 55,000 males and at least 10,000 females, produced from a pup crop of 360,000 pups. However, despite the care which had gone into developing this strategy and analyzing the data, the population failed to yield the

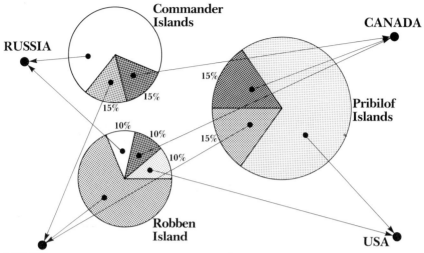

Figure 3.7.   Distribution of northern fur seal harvests under the formula drawn up by the North Pacific Fur Seal Convention of 1911.

Figure 3.8.   Average yearly kill of male northern fur seals on the Pribilof Islands, 1936–79 (five-year averages).

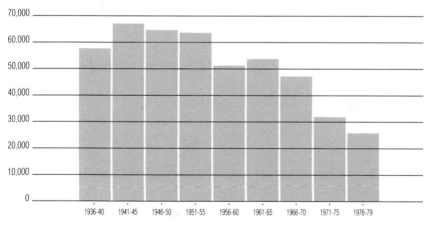

Figure 3.9.   Harems of northern fur seals on shore. (Photo: National Marine Fisheries Service, Pribilof Islands Program.)

expected harvests. From averages of over 50,000 male seals per year for the period 1951–65, the catch fell gradually to yearly averages of about 25,000 males in 1976–79 (Figure 3.8). This was interpreted by Lander and Kajimura (1976) as a lessened survival to harvestable age since the numbers of pups born in 1929–33 and in 1962–66 were very similar.

However, it is not easy to make direct comparisons, since there have been major changes in harvesting effort between the two periods under comparison. The designation of St. George Island in 1973 as a research sanctuary where no commercial sealing would take place reduced the stocks available to the sealers, while changes in season length, length of the working week for the harvest crews, and length limits of harvestable animals have all combined to complicate the picture (Engel et al., 1980). George Harry (personal communication) concluded that about 185 males were harvested per 1,000 pups born in 1926–37, and 180 males harvested per 1,000 pups born in 1965–75, indicating a very slight increase (if any) in natural mortality. York and Hartley (1980) showed that about two-thirds of the decline in estimated pup production could be attributed to a loss of reproductive females from the stock as a consequence of the female harvest. These included females removed directly, those that would have been born and survived to reproduce if the harvest had not taken place, and the progeny of both these groups. The remaining one-third of the decline might be due to systematic bias in the estimating procedure, though further research and analysis are needed to test this possibility.

The question is not yet resolved, but it is clear that the expected increase in productivity has not taken place and it is tempting to associate this with food availability. It has been suggested that changes in the species composition and reduction in stock size of the fur seals' food, caused by extensive commercial fishing in the Bering Sea, are responsible for the failure of the herd to increase its productivity in the expected way, perhaps because of the extra expenditure by nursing females of energy and time in search of food (ACMRR, 1978). However, as has been pointed out by Engel et al. (1980), this hypothesis of a reduced carrying capacity has not been proven, and the best explanation for declines in the population since 1957 remains the female harvest itself, coupled with changes in the male harvest effort. Since 1968, management policy at the Pribilof Islands has been to increase the escapement of young seals into the breeding stock.

Sealing at the Pribilofs is greatly facilitated by the habits of the seals and the topography of the islands. Some 80 percent of the herd is found on the southern and eastern beaches of St. Paul Island. The bachelor males, the segment of the herd from which the harvest is currently taken, haul out separately from the breeding seals, and it is a comparatively easy matter to drive groups from the beaches over the low grassy country to the killing fields.

The Aleut inhabitants of the islands (whose ancestors were brought over from the Aleutian Islands by the Russians) are employed in the sealing. Work starts at about three o'clock in the morning, when a crew of from 20 to 50 sealers proceed in trucks to a hauling ground. They work cautiously upwind between the seals and the water until several thousand are cut off and then drive the whole group to the killing ground. The seals must be driven slowly, as they are prone to heat exhaustion in the humid atmosphere of the Pribilofs.

At the killing ground the main group of seals is rested and small pods are separated. Seals outside the permitted limits are allowed to escape; the remainder are killed by a blow from a heavy hardwood pole or club, followed by exsanguination. The skin is slit open down the belly and cut around the head, tail, and foreflippers, and the carcass is then turned over on the grass to bleed. To remove the skin, one sealer pins the dead seal to the ground over the neck with a tool resembling a large fork, while other sealers using tongs rip off the skin, a technique that avoids knife cuts in the pelt.

Skins are transported by truck to the village processing plant, where they are washed in cold sea water, deblubbered, brined, and packed in salt. The carcasses are ground and frozen for use as ranch-mink food. Final processing of the skins, which involves further washing, dehairing, tanning, and dyeing, is done at the Fouke Fur Company's plant at St. Louis.

The dressed skin of the Pribilof fur seal is a valuable fur, but the economics of the sealing operation are not simply explained in terms of the product produced. Overhead and associated costs are high, and the situation is complicated by the fact that there is no other obvious employment available for the Aleut inhabitants of the islands.

The management of the Pribilof fur seal herd in the past has rightly been an object of admiration by wildlife biologists. Colin Bertram in 1950 wrote: "One can give no higher praise than sincerely to hope that planning and agreement for the future may be as benificent and rational as has been the administration and conservation of the herd during the last forty years." Bertram's hopes have been well fulfilled in the thirty years since he wrote those words.

References

ACMRR. 1978. Report of the Advisory Committee on Marine Resources Research Working Party on Marine Mammals, 1. FAO. Rome.

Beddington, J.R. and Williams, H.A. 1979. The structure and management of the N.W. Atlantic harp seal. Draft Rep. to the U.S. Marine Mammal Commission. 141pp.

Benjaminsen, T. and Øritsland, T. 1975. Adjusted estimates for year class survival and production with estimates of mortality for northwest Atlantic harp seals. ICNAF Working paper 75/XII/3.

Benjaminsen, T. and Øritsland, T. 1976. Age group frequencies, mortality and production estimates for NW Atlantic harp seals updated from samples collected off Newfoundland-Labrador in 1976. ICNAF Working Paper 1976/X/1.

Bertram, G.C.L. 1950. Pribilof fur seals. J. Arctic Inst. America 3(2):75–85.

Burns, J.J. and Fay, F.H. 1970. Comparative morphology of the skull of the ribbon seal, *Histriophoca fasciata*, with remarks on the systematics of Phocidae. J. Zool., Lond. 161:363–394.

Capstick, C.K., Lavigne, D.M. and Ronald, K. 1976. Population forecasts for northwest Atlantic harp seals, *Pagophilus groenlandicus*. Int. Comm. Northwest Atl. Fish. Res. Doc. 76/X/132. 25pp.

Chapman, D.G. 1964. A critical study of Pribilof fur seal population estimates. Fish. Bull., U.S. Fish. Wildl. Serv. 63:657–669.

Chapman, D.G. 1973. Spawner-recruit models and estimation of the level of maximum sustainable catch. Rapp P.-v. Réun. Cons. Int. Explor. Mer 164:325–332.

Colman, J.S. 1937. The present state of the Newfoundland seal fishery. J. anim. Ecol. 6:145–159.

Colman, J.S. 1949. The Newfoundland seal fishery and the second World War. J. anim. Ecol. 18:40–46.

Elliott, H.W. 1884. Report on the seal islands of Alaska. U.S. Govt. Printing Office. Washington. 188pp.

Engel, R.M., Lander, R.H., Roppel, A.Y., Kozloff, P., Hartley, J.R., and Keyes, M.C. 1980. Population data, collection procedures, and management of the northern fur seal, *Callorhinus ursinus*, of the Pribilof Islands, Alaska. National Marine Mammal Laboratory, Northwest and Alaska Fisheries Center, Nat. Mar. Fisheries Serv., NOAA, Seattle.

Fisher, H.D. 1952. Harp seals of the northwest Atlantic. Fish. Res. Bd. Can. Atlantic Biol. Stn. Circ. 20.

Fisheries and Environment Canada. 1978. Conservation concern prompts closure of North Atlantic capelin fisheries. News Release FMS-HQ-NR-35, November 23, 1978. Fisheries and Ocean, Information Branch, Ottawa. 2pp.

ICNAF. 1976. Report of special meeting of Panel A (Seals). 9th Special Commission Meeting, December 1976. ICNAF Summary Doc. 76/XII/47.

Innes, S.R., Stewart, E.A. and Lavigne, D.M. 1978. Growth in northwest Atlantic harp seals, *Pagophilus groenlandicus*: density-dependence and recent changes in energy availability. Can. Atl. Fish. Sci. Advisory Comm. Working Paper 78/46.

Lander, R.H. and Kajimura, H. 1976. Status of northern fur seals. Advisory Committee on Marine Resources Research, Scientific Consultation on Marine Mammals, Bergen. ACMRR/MM/SC/34, 50pp.

Lavigne, D.M. 1979. Management of seals in the northwest Atlantic Ocean. Trans. 44th N. Amer. Wildl. Conf. Pp. 488–497.

Lett, P.F. and Benjaminsen, T. 1977. A stochastic model for the management of the northwestern Atlantic harp seal (*Pagophilus groenlandicus*) population. J. Fish. Res. Bd. Can. 34:1155–1187.

Mercer, M.C. 1977. The seal hunt. Information Branch Fish. and Mar. Serv., Dep. Fish. Envir. Ottawa. 25pp.

NAFO. 1979. Report of the standing committee on fishery science (STACFIS). Special meeting on shrimp and seals. November 1979. NAFO SCS Doc. 79/XI/2. HS/WP 25.

Osgood, W.H., Preble, E.A. and Parker, G.H. 1915. The fur seals and other life of the Pribilof Islands, Alaska, in 1914. U.S. Bur. Fish., Bull. 34.

Riley, F. 1961. Fur seal industry of the Pribilof Islands, 1786–1960. U.S. Fish. Wildl. Serv., Fish. Leaflet 516. v + 14pp.

Roppel, A.Y. and Davey, S.P. 1965. Evolution of fur seal management in the Pribilof Islands. J. Wildl. Manage. 29(3):448–463.

Rowsell, H.C. 1975. Harp and hooded seal fisheries on the Front, March 17th–30th 1975. Report to the Committee on Seals and Sealing. 88pp.

Scheffer, V.B. 1950. Growth layers on the teeth of Pinnipedia as an indication of age. Science, N.Y. 112:309–311.

Sergeant, D.E. 1973a. Feeding, growth and productivity of the northwest Atlantic harp seals (*Pagophilus groenlandicus*). J. Fish. Res. Bd. Can. 30:17–29.

Sergeant, D.E. 1973b. History and present status of populations of harp and hooded seals. Biol. Conserv. 10:95–117.

Sergeant, D.E. 1976. Transatlantic migration of a harp seal, *Pagophilus groenlandicus*. J. Fish. Res. Bd. Can. 30:124–125.

Sims, E.W. 1906. Report on the Alaska fur seal fisheries. U.S. Congress House, 59th Congr., 2nd Sess. Doc. 251. Govt. Printing Office, Washington. 59pp.

Winters, G.H. 1978. Production, mortality and sustainable yield of northwest Atlantic harp seals (*Pagophilus groenlandicus*). J. Fish. Res. Bd. Can. 35:1249–1261.

Yablokov, A.V. and Sergeant, D.E. 1963. Cranial variation in the harp seal (*Pagophilus groenlandicus* Erxleben 1777). Zoologicheskii Zhurnal 42:1857–1865. (Fish. Res. Bd. Can. Transl. Serv. No. 485).

York, A.E. and Hartley, J.R. 1980. The effect of a female fur seal harvest on pup production. Unpubl. Manuscr. 19pp. National Marine Mammal Laboratory, Northwest and Alaska Fisheries Center, Nat. Mar. Fisheries Serv. NOAA, Seattle.

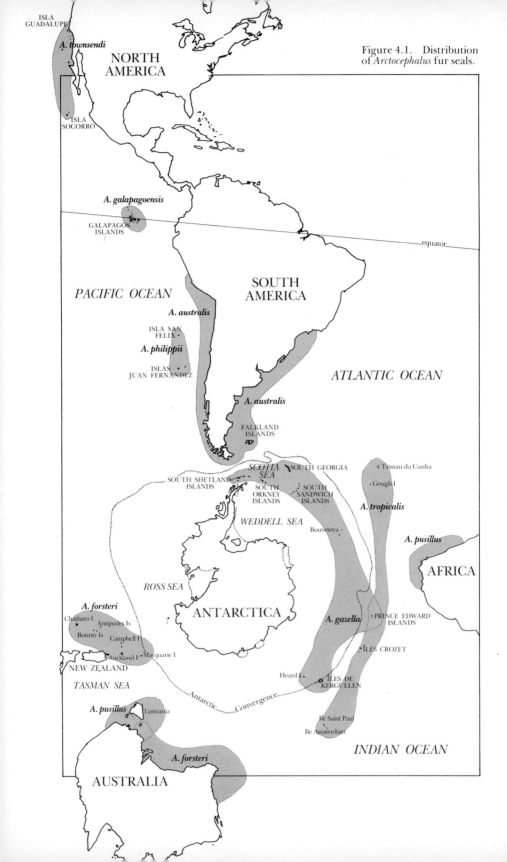

Figure 4.1. Distribution of *Arctocephalus* fur seals.

CHAPTER FOUR

The Fur Seals
Of the Southern Hemisphere

The fur seals of the genus *Arctocephalus* form a fairly compact group of eight species, all but one of which are found in the Southern Hemisphere. For that reason they are often referred to as the "southern fur seals"—an unfortunate term, as it leads to confusion with one of the species, *Arctocephalus australis*, the southern fur seal in the strict sense.

Confusion is indeed a characteristic of man's study of these seals. There can scarcely have been a group of large mammals (except perhaps for some of the odontocete genera such as *Stenella* or *Mesoplodon*) whose taxonomy has been more involved. Readily distinguishable species have been lumped together under the same name, and the conspecificity of two populations of the most aberrant member of the genus ignored. The animals themselves seem determined to puzzle the taxonomists further by producing natural hybrids between very distinct species (see Condy, 1978). It was not until 1971, when a joint paper by Repenning, Peterson, and Hubbs (Repenning et al., 1971) was published, that the matter was finally resolved and we can now with reasonable certainty correctly assign a member of the genus *Arctocephalus* to its species.

Fortunately the distribution of the eight species is reasonably exclusive, though *A. tropicalis* and *A. gazella* breed sympatrically (and hybridize) on Marion Island (in the Prince Edward Islands), while South Australia has populations of both *A. forsteri* and *A. pusillus doriferus*. At Macquarie Island in the Indian Ocean the majority of fur seals are *A. forsteri*, but *A. tropicalis* has been described from there and may have been the original inhabitant (Csordas, 1962).

The *Arctocephalus* seals are found in their greatest abundance in regions where cool, nutrient-rich water currents promote high primary productivity and hence large stocks of the fish and invertebrates on which the seals feed. Thus the vast stocks of the Juan Fernandez fur seal, *A. philippii*, were once found in the Humbolt Current; the South African fur seal, *A. pusillus pusillus*, in the Benguela Current; and the antarctic fur seal, *A. gazella*, around South Georgia. The general distribution is shown in Figure 4.1.

Four species are associated with the Pacific coast of the Americas. *A. townsendi* is now known only from Isla Guadalupe as a breeding species, but old sealing records and subfossil remains indicate a distribution on the mainland coast as well. *A. galapagoensis* is confined to a few sites at the Galapagos; though it was once much more abundant than it is now, there is no indication that it ever had a wider distribution. *A. philippii* lingers on as a few individuals on the Juan Fernandez archipelago. Alone of this group *A. australis*, the southern or South American fur seal, has a wider distribution, stretching from Peru around Cape Horn up to southern Brazil, taking in the Falkland Islands.

The other four species all have wide distributions. *A. pusillus*, the largest and most distinct member of the group, occurs as a western population on the south and southwest coast of southern Africa. Another population of the same species is found in Australia in New South Wales, around Tasmania, in the Bass Straits, and along the coast of Victoria. This subspecies has been described variously as *A. forsteri*, *A. doriferus*, and *A. tasmanicus*; it is now recognized as *A. pusillus doriferus*. The real *A. forsteri*, the New Zealand fur seal, is found in the southern part of South Island, New Zealand, and its associated offshore islands; on Macquarie Island; and from Western Australia to South Australia, where it meets *A. pusillus doriferus*.

The remaining two species have complementary distributions around oceanic islands in differing climatic zones. *A. tropicalis*, the Amsterdam Island fur seal, is found at Gough Island in the South Atlantic, the Prince Edward Islands, and the Crozet Islands in the Indian Ocean, with an occasional extension to Macquarie Island, where, as noted, it may have been the indigenous fur seal. *A. gazella*, the antarctic fur seal, is found in greatest abundance at South Georgia, with other populations at the South Shetlands, South Orkneys, South Sandwich Islands, and Bouvetøya, Kerguelen, and Heard islands. Its distribution thus lies south of the Antarctic Convergence within the cold antarctic surface water, except for the population at Kerguelen and the few individuals that breed on Marion Island.

Prior to the eighteenth century these seals were all but undisturbed by man. There is evidence that the substantial population of Guadalupe fur seals existing in pre-Columbian times were regularly hunted, together with other pinnipeds, by the aborigines living in the Channel Islands area (Walker and Craig, 1979). In South America the sparse populations of Indians used *A. australis* as a source of food and skins as the Tasmanian aborigines used *A. forsteri*. Many of the seal populations were established on remote oceanic islands unknown to primitive man. Gough Island, the Falklands, South Georgia, the Juan Fernandez Islands: these places and many others supported vast colonies of fur seals which, since the time their forebears first gathered to form the initial breeding nuclei, had been totally undisturbed by man.

This situation, of course, was unlikely to continue. We cannot be sure when the first organized hunting of *Arctocephalus* fur seals began on a commercial basis. In Uruguay sealing began shortly after the discovery of the country by Juan Diaz de Solfs in 1515. After his death his crew made a cargo of fur seal skins to be sold in the market in Seville (Vaz Ferreira, 1979). Thus began the longest commercial exploitation of any fur seal—the Uruguayan fur sealing industry is still operating today. In South Africa commercial hunting of fur seals began about three hundred years ago (Rand, 1972). These operations were relatively small-scale affairs. The real onslaught was to begin when the ships of the South Sea whalers began to roam the oceans of the Southern Hemisphere and located the fur seals in their hitherto secure breeding haunts.

Yankee whalers first crossed the equator in search of fresh sperm whaling grounds in 1774. A few years later their vessels were cruising along the South American coast as far south as Patagonia, and around Tristan da Cunha and the Falkland Islands. It was here that the first itinerant southern sealing began. The first recorded vessel to fit out especially for sealing was the ship *States*, owned by a lady named Haley of Boston. The *States*, a huge ship of 1,000 tons, set out soon after the end of the Revolutionary War in 1775 and secured a cargo of 13,000 fur seal skins from the Falklands. These were sold in New York for 50 cents apiece, but resold in China for five dollars (Eben Townsend, quoted in Clark, 1887). The success of the *States* naturally attracted others to this enterprise, and by the end of the eighteenth century the main sealing grounds of the Falklands, South America, the Juan Fernandez Islands, New Zealand, the Bass Straits, South Georgia, and Kerguelen had been discovered and heavily exploited (Clark, 1887; summary in Bonner, 1968).

Prior to about 1815 the trade consisted of carrying the skins to Canton, where they were sold and cargoes of Chinese goods (often tea and porcelain) purchased with the proceeds. For the "China trade" the seals were flayed and the skins pegged out on the ground to dry. After drying they were packed in the hold. "While aboard ship [the skins] must be frequently shifted and beat to keep the worms out," wrote Eben Townsend in 1797. According to Clark (1887), in China the skins were used in the manufacture of leather and "the fur was cut off clean and thrown away as useless." I think this is a misunderstanding. Air-dried skins that had crossed the equator in slow sealing vessels would not have been likely to produce good leather, no matter how assiduously they had been beaten to keep the worms out! It seems more probable that the Chinese were interested primarily in the fur for manufacturing felt garments, just as beaver skins were used for felt in Europe. For this purpose air-dried skins would have served adequately; the mixture of long, stiff guard hairs and fine underfur fibers would have made a strong felt.

The development of southern fur sealing in the last two decades of the eighteenth century showed the effects of the market governing the trade. The existence of one of the largest colonies—that at Juan Fernandez—had been known since 1683, when Dampier (1729) wrote:

> Seals swarm around the island of John Fernando as if they had no other place in the world to live in; for there is not a Bay nor Rock that one can get ashoar on, but is full of them. . . . those at John Fernando's have a fine thick, short furr; the like of which I have not taken notice of anywhere but in these Seas. Here are always thousands, I might say possibly millions of them, either sitting in the Bays or going or coming in the Sea around the Island, which is covered with them (as they lie at the top of the Water playing and sunning themselves) for a Mile or two from the shore. . . . A blow on the Nose soon kills them. Large ships might here load themselves with Seals Skins, and Trane-oyl; for they are extraordinary fat.

Dampier's account of the seals does not seem to have attracted much attention until after the first Nantucket whalers rounded the Horn into the Pacific in 1791 (following the English whaler *Emelia*, which had led the way in 1789), by which time a good market for the seals had been established in China. In the same year the sealing brigantine *Hancock* sealed at Masafuera, the main island of the Juan Fernandez group. The main slaughter commenced in 1797. In 1798 Captain Edmund Fanning of the ship *Betsy* sold 100,000 skins in Canton, nearly all from Masafuera, and estimated that between 500,000 and 700,000 seals still remained (Fanning, 1924). Delano (in Clark, 1887) estimated that more than 3 million skins had been carried to Canton from Juan Fernandez in the space of seven years, and that 14 vessels had been at the island at one time killing seals. By 1807 the business of fur sealing was said to be scarcely worth following at Masafuera, and by 1824 the island, together with its neighbor Mas a Tierra, "was almost entirely abandoned by the animals" (Morrell, 1832).

Perhaps I could pause here to consider this phrase. It is strange to read again and again in sealers' accounts that the seals had abandoned the rocks. Clearly, what had happened in these cases was that the seals, remaining faithful to their now-insecure breeding grounds returned to be greeted with a sealer's club and death. Perhaps by their euphemism the sealers salved their consciences and kept alive the hope that they yet might find the rocks whither the seal herds had departed.

A few more seals were taken from the Juan Fernandez Islands through the nineteenth century (Hubbs and Norris, 1971), but by 1968 Rice and Scheffer (1968), in preparing their list of marine mammals of the world, considered the Juan Fernandez fur seal as perhaps extinct.

Although the Juan Fernandez Islands and their fur seals were known long before major exploitation began, this was not generally the case elsewhere; as a rule exploitation swiftly followed discovery. The invention around 1812 of a means of dressing the skins in London so as to produce furs of high quality, was an added inducement to the sealers in their search for new seal colonies.

Secrecy was an important ingredient for success (and has considerably hampered research into the history of the industry). When Captain Fanning, using the original discoverer's map, rediscovered the Crozet Islands and their fur seal herds, he left at the Prince Edward Islands information regarding their location for the use of another vessel of the same owners. Following instructions from his owners, he erected a marker of stones but buried the record thirty feet to the northeast of it. The ruse was successful. When the ship for whom the information was intended arrived, the crew found that the cairn had been demolished and a deep hole excavated in the place where it had been, but they were able to find the packet easily enough.

As another example I may cite Captain Althearn (in Clark, 1887), writing to a friend about to set off on his first sealing voyage to the Bounty Rocks (Bounty Island), probably around the late 1870s. Althearn instructed his friend what he should do should he have the good fortune to discover an undisturbed colony of seals:

> If you got out there early and saw a great show of seals, I should get as many on board as I could without running any risk of not getting back in time. I would leave on the rocks all the men that I thought would blab; go to the most convenient port, ship my skins, get what I needed [more salt] and go back to the rocks, and finish up the season and go to Valparaiso without touching at New Zealand, and I should expect to have another season without company. . . . You will remember that you cannot get all the seal from a rookery in one season. If you get 3000 the first season you may expect to get 1000 or more the next, and in the same proportion for a larger or smaller number.

Many men were left on rocks as Althearn suggested, and in some cases their ships never returned for them. Althearn, despite his seeming callousness, was a kind and considerate captain who gave careful instructions on avoiding sickness by having the men eat plenty of seal meat. If they showed overt symptoms of scurvy they were to be given raw seal meat, soaked in vinegar.

No major discoveries of fur seals were made after the second decade of the nineteenth century, and the trade declined, though occasional successful voyages were made when a rookery that had been left undisturbed for several years was revisited. Fur sealing at the islands died out with the disappearance of the last whaling ships.

The cycle of discovery, near-extermination, and subsequent recovery can be illustrated by the history of the exploitation of the antarctic fur seal, *A. gazella*, at South Georgia and the islands farther south. South Georgia was first visited by Captain James Cook on January 17, 1775: "Seals, or sea-bears, were pretty numerous. They were smaller than those at Staten Island; perhaps the most of those we saw were females, for the shore swarmed with young cubs" (Cook, 1777). The first sealing voyage to South Georgia of which anything definite is known (although Roberts [1958] mentions voyages from 1778) was some time between

1790 and 1792, when two vessels under Captains Daniel Green and Roswell Woodward were fitted out for a sealing voyage to the Falklands and obtained part of their cargos at South Georgia (Clark, 1887). In 1791 an English sealer, the *Ann*, with Captain Pitman, visited South Georgia, and there may have been other vessels there that year. Sealing developed rapidly and reached a peak in the 1800–01 season, when 17 American and British vessels were working the island (Fanning, 1924). The total catch that year was 112,000 skins, of which Fanning's ship *Aspasia* succeeded in obtaining no less than 57,000. By 1822 Weddell (1825) calculated that at least 1,200,000 fur seal skins had been taken from South Georgia alone and that the species was virtually extinct there.

Meanwhile, however, another great refuge of the species was to be found some 1,300 km to the southwest. On February 18, 1819, the brig *Williams* of Blyth in Northumberland (Captain William Smith), blown off her course while on a trading voyage between Buenos Aires and Valparaiso, discovered the New South Shetland Islands (Jones, 1975). This was to be the last major discovery of any group of *Arctocephalus* fur seals. News of the discovery soon leaked out, and by the subsequent sealing season (1819–20) three vessels—the Argentinian *San Juan Nepomuceno*, the British *Espirito Santo*, and the Stonington sealer *Hersilia*—all made good hauls (Clark, 1887; Bruce, 1920). The following season sealers flocked to the South Shetlands, at least 47 American and British vessels working the beaches in 1820–21. (It is pleasing to note that Smith managed to get a cargo of 38,000 for his share.) The next season there were 44 vessels, though by that time the stock had so declined that many went back practically empty-handed. The highest catch was in 1820–21, when about a quarter of a million seals were taken and many thousands killed and lost. Weddell (1825) wrote:

> The quantity of seals taken off these islands, by vessels from different parts, during the years 1821 and 1822, may be computed at 320,000, and the quantity of sea-elephant oil at 940 tons. This valuable animal, the fur seal, might, by a law similar to that which restrains fishermen in the size of the mesh of their net, have been spared to render annually 100,000 furs for many years to come. This would have followed from not killing the mothers till the young were able to take the water; and even then, only those which appeared to be old, together with a proportion of the males, thereby diminishing their total number, but in slow progression. This system is practised at the River of Plata. The island of Lobos, in the mouth of that river, contains a quantity of seals, and is farmed by the Governor of Monte Video, under certain restrictions, that the hunters shall not take them but at stated periods, in order to prevent the animals from being exterminated. The system of extermination was practised, however, at Shetland; for whenever a seal reached the beach, of whatever denomination, he was immediately killed, and his skin taken; and by this means, at the end of the second year the animals became nearly extinct; the young, having lost their mothers when only three or four days old, of course all died, which at the lowest calculation exceeded 100,000.

We can see in Weddell's complaint and suggested remedy the foundation for some sort of controlled sealing on a sustainable basis. The problem, of course, was that the sealers at the South Shetlands, unlike those at Montevideo, recognized no authority competent to impose a law. Had one gang refrained from killing a suckling cow, another would certainly have taken her. Weddell realized this, abandoned restraint, and played his part in hastening the destruction of the seals.

A visitor to the South Shetlands in 1829 was greatly impressed with the wanton destruction of the seal stocks. Webster (1834) wrote:

> The harvest of the seas has been so effectually reaped, that not a single fur seal was seen by us, during our visit to the South Shetland group; and although it is but a few years back since countless multitudes covered the shores, the ruthless spirit of barbarism slaughtered young and old alike, so as to destroy the race. Formerly 2000 skins a week could be procured by a vessel; now not a seal is to be seen.

The more enterprising of the sealers, unable to obtain a cargo at the South Shetland Islands, searched farther afield and discovered and depleted the smaller stocks of fur seals at the South Orkney Islands, South Sandwich Islands, and Bouvetøya.

In South Georgia there was a brief recrudescence of fur sealing in the 1870s. The schooner *Flying Fish* took 500 skins in 1870 and the *Franklin* 1,450 in 1874. The following season five vessels could obtain only 600. In 1876 the situation was even worse, with four vessels securing 110. In 1892 the *Franklin* revisited South Georgia and took 135 fur seals, "none, however, coming from the old rookeries" (Buddington, in Allen, 1899). George Comer visited South Georgia in 1885 and 1886, either in the *Express* (Roberts, 1958) or the *Era* (Murphy, 1948), or perhaps in both, but "did not get a seal and saw only one" (Comer, in Allen, 1899). The following season he had better luck. He got three. The last of the old fur sealers to visit South Georgia seems to have been the brig *Daisy* of New York (Captain Benjamin Cleveland) in 1907 (Murphy, 1948), which took a cargo of 170 furs (Larsen, 1920).

There was a similar revival at the South Shetlands. In 1852 a vessel took 500 fur seals there, but there were no further recorded voyages until 1871–72, when three schooners took 8,000 furs; the following season eight vessels took 10,000. Williams (1888) wrote:

> In 1872, fifty years after the slaughter in the South Shetland Islands, the localities before mentioned were all revisited by another generation of hunters, and in the sixteen years that have elapsed they have gleaned every beach and searched every rock known to their predecessors and found a few secluded and inhospitable places before unknown, and the result of all the toil and daring for the years scarcely amounted to 45,000 skins and not even a remnant now remains save on the rocks off the pitch of Cape Horn. . . . So in wretched and wanton destruction has gone forever from the southern seas a race of animals useful to man and a possible industry connected with them.

Fortunately for the seals, Williams was wrong in his gloomy predictions. We now know that not one species of the *Arctocephalus* fur seals was exterminated by the sealers, though some isolated populations appear to have been totally wiped out. Even the South Shetlands were not stripped quite bare in the harvesting to which Williams refers; Clark lists another cargo of 1,860 furs brought back from there in 1879. However, this seems to have been the last record of fur seals at the South Shetlands for three-quarters of a century.

Both South Georgia and the South Shetlands were visited by the modern generation of steam whalers early in the twentieth century, so that opportunities for sighting those fur seals that remained were good. It is fairly certain that at South Georgia the lingering remnants of those fur seals that survived the most recent harvesting in 1907 were located at Bird Island and the Willis group, which lie off the northwestern extremity of the mainland of South Georgia. Despite searches for fur seals in likely places none was found until 1915, when a young male was "accidentally" shot by a party of elephant sealers at the southeastern end of the island (Bonner, 1968). In 1919 five fur seals were seen on Bird Island. Further sightings occurred, the most significant of which were in 1933, when 38 fur seals were seen on Bird Island, including what was probably a moulted pup of the year, and in 1936 when 59 fur seals, of which 12 were pups, were sighted in the same place (summary in Bonner, 1968).

Thereafter interest waned in fur seals at South Georgia, until in 1956 I was fortunate enough to be given the opportunity to make another search for their breeding places. I managed to locate thriving colonies of fur seals at both Bird Island (Figure 4.3) and on Main Island in the Willis group (Bonner, 1958). In subsequent seasons regular visits were made to Bird Island and pup production carefully monitored until 1963–64, during which period it approximately doubled (Figure 4.2). After an intermission in active field work, pup production monitoring began again in 1971–72 and has since continued as part of the research program of British Antarctic Survey. The background of existing knowledge of the biology and previous history of these animals, together with the accessibility of their colonies at South Georgia and the fact that the seals show very little fear of man and so are easy to observe, make the South Georgia fur seals a good subject for the study of the dynamics of an expanding large mammal population (Payne, 1977).

In the early stages of this work there was little difficulty in assessing the annual production of pups. Over 90 percent of the births occur in a three-week period and the date by which 50 percent are born varies by not more than one day. However, with increasing numbers of pups born on the beaches, density-dependent errors (those associated with the difficulty of finding all the pups, or of counting them on densely crowded

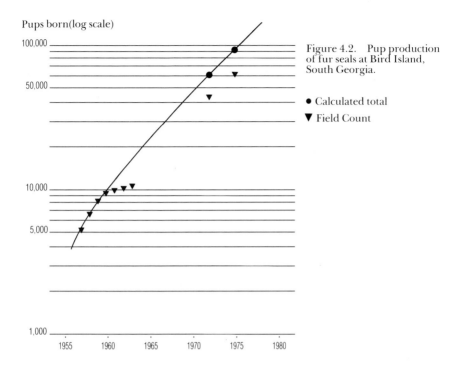

Pups born(log scale)

Figure 4.2. Pup production of fur seals at Bird Island, South Georgia.

● Calculated total
▼ Field Count

beaches) began to creep in, leading to counts below the proper total. Initially in the 1956–62 series of counts I interpreted this as an indication that the rate of increase was beginning to fall off with increasing density (Bonner, 1968). In fact, however, more careful counts later showed that the first observed rate of increase had been largely maintained.

In 1972 Payne used a capture-recapture method, derived from that of Chapman and Johnson (1968), to make an estimate of the under-counting error in direct field counts. A well-defined study area in which about 10,000 pups were born was selected. Pups were marked by shearing a patch of guard hair from the top of their heads to expose the pale grey underfur. After marking about 40 percent of the pups present (in an unselective manner), a week was allowed to elapse to permit the marked pups to disperse evenly. Observers then counted the numbers of marked pups in blocks of 25 animals, allocating the blocks in proportion to the overall distribution of pups.

The degree of undercount of live pups (K) was estimated by adjusting the capture-recapture estimate of the live pup population ($\bar{N}$) at the time of marking for the mortality which had taken place since the counts were made:

$$K = \frac{\bar{N}}{N_c} + \frac{A}{N_m}$$

65

where N_c is the number of pups counted in the area, N_m is the number of pups counted in mortality study area, and A is the number of pups dying in mortality study area between count and date of marking. $\bar{N}$ is estimated by

$$\bar{N} = \frac{M}{\bar{p}}$$

where M is the number of animals marked (less those lost to the area by exchange with other areas) and $\bar{p}$ is the proportion of pups marked from recapture counts.

Using this method Payne found that the best counts of live pups must be multiplied by a factor of 1.541 (95 percent confidence interval ± 0.082) to obtain the number actually present. (This result may surprise those not used to counting seal pups, but the task is less easy than one might suppose.) Applying this factor to the counts available, Payne found that between 1958 and 1972 the South Georgia population increased at an average annual rate of 16.8 percent (Payne, 1977). At this rate of growth the doubling time for the number of pups born is 4.5 years. This would be a high figure for a population of large mammals where the females can produce at most only one young each year. From age structures derived from the examination of thin sections of canine teeth, and observations on recruitment, Payne concluded that female fur seals in the South Georgia herd first produce pups at age 3, when 5 percent are pregnant, and are fully recruited by age 5. The South Georgia fur seals are thus about a year in advance of the northern fur seal in the western Pacific, and two years in advance of the Pribilof seals (North Pacific Fur Seal Commission, 1965).

Such a high rate of increase naturally cannot be expected to continue indefinitely. Payne felt it was unlikely to continue for more than about another ten years before density-dependent effects would reduce it. These effects might include the reduction of pup survival because of greater difficulty in establishing the mother-pup bond (necessary for the cows to locate their pups on returning from a feeding expedition); reduced fecundity rates resulting from increased competition for food, with consequent slower growth rates and postponement of puberty in the females (and perhaps a lessened ability to maintain viable fetuses); and lessened survival of pups because of poorer nutritional status associated with competition for food by their mothers during the lactation period. A comparative study currently being carried out at South Georgia of pup mortality on beaches of widely differing density is expected to throw light on some of these density-dependent effects.

Density-dependent factors need not manifest themselves if the population spreads out so as to maintain its density below critical values.

The expansion of the South Georgia fur seal herd is well documented. Local expansion was first noted as more and more of the available beaches at Bird Island were colonized by the seals in the 1950s. In the same period a small group of seals established itself on the northwest mainland coast, and this movement has continued in an eastward direction along both north and south coasts of South Georgia until in 1975–76 more than half of the corrected estimate of 90,000 pups born were on the mainland beaches of northwest South Georgia (Figure 4.3). It is always rash to prophesy trends in animal populations, but if present rates continue, the fur seals of South Georgia may regain their former abundance, measured in millions, in 15–20 years.

It is not only at South Georgia that the antarctic fur seal is increasing (Figure 4.3). Small but increasingly larger breeding groups are now present in the South Shetlands and South Orkneys; they almost certainly represent overspill from the South Georgia population. When Øritsland (1960) found fur seals breeding at Michelsen Island in the South Orkneys in 1956, he noted that among the animals was one with an almost white coat. Similarly, Aguayo (1978), in recording the increase of fur seals at the South Shetlands between 1957 and 1972, mentions that at Snow Island two yellowish-white pups were seen. R. W. Vaughan reports seeing white fur seals at the South Sandwich Islands when he visited them in 1964 (Vaughn, personal communication). I had recorded this color morph (Figure 4.4) at a level of about 0.1 percent in the animals at Bird Island in the 1950s (Bonner, 1958, 1968), and one of the 60 animals seen there in 1933 was described as pale golden. Since such color variations have not been reported elsewhere in *Arctocephalus* species (with one exception that I shall come to later), it seems likely that this anomaly was fixed in the small relic population at South Georgia, and that its occurrence at the South Orkneys, South Shetlands, and South Sandwich Islands is a consequence of dispersal from South Georgia to these localities.

Further evidence that these fur seal colonies are being reinforced by stock from elsewhere is provided by the age and sex composition and rates of increase in some places. At Signy Island (South Orkneys) male fur seals, predominantly juveniles, are observed in hundreds, yet there is no established breeding stock. Aguayo (1978) recorded that the number of pups born at Livingstone Island (South Shetlands) had shown an average rate of increase of 34 percent per year. Such a rate would be beyond the physical capabilities of the animals, supposing them to produce their first pups at age 3 (no animals have been age-sampled from the Livingstone Island population), so it is necessary to postulate immigration from another source, most probably South Georgia.

It is less likely that groups of the same species breeding at Bouvetøya and Heard Island are derived from the South Georgia stock. In-

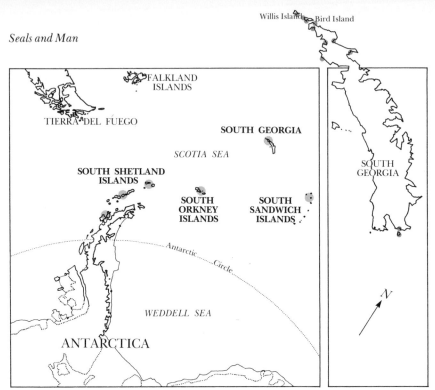

Figure 4.3.   Current breeding localities of antarctic fur seals at South Georgia and in the Scotia Sea region.

Figure 4.4.   Juvenile male antarctic fur seal, showing white color variety. Bird Island, South Georgia. December 1977.

deed, it seems probable that some of these islands supported their own relic populations after the depredations of the sealers. Possibly the Heard Island seals are derived from Kerguelen—where there is little information regarding the status of the species—but, interestingly, one of the bulls seen at Heard Island was a pale-colored morph (Budd, 1972), and this might imply that wanderers from South Georgia had been at least partly responsible for the increase noted there. Information from these island groups is less complete than that for the South Georgia seals and those at the South Orkneys and South Shetlands, but the general trend seems to have been for increase (Budd and Downes, 1969; Bonner, 1979).

As we have seen, other species of fur seals were similarly reduced by sealers in the nineteenth century. Most of these have been effectively protected and most populations are now recovering, but none of them has shown such a remarkable increase as the seals at South Georgia. *A. tropicalis*, at Marion Island, for example, has increased by 10.5 percent per year between 1952 and 1975 (Condy, 1978). The question presents itself: What is the factor that has led to this unparalleled rate of increase in *A. gazella*?

It seems likely that it is the availability of food. The antarctic fur seal feeds on the planktonic crustacean krill, *Euphausia superba* (Bonner, 1968), and the commercial depletion of the antarctic krill-eating whales to around 16 percent of their original biomass (Laws, 1977) will have reduced the competition for krill. Marr (1962) has shown that the sea around South Georgia is a region with a particularly dense concentration of krill, while whales are now extremely scarce there. It is thus probable that lactating female fur seals, when making their feeding excursions between bouts of suckling their pups, have benefited greatly from this reduced competition. If this improved pup growth and reduced juvenile mortality, the observed rates of increase could be the consequence.

We thus see how overexploitation of natural resources by man first of all brought the antarctic fur seals to the verge of extinction and then, the exploitation being directed to another group of predators competing for the same food resource, created the conditions by which the surviving fur seals could recover at a rate scarcely attainable had the trophic environment remained unchanged. The interaction of species at the higher trophic levels is a matter of main concern to ecologists and fishery biologists alike. The whales-seals-krill system is one to which I shall return later.

References

Aguayo, A. 1978. The present status of the antarctic fur seal *Arctocephalus gazella* at the South Shetland Islands. Polar Rec. 19(119):167–176.

Allen, J.A. 1899. Fur seal hunting in the Southern Hemisphere. Pp. 307–319 in Jordan, D.S. The fur seals and fur-seal islands of the North Pacific Ocean. Washington, Government Printing Office, Doc. 2017, 3, chap. 12.

Bonner, W.N. 1958. Notes on the southern fur seal in South Georgia. Proc. zool. Soc. Lond. 130:241–252.

Bonner, W.N. 1968. The fur seal of South Georgia. Brit. Anarct. Surv. Sci. Rep. 56, 81pp.

Bonner, W.N. 1979. Antarctic (Kerguelen) fur seal. Pp. 49–57 in Mammals in the Seas. F.A.O. Fisheries Ser. No. 5, Vol. 2.

Bruce, W.S. 1920. In Report of the Interdepartmental Committee on Research and Development in the Dependencies of the Falkland Islands, Appendix 2, 38–41. Command 657. London, His Majesty's Stationary Office.

Budd, G.M. 1972. Breeding of the fur seal at McDonald Islands, and further population growth at Heard Island. Mammalia 36(3):423–427.

Budd, G.M. and Downes, M.C. 1969. Population increase and breeding in the Kerguelen fur seal, *Arctocephalus tropicalis gazella*, at Heard Island. Mammalia 33:58–67.

Chapman, D.G. and Johnson, A.M. 1968. Estimates of fur seal population by randomised sampling. Trans. Am. Fish. Soc. 97:264–270.

Clark, A.H. 1887. The antarctic fur seal and sea-elephant industry. Pp. 400–467, Sect. 5, Vol. 2 in The Fisheries and Fishery Industries of the United States, ed. G.B. Goode. Washington, Government Printing Office.

Condy, P.R. 1978. Distribution, abundance, and annual cycle of fur seals (*Arctocephalus* spp.) on the Prince Edward Islands. S. Afr. J. Wildl. Res. 8:159–168.

Cook, J. 1777. A Voyage Towards the South Pole and Around the World . . . . In the Years 1772, 1773, 1774 and 1775. W. Strahan and T. Cadell, London.

Csordas, S.E. 1962. The Kerguelen fur seal on Macquarie Island. Victorian Nat. 79:1–4.

Dampier, W. 1729. (Quoted in Hubbs and Norris, 1971.) New Voyage around the World, Describing Particularly the Isthmus of America . . . . 2. James and John Knapton. London.

Fanning, E. (1924.) Voyages and Discoveries in the South Seas 1792–1832. Marine Research Society, Massachusetts.

Hubbs, C.L. and Norris, K.S. 1971. Original teeming abundance, supposed extinction, and survival of the Juan Fernandez fur seal. Pp. 35–52 in Antarctic Pinnipedia, ed. W.H. Burt. Anarct. Res. Ser. 18. Am. Geophys. Union.

Jones, A.G.E. 1975. Captain William Smith and the Discovery of New South Shetland. Geog. J. 141(3):445–461.

Larsen, C.A. 1920. Statement on fur seals. In Report of the Interdepartmental Committee on Research and Development in the Dependencies of the Falkland Islands, para. 18, Appendix 11 (p. 92), Command 657. His Majesty's Stationery Office, London.

Laws, R.M. 1977. Seals and Whales of the Southern Ocean. Phil. Trans. R. Soc. Lond. B. 279:81–96.

Marr, J. 1962. The natural history and geography of the antarctic krill (*Euphausia superba* Dana). Discovery Rep. 32:33–464.

Morrell, B. 1832. A Narrative of Four Voyages, etc., From the Years 1822 to 1831. J. and J. Harper, New York.

Murphy, R.C. 1948. Logbook for Grace: Whaling Brig "Daisy," 1912–1913. Robert Hale Limited, London.

North Pacific Fur Seal Commission, 1965. Report on Investigations 1958 to 1961. Tokyo, Kenkyusha.

Øritsland, T. 1960. Fur seals breeding in the South Orkney Islands. Norsk Hvalfangst Tid. 49(5):220–225.

Payne, M.R. 1977. Growth of a fur seal population. Phil. Trans. R. Soc. Lond. B. 279:67–79.

Rand, R.W. 1972. The Cape fur seal *Arctocephalus pusillus*. 4. Estimates of population size. Invest. Rep. Div. Sea Fish. S. Afr. 89:1–28.

Repenning, C.A., Peterson, R.S. and Hubbs, C.L. 1971. Contributions to the systematics of the southern fur seals, with particular reference to the Juan Fernández and Guadalupe species. Pp. 1–34 *in* Antarctic Pinnipedia, ed. W.H. Burt. Antarct. Res. Ser. 18. Am. Geophys. Union.

Rice, D.W. and Scheffer, V.B. 1968. A list of the marine mammals of the world. Spec. Scient. Rep. U.S. Fish. Wildl. Serv. 579. 16pp.

Roberts, B.B. 1958. Chronological list of antarctic expeditions. Polar Rec. 9(59):97–134 and (60):191–239.

Walker, P.L. and Craig, S. 1979. Archaeological evidence concerning the prehistoric occurrence of sea mammals at Point Bennett, San Miguel Island. Calif. Fish and Game. 65(1):50–54.

Webster, W.H.B. 1834. Narrative of a Voyage to the Southern Atlantic Ocean in the Years 1828, 29, 30 Performed in H.M. Sloop *Chanticleer*, Under the Command of the Late Captain Henry Foster. London, Richard Bentley.

Weddell, J. 1825. A Voyage towards the South Pole, Performed in the Years 1822–24. London, Longman, Hurst, Rees, Orme, Brown and Green.

Williams, C.A. 1888. *In* Report to the Committee of Congress on Merchant and Marine Fisheries, Washington, Government Printing Office.

Vaz Ferreira, R. 1979. South American fur seal. Pp. 34–36 *in* Mammals in the Seas. F.A.O. Fisheries Ser. No. 5, Vol. 2.

Figure 5.1. Breeding grounds of southern elephant seals. The size of the circle is proportional to the size of the colony, except in cases of colonies of less than 5,000. After Laws, 1960.

Figure 5.2. The build-up of an elephant seal breeding group. **a.** Early in the season a dominant bull lies on the beach in the center of a group of cows; subordinate bulls lie on the periphery of the group and at the water's edge. **b.** Later the group of cows has become so large that one bull may be unable to control them all, and other bulls of lower rank in the hierarchy appear among the cows and maintain areas of influence around them. Subordinate bulls are found, as before, around the main mass of cows. A subordinate bull is shown swimming in the shallows, seeking a chance to establish itself elsewhere.

- ● adult bull
- ○ adult cow
- • pup

Figure 5.3. A dominant bull elephant seal challenges a rival.

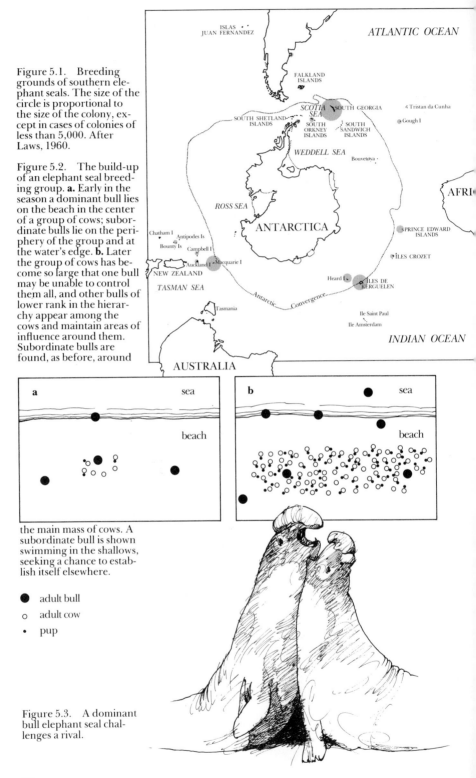

CHAPTER FIVE

The Southern Elephant Seal
And the Elephant Oilers

Early in the southern spring, in September, the bull elephant seals begin to haul out to breed on the beaches of the sub-Antarctic islands. Currently, the largest groups are found at South Georgia (including South America, the Falkland Islands, and the islands of the Scotia Arc), Kerguelen and Heard Island, and Macquarie Island (together with the New Zealand sub-Antarctic islands) (Figure 5.1), but in earlier times substantial breeding populations were probably found on most of the temperate oceanic islands and along some mainland coasts in the Southern Hemisphere.

The bulls are massive creatures, about 4.5 m long from nose to tail tip and weighing around three or four tonnes (perhaps as much as five tonnes) when they emerge from a winter spent feeding at sea, having accumulated a blubber layer up to 17 cm thick. Soon after the arrival of the first bulls the much smaller cows begin to haul out. They are only some 2.8 m long and weigh around 900 kg. The cows are gregarious and form small groups, usually on broad sandy beaches or on level ground (perhaps a raised beach) behind the shore. The largest bulls associate with the groups of cows, and in this way a harem system is built up. It is not a harem in the sense that the northern fur seal keeps a harem, defending a territory and actively accumulating cows; the bull elephant seal relies on the cows' gregariousness to form themselves into groups, and then moves in to keep the other males away. One finds a dominant bull in the middle of a group of cows, on the periphery of which lurk a number of subordinate bulls (Figure 5.2a).

When any new male appears, the dominant bull, or beachmaster, challenges him by roaring, the sound resonating in the grotesque proboscis that earned the species its vernacular name (Figure 5.3). If a vocal threat is not sufficient to make the newcomer retreat, the beachmaster attempts to intimidate him further by rearing the front two-thirds of its body off the ground until it is perhaps three meters into the air. If the newcomer persists, a fight ensues, the seals whacking away at each other's chest and shoulders with their large canines.

This behavior pattern is developed very early as a play activity, and young males only a few weeks old can be seen pushing and worrying at each other's neck. The result is to build up a heavy shield of scar tissue around the parts most vulnerable to wounds. In the southern species this dermal shield is not as impressive as in the northern elephant seal, but its effect is the same. Severe injuries are not as common as in fur seals, perhaps because of the almost incredible cumbersomeness of the contestants. Fights do not usually last long, and the bull that loses the encounter (almost always the newcomer) backs off to reach the safety of the sea, while the beachmaster lies down again among his cows.

As the season wears on, the groups of cows become very large. At one beach on South Georgia I found a patch of cows, unbroken except by a small stream, that numbered nearly four thousand. In such circumstances there will be many bulls in the crowd. Except in the very largest assemblies, one bull is dominant over all the rest, but others are present among the cows and maintain areas of influence around them. On the periphery of the harem crowd are bulls lower in the hierarchy; still farther off, cruising in the shallows, are the lowest bulls in the hierarchy. The bulls excluded from the harems are highly mobile and move from one beach to another, seeking a chance to establish themselves with a group of cows (Figure 5.2b).

About eight days after hauling out ashore the cow produces a pup weighing around 46 kg. Fed on an exceedingly rich milk, it quickly gains weight, doubling its birth weight in 11 days and quadrupling it by the end of lactation (Laws, 1953a). The cow, which remains with her pup on shore for the duration of lactation, comes into estrus about 19 days postpartum and remains receptive for about 4 days (McCann, 1980), during which time she mates several times with one or more bulls. Usually the dominant bull of the group is the first to detect and mate with an estrous cow; on her final departure from the beach, she may be mated by one of the aquatic bulls at the water's edge or in the sea itself.

During the breeding season cows are on shore for around 30 days; bulls stay much longer, perhaps up to 90 days. During this time both sexes lose much weight by depleting their blubber layer. The cows transfer much of this loss to their pups in the form of milk, while the bulls use their fat to provide energy for the violent activities of maintaining their position on the beach and mating with the cows, both of which involve a good deal of locomotion on land for which these huge animals are ill equipped.

The strain of maintaining these activities for such a long period ensures that a bull is unlikely to have more than one or two seasons as a beachmaster. Probably most old beachmasters perish at sea after the end of their final active breeding season, since dead seals are rarely seen ashore and old bulls do not appear as subordinate males on the breeding beaches.

By the end of November, most of the adult breeding seals have left the beaches. Juvenile seals of both sexes (the males predominating, since they take longer to reach sexual maturity) haul out to moult in late November and December, having been absent from the beaches since the previous April. The breeding cows return to moult in January and February and the breeding bulls in March and April. Moulting seals tend to avoid the beaches and haul out behind the shore, often in peaty mud wallows, where they lie in large heaps. At this season the aggressive tendencies of the bulls are subdued, and actual bodily contact seems not only to be permitted but even sought after.

The annual cycle of the southern elephant seal (Figure 5.4) thus ensures that from early in September to late in April there are always some animals ashore, with a great concentration during the breeding months of September to November. The newest arrivals always have a great store of blubber.

Not surprisingly, the sealers of the eighteenth and nineteenth centuries who came to hunt the fur seals did not ignore this potential resource. Furs were preferred to elephant seal oil, since the former were less trouble to obtain, took less space on board, and, above all, were more valuable. On the other hand, elephant oiling could be carried on before the fur sealing began, and once the fur seal population had been reduced, elephant oiling offered a profitable pastime while the search went on for the surviving fur seals.

Sealing vessels usually started life as whalers and thus had the technology and apparatus on board for processing blubber, whether it came from a whale or a seal. A large elephant seal could easily yield two barrels of oil, or a third of a ton, and that probably with less effort than was required to find, hunt, flense, cook out, and stow away an equivalent amount of right whale or sperm whale blubber at sea. Certainly many whale ships took partial cargoes of elephant seal oil (and fur seal skins, too, if they could find them), while some vessels were fitted out especially for elephant oiling.

The sealers started in mid-October and were quite indiscriminate in what they killed. Cows and pups were stunned with a blow to the snout from a heavy club and then lanced; the largest bulls were killed by a rifle ball fired up through the palate when the bull reared up and roared. Once killed, the animals were skinned and the blubber removed in "horse-pieces" (also known as "blanket-pieces"), usually about 45–60 cm long and 40 cm wide. These were then either strung on backpoles or loaded into barrows and taken off to the tryworks. In many cases horse-pieces were floated off to the parent vessel to be tried out.

If seals were very numerous, a tryworks was set up ashore, together with rough living quarters for the sealers. The tryworks consisted of the ordinary cast-iron pots generally in use on whaling vessels, of about 100 gallons capacity, set up in pairs on a brick hearth, usually near a small stream, for it was the custom to soak the blubber for 24–48 hours before

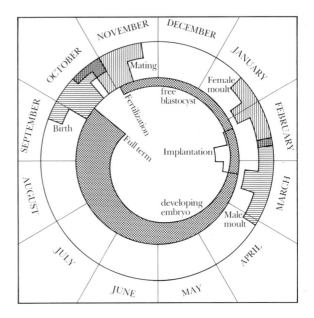

Figure 5.4.   Annual cycle of the elephant seal in South Georgia.

Figure 5.5.   A breeding beach of elephant seals in South Georgia. (Photo: R.W. Vaughan.)

mincing and boiling. Such ruined tryworks can still be found in sheltered anchorages on islands such as South Georgia.

The blubber of elephant seals was said to be harder to boil than whale blubber and so was minced more finely. The sealers claimed that a barrel of blubber would make a barrel of oil. A tryworks of 100 gallons capacity could produce about 900 gallons of oil a day (Clark, 1877). According to Scammon (1874) the oil so produced was superior to whale oil for lubricating purposes, though in fact elephant seal oil is very similar to whale oil in its properties.

After extraction, the oil from the try pots was bailed off to a cooler and then into casks which were rafted out to the ship. The scraps left after boiling blubber were used for fuel, sometimes after passing through a press to extract more oil, just as on a whale ship.

As in sperm whaling, the Yankees were pre-eminent in elephant oiling. Scammon (1874) claimed that American vessels had a monopoly of the business. Some British ships were no doubt also involved (a common design of try pot at South Georgia bears the inscription "Johnson & Co, Wapping Dock"), but the British gradually withdrew from both southern whaling and sealing, leaving the field to the Americans in the last quarter of the nineteenth century.

The indiscriminate hunting methods adopted soon reduced the stocks of elephant seals to a low level, but they were not so relentlessly pursued as the fur seals. First, elephant seals were intrinsically less valuable than fur seals, and so small cargoes were unprofitable (small parcels of furs could be profitably sought as long as there were sufficient elephant seals to make up a cargo of oil). Second, since the produce was bulky in either a raw or a refined state, it was often impossible to seal on beaches that lacked a good boat landing. At Heard Island one very large beach, Long Beach, was covered with elephant seals in the breeding season, but though it could be approached by land across a glacier, no boat could land on it. Consequently, men were stationed at Long Beach to drive the seals back into the water as they hauled out, in the hope that they would haul up on some more accessible beach where they could be killed and their blubber taken and boiled down. There must have been many smaller beaches where the seals could breed unmolested by the sealers. As elephant seals became scarcer, the practice developed of landing a party to live ashore, perhaps for several years (Moseley, 1879), to kill the seals as they hauled out through the year and thus make up a few barrels of oil.

Records are scarce, but it is likely that as the southern whaling trade declined with the decrease of right whales and the introduction of petroleum (which depressed the market for whale oil), so too did the elephant seal industry. The 1870s were the last decade in which elephant oiling was carried on to any great extent. A few old brigs and schooners continued sealing through the closing years of the nineteenth century and even into the twentieth. The last of the old whaler/sealers, the brig *Daisy*, visited South Georgia in 1907 and again for the last time in 1912–13. Fortunately she had on board an outstanding chronicler for her last trip. This was Robert Cushman Murphy, who left a charming and valuable account in his *Logbook for Grace* (1947).

Murphy, newly graduated and on his first collecting expedition for the American Museum of Natural History, was appalled at the wanton slaughter of the cow and pup seals. Captain Benjamin Cleveland, the master of the *Daisy*, was equally appalled to discover that between his visits of 1907 and 1912 a legal administration had come to South Georgia and he had to apply for a license to take the seals he regarded as his by right. A condition of the license he was issued (on payment of £50) was that only male seals might be taken and the young were to be left undisturbed. Cleveland, by Murphy's account, ignored these conditions and avoided any consequences by sailing direct from South Georgia, forgoing the formality of clearing his ship officially and leaving behind him an unpaid bill for £1 3s. for (probably unwanted) customs services.

The changes that Cleveland deplored were consequent to the development of the modern antarctic steam whaling industry which was established in South Georgia by C. A. Larsen in December, 1904. On discovering that their hitherto neglected colony was the site of a flourishing commercial enterprise, the British, who claimed South Georgia by right of Captain Cook's first landing in January, 1775, sent an administrative staff to control the activities of the whalers.

The British administration was aware of the damage that uncontrolled sealing and whaling could do, and the Falkland Islands, of which South Georgia was a Dependency, already had legislation (the Seal Fishery Ordinance of 1899) which provided protection for seals. This was modified and extended in 1909 to cover the seals in South Georgia. Fur seals were protected absolutely, but the whaling company set up by Larsen was granted a license to take elephant seals in 1910.

By 1910 the elephant seal stock at South Georgia had largely recovered from the depredations of the nineteenth century—the occasional sealing voyages of the 1880s and 1890s and Captain Cleveland's two expeditions notwithstanding. Initially, restrictions on sealing were on an ad hoc basis, but fortunately the British administrator, who was responsible for drafting the conditions of the sealing licenses, drew up a set of rules which formed the basis for rational exploitation.

.The coast of South Georgia was divided into four sealing divisions (with several areas where sealing was not permitted), of which only three were to be worked in any one year. A license fee of £50 was charged for the right to kill up to 2,000 adult male elephant seals in each division so licensed. At first, leopard and Weddell seals, which appeared in small numbers at South Georgia, were included in the permitted total, but Weddell seals were protected in 1917 and leopard seals made up a negligible proportion of the seals killed. The maximum number of seals that could be taken in any one year was thus 6,000, though it was not until controlled sealing had been in progress for more than twenty years that this figure was approached, and it was not achieved until 1937. In the early years of controlled sealing a closed season from October 1 to the last day of February protected the seals for much of the breeding season, but by 1921 the start of the closed season was changed to November 1, and extensions to allow sealing in November were regularly approved. Most seals were killed in the spring, during the breeding season, but some were taken in March and April during the moulting of the bulls.

Techniques differed markedly from those of the old-time sealers; good accounts are available by Matthews (1929) and Laws (1953c). Modern sealing was run as an ancillary industry to a whaling shore factory. Obsolete whale catchers were used to take the sealing crews around the island to hunt the seals and ship the blubber back to the whaling station, where it was cooked in the same way as whale blubber. When I first visited South Georgia in 1953 there were three sealing vessels at work. The most modern had been built in 1921 and had a gross tonnage of 210; the oldest had been built in 1884 and was 77.5 tons gross.

On reaching a beach where seals were to be taken, the sealing crew was sent ashore in a heavy Norwegian pram dinghy. The crew consisted of the gunner (the mate of the sealing vessel), a beater, three flensers, and three hookers. The pram was either rowed by one of the seamen from the sealer or towed close inshore by the motor lifeboat of the sealer. The master, chief engineer, and one seaman remained on board the sealer to receive and load the skins as they were brought out.

On reaching the shore the sealers had to maneuver their heavy boat so as to make a safe landing, usually a difficult matter during the equinoctial seasons in those latitudes, so that wettings were frequent and unremarked. The gunner was in charge ashore and indicated where operations were to begin and which bull was to be taken first. The beater was equipped with an old brass condenser tube, about 2 m long, from one of the whale boats, with which he struck the bull about the head, usually over the eye. This usually caused even a large bull to back away—not as a result of the strength of the blows, which were trivial compared with those received in intraspecific fighting, but because despite its roars and challenges it continually received blows on what in a normal contest would be a very vulnerable area. Beaters also shouted at the bulls, but I doubt if this had any effect at all. Shaking pebbles vigorously in a tin container was a useful way of driving off cows that encroached on the scene of operations.

Occasionally a bull proved impossible to drive and had to be shot where it was or abandoned, but this was rare. If, as normally happened, the bull backed off, it usually turned about and lumbered headfirst down to the sea. The beater then jabbed at its hindquarters just as it was about to enter the water, causing it to swivel around and back the last few meters down to the water with its head raised. A clever beater would arrange for the bull to be slightly oblique to the slope of the beach at this point so that, just as the hindquarters entered the water, the gunner could shoot the bull in the head with a soft-nosed bullet. Usually the shot was placed just in front of the ear, but, at a range of only two or three meters, the exact site of impact was not very important.

The gunner and beater then went off for the next bull and the flensers took over. Their first task was to drive a long-bladed knife into the heart, not to ensure the death of the seal (a second shot directly into the cranium was the usual means of doing this if there was any doubt) but to arrest the action of the heart, which was usually still pumping strongly despite the total destruction of the brain. If arterial pressure were not relieved, each minor artery cut in the course of flensing would jet a fine spray of blood, as often as not (it seemed) right into the eyes of the flenser.

In the early years of controlled sealing the flensers followed the practice of the nineteenth-century sealers and took the blubber off in eight blanket-pieces (Matthews, 1929), but since 1935 the skin and blubber were removed together in one almost circular sheet, a technique that saved much labor and loss of oil. To do this, the first move was to cut around the foreflipper on one side (the side that was lower on the beach, if the bull was lying obliquely, as it should). The cut was extended posteriorly, right through the thickness of the blubber, about the length of the flipper. Similar cuts were made around the other flipper, the head, and the tail, and one longitudinal cut along the ridge of the back (Figure 5.6). In making these cuts, the flensers were always careful to keep the edge of their knife upwards so that they slit through the skin from beneath, thus avoiding dulling their knives on the grains of sand that usually lodged among the coarse hairs of the hide. Even so, they paused after every two or three cuts to whet their knives on steels that hung from their belts.

Once these first cuts had been made it was an easy task to flense the dorsal skin and blubber away from the carcass, using small hand hooks to hold the blubber. When the two flaps of dorsal blubber were spread on either side of the carcass, the flipper on the lower side was passed through the long slit cut in the blubber, cut away with its scapula, and discarded. The flipper on the upper side was passed through the skin in the same way. Then the hookers struck their long blubber hooks into the flipper and, heaving on them, rolled the carcass over down the slope of

Figure 5.6.   The flensing cuts on a bull elephant seal. After the seal is stabbed in the heart, the cuts are made in the order indicated. Modified from Laws, 1953c.

Figure 5.7.   Stages in flensing a bull elephant seal. South Georgia, October 1961.

the beach. As the carcass turned, the flensers, on the other side, cut it away from the skin and blubber, on which was left much of the superficial musculature, including the whole of the abdominal wall. If the carcass lay obliquely, as it should, it would almost roll down the beach under its own weight, saving much labor. There it was left to rot. The whole process, from shooting to cutting the skin and blubber completely free, was normally accomplished in a little less than four minutes.

The upper edge of the skin (usually the head end) was then doubled over its lower part, and the loose bundle was rolled smoothly into the sea, where it floated. A 4–4.5 m strop of stout rope with an eye splice at each end was then threaded through one of the flipper holes and the eyes looped over a toggle, one of eight on a long line. When all the toggles had skins attached, the pram passed the end of the toggle line to the motor boat, which towed the bundles out to the sealer. If seals were plentiful, about fifty—and perhaps as many as seventy—could be taken in a day's work.

On board, the skins were stowed in what had been the line box when the vessel was a whaler. As this lay rather far forward, it was usually necessary to take a deck cargo aft, to trim the ship a little. A full cargo was from 70 to 230 skins, depending on the size of the ship and the time of year the seals were taken. The ship then returned to the whaling station, where the skins were unloaded, drawn up on the flensing plan (the area where the whales were cut up), chopped up, and cooked under steam at a pressure of 60 psi for six hours. Despite the high proportion of skin and muscle tissue present with the blubber, a high-grade oil, equivalent to No. 1 whale oil, was produced.

This sealing was highly profitable; for comparatively little investment, up to two thousand tons of oil of the same value as whale oil could be obtained from one season. In an attempt to increase the returns even further, it was rashly decided to increase the quota from 6,000 seals to 7,500 in 1948, and to 9,000 in 1949. This highest quota was never achieved in fact, the greatest take being 7,877 seals in 1951. Fortunately for the future of the stock, in that year R. M. Laws, who had been studying the biology of the small breeding colony of elephant seals at Signy Island in the South Orkneys, came to South Georgia.

Laws detected signs of deterioration in the condition of the herd, which had progressively worsened from the late 1930s onward (Laws, 1960). The first sign had been the seals' vacating the large open beaches for smaller, rockier ones, often inaccessible to the sealers. Laws also suspected that a "refugee" movement of elephant seals from South Georgia to other island groups—which began in the Falkland Islands some time in the late 1920s, and in the South Orkney's perhaps in the 1940s—might be a symptom of overharvesting. It is hard to see why this movement from South Georgia, which mostly involved moulting seals of both

Figure 5.8. Section of canine tooth of an elephant seal aged 10 years, showing the annual growth zones. From a preparation by T.S. McCann.

sexes at a time of year when hunting was in abeyance, should be associated with excessive sealing, but there is no more obvious explanation, though possibly minor climatic changes might be involved. There was less controversial evidence of a decrease in the male component of the stock from about 1940 onward. Using the catch per catcher's day's work (CDW) as a unit of effort and taking the seasons in groups of four (to eliminate variations caused by the rotation of the divisions sealed), Laws showed that the catch at South Georgia declined from 38.3 seals per CDW in the 1930s to 29.4 seals per CDW in 1951–54, a drop of 23.2 percent.

Perhaps the most powerful tool Laws was able to bring to this study was a means of determining accurately the age of the seals killed. During his work at Signy, he had noted that the pulp cavity of the elephant seal canine remains open throughout life and that dentine is laid down seasonally, resulting in a pattern of bands of differing optical properties associated with feeding and fasting periods (Figure 5.8). By counting the number of these cycles and knowing that all births took place in a few weeks each year, he could determine age with great accuracy. As the pattern of the layers changed on the attainment of sexual maturity, age not only at death but also at puberty could be determined (Laws, 1952, 1953a, 1953b). Laws's hypothesis of age determination from tooth structure was subsequently confirmed from known-age branded animals by Carrick and Ingham (1962). Applying this method, Laws was able to show that in 1951 the average age of the bulls killed by the sealers at South Georgia was 6.6 years (range 2–10), and not one of 100 bulls examined was older than 10 years, while at Signy the average age of breeding bulls was 10 years and some were as old as 20 (Laws, 1953c).

As a result of his observations, Laws made recommendations for the future control of the sealing. These included setting quotas for the various divisions calculated on the basis of the available stock, restricting the kill to bulls of more than 3.5 m nose to tail length, and ensuring that 10 percent of the bulls above this size were left on each beach. An additional important recommendation was that a lower canine tooth be collected from every twentieth bull killed, so that a check could be kept on the average age of the seals killed in each division. In calculating the divisional quotas, Laws worked on the assumption that an appropriate ratio would be one breeding bull to every twelve cows. On this basis the calculated surplus accession of bulls amounted to 5,842, so that it seemed the original arbitrarily chosen quota of 6,000 was very near the mark, provided it was divided among the divisions in proportion to the available stock.

Laws's recommendations were adopted in 1952 with marked success. I had the privilege of working with the sealing industry to ensure that the regulations were properly observed and that later quotas were further adjusted to take account of variations observed in the average age of the catch. The yield of seals per CDW rose as a response to increased stocks, as did the average age of the catch and the oil production, this last being affected not only by the greater size of the older seals being killed but also by the advance of the date of the midpoint of the season—another consequence of more abundant seals, since the earlier a bull is taken, the more oil it yields.

Laws was able to draw age/biomass curves for the seals from calculated mortalities and length/weight relationships. These showed that in the male the biomass of a year class increases from birth to age 1 as a result of growth, declines from then to age 3 through mortality of the young seals, reaches a peak at age 6 with the rapid growth to sexual maturity, and then declines steadily as mortality gradually extinguishes the year classes (Figure 5.9). If the estimated weight of the catch in each age group is plotted on the same graph, it can be seen that this would be equivalent to taking the entire 8-year class, leaving no escapement. It would be theoretically possible to obtain a catch about 17 percent greater by taking the entire 6-year class, but this would involve handling an increase of about 45 percent in the number of seals taken and would leave no fully mature bulls for breeding. The general conclusion is that the average age of the catch should be kept around 7.5–8 years for maximum sustainable yield exploitation. In fact, by the time the South Georgia sealing industry ceased (for reasons quite unconnected with the availability of seals), the average age of the catch had leveled off at 7.7 years (Laws, 1979) (Figure 5.10), exactly fitting the requirements postulated by Laws for rational exploitation.

Inevitably, exploitation at this level, which Laws calculated to be about 6 percent of the standing crop per year (Laws, 1960), had a marked effect on the seals. As it was possible to confine the kill to males only, the main change in the stock was not a general reduction in stock

Figure 5.9. Variation of biomass with age in South Georgia elephant seals. After Laws, 1960.

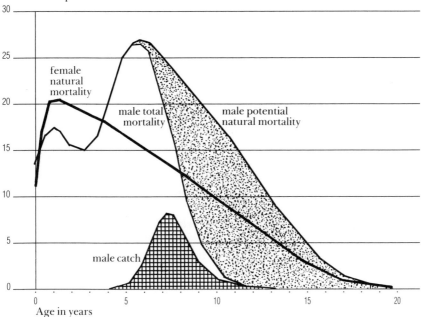

Biomass
in millions of pounds

female
natural
mortality

male total
mortality

male potential
natural mortality

male catch

Age in years

Figure 5.10. Average age of commercial catch of elephant seals at South Georgia. From Laws, 1960.

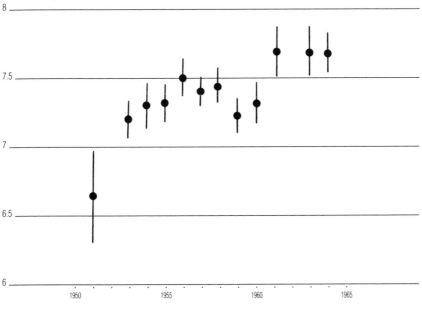

Average age
of catch in years

size, as would be the expected response from a virgin stock to unselective exploitation, but a change in sex ratio and age distribution of the breeding males, which had consequential effects on the females and the social behavior of the seals. McCann (1980) has studied these changes by comparing conditions at South Georgia about 12 years after the ending of commercial sealing (adequate time for a new bull class to appear) with those recorded by Laws. McCann found that following the cessation of sealing there were at least three times as many adult bulls of 6 years and over in the population in 1976–77 and that most harem bulls were 10 or 11 years old, compared with an average of 8 years found by Laws in 1951 (Laws, 1953a). In McCann's study area, he found that although the cow:bull ratio had declined (because of the greater survival of bulls), the average harem size had increased, because there were now greater numbers of experienced, dominant bulls able to exclude other bulls from larger groups of cows.

One conspicuous difference between exploited and unexploited elephant seals was noted when Carrick et al. (1962) showed that at Macquarie Island (where elephant seals had not been hunted commercially since 1920), the females first pupped at age 4 and attainment of sexual maturity continued until age 7, whereas Laws (1956) showed that South Georgia females pupped mostly at age 3. This difference was attributed to lessened competition for food from a reduced stock of males in the exploited population, which allowed faster growth, and hence earlier pregnancy, in the females at South Georgia. However, when a random sample of females was collected at South Georgia in 1978 (McCann et al., 1979) no significant difference could be found in the age at first pupping in females born in 1964 and earlier (i.e., during the time of sealing) and those born later (Table 5.1).

Table 5.1.   Distribution of year of birth and age at first pup for 71 elephant seals aged 5 years and older (McCann et al., 1979)

Age at first pup (years)	Year of birth 1964 or before	Year of birth 1965–1969	Year of birth 1970–1973
3 or 4	20	25	11
5 or 6	2	8	5

This finding does not necessarily mean that the relationship between competition for food and age at first breeding does not exist. Other factors besides the intensity of sealing have changed at South Georgia since 1964. The very great reduction of whales in the waters around the island may have altered the trophic balance. Elephant seals feed on squid and fish, which probably both feed on antarctic krill, *Euphausia superba*. The reduction of both krill-eating baleen whales and squid-eating sperm whales may have made more krill and squid available to other predators. An increase in king penguins (*Aptenodytes patagonica*), which like elephant seals are squid-eaters, has been noted in South Georgia (Smith and Tallowin, 1980). If the increase in elephant seals as a result of the cessation of sealing was enhanced by an increase in the available food base, there need be no compensatory postponement of puberty in the females. This example demonstrates the futility of examining in isolation a single species in a complex web of trophic relationships. A multispecies approach is needed, though currently there is no adequate data base to support one.

In summary, we can see how the elephant seal industry at South Georgia went through the stages of initial uncontrolled exploitation and subsequent depletion, followed by spontaneous recovery when the sealing pressure lifted. Controlled sealing was successful until damage was done first by failing to set quotas in proportion to the stocks, and then by increasing quotas to beyond the combined maximum sustainable yield. This situation was saved by adopting appropriate management policies with which it was possible to maintain the original quotas while bringing the stock back to stability with a substantially higher production for the sealing company.

Like the fur seal in the Pribilofs, the southern elephant seal provides an outstandingly good example of successful scientific management of a natural resource. Their basic pinniped characteristics had, as it were, pre-adapted them for this role. Their polygynous habit meant that the natural ratio of males to females could safely be reduced without risking a drop in the impregnation rate; the eagerness of the mobile aquatic bulls to get ashore ensured that even a beach completely cleared of adult bulls would soon be repopulated. Because of the great sexual dimorphism, there was no difficulty in picking out the bulls, while their huge absolute size meant the sealers were handling economically sized packages of the stored fat.

This valuable industry could have been preserved had it existed independently rather than as an adjunct of a whaling company. When the whaling collapsed from gross overexploitation, the rationally managed sealing industry was dragged down with it.

References

Carrick, R. and Ingham, S.E. 1962. Studies on the southern elephant seal, *Mirounga leonina* (L). II. Canine tooth structure in relation to function and age determination. CSIRO Wildl. Res. 7(2):102–118.

Carrick, R., Csordas, S.E. and Ingham, S.E. 1962. Studies on the southern elephant seal, *Mirounga leonina* (L.). IV. Breeding and development. CSIRO Wildl. Res. 7(2):161–197.

Clark, A.H. 1877. The antarctic fur seal and sea-elephant industry. Pp. 400–467 *in* The Fisheries and Fishery Industries of the United States, ed. G.B. Goode. Sect. 5, Vol. 2. Washington, Government Printing Office.

Laws, R.M. 1952. A new method of age determination for mammals. Nature, Lond. 169:972.

Laws, R.M. 1953a. The elephant seal (*Mirounga leonina* Linn.). I. Growth and age. Sci. Rep. Falkland Islands Dependencies Survey. No. 8:1–62.

Laws, R.M. 1953b. A new method of age determination for mammals with special reference to the elephant seal, *Mirounga leonina*, Linn. Sci. Rep. Falkland Islands Dependencies Survey. No. 2:1–11.

Laws, R.M. 1953c. The elephant seal at South Georgia. Polar Rec. 6:746–754.

Laws, R.M. 1956. The elephant seal (*Mirounga leonina* Linn.). II. General, social and reproductive behaviour. Sci. Rep. Falkland Islands Dependencies Survey. No. 13:1–88.

Laws, R.M. 1960. The southern elephant seal (*Mirounga leonina* Linn.) at South Georgia. Norsk Hvalfangsttid. 10 & 11:466–476, 520–542.

Laws, R.M. 1979. Monitoring whale and seal populations. Pp. 115–140 *in* Monitoring the Marine Environment, ed. D. Nichols. London, Institute of Biology.

Matthews, L.H. 1929. The natural history of the elephant seal. "Discovery" Rep. 1:233–256.

McCann, T.S. 1980. Population structure and social organisation of the southern elephant Seal, *Mirounga leonina* (L.). Biol. J. Linn. Soc. Lond. 14(1):133–150.

McCann, T.S., Bonner, W.N., Prime, J. and Ricketts, C. 1979. Age distribution and age at first pregnancy of South Georgia elephant seals. ICES C.M. 1979/N:13. 6pp. (mimeo).

Moseley, H.N. 1879. Notes by a Naturalist . . . . Made during the Voyage of H.M.S. "Challenger" . . . . 1872–76. London, Macmillan.

Murphy, R.C. 1947. Logbook for Grace: Whaling Brig "Daisy," 1912–13. New York, Macmillan.

Smith, R.I.L., and Tallowin, J.R.B. 1980. The distribution and size of king penguin rookeries on South Georgia. Br. Antarct. Surv. Bull. No. 49:259–276.

Scammon, C.M. 1874. The Marine Mammals of the North-western Coast of North America. J.H. Carmony, San Francisco and G.P. Putman's Sons, New York.

CHAPTER SIX

The Antarctic Seals
An Unexploited Resource

The true antarctic seals comprise four well-defined monotypic genera which together make up the tribe Lobodontini. Ancestral phocids evolved in the Northern Hemisphere, and some time early in the initial radiation in the Miocene a stock split off that was associated with the temperate rather than the cold polar waters. This was the subfamily Monachinae, a group that eventually split into three.

One part, comprising the monk seals, *Monachus*, remained in temperate and even tropical waters. In recent times there have been three species of *Monachus*, but one of these, the Carribean monk seal (*M. tropicalis*), became extinct when the last colony on the Serranilla Bank (about halfway between northern Nicaragua and Jamaica) disappeared some time after 1952. The Mediterranean monk seal (*M. monachus*) and the Hawaiian monk seal (*M. schauinslandi*) represent two relic populations each numbering less than a thousand individuals. All three species of monk seal suffered at the hand of man, but none of them seems to have ever supported a very large population. The reasons for this are obscure, but it would appear that phocids are less well able to compete in warm-water ecosystems.

The elephant seals, *Mirounga*, are another group of monachine seals (King, 1966) which have established themselves in temperate and subpolar habitats. The more numerous and older southern species (*M. leonina*), as we have seen, has its headquarters in the subantarctic islands. The more recently evolved northern elephant seal, *M. angustirostris*, breeds on off-shore islands from central Baja California, Mexico, to central California, but its main feeding grounds lie northward in the cool waters off Washington State, British Columbia, and southeast Alaska.

The remaining group of phocids, the Lobodontini, colonized the Antarctic during the late Miocene or early Pliocene (Laws, 1964), at which time the Antarctic enjoyed a more temperate climate. With the drift of the continents, Antarctica moved toward the pole, and during the subsequent cooling and glaciation the Lobodontini became adapted to low temperatures. An evolutionary radiation occurred, giving rise to the four rather distinct and highly successful forms of antarctic seal that we know today. These are the Weddell seal, *Leptonychotes weddellii*; the crabeater seal, *Lobodon carcinophagus*; the leopard seal, *Hydrurga leptonyx*;

and the Ross seal, *Ommatophoca rossii**. These four species, together with
the southern elephant seal and the antarctic fur seal in the northern part
of their range, divide up the available niches among them. They provide
a good example of morphological and ecological radiation derived from
food utilization. Where two or more species occur side by side, they exploit different food resources (for example, *Lobodon/Ommatophoca/
Hydrurga*)**; where they feed on the same food they are geographically
separated (*Mirounga/Ommatophoca, Arctocephalus/ Lobodon*).

Weddell Seal

The Weddell seal is a coastal species inhabiting the fast ice surrounding the continent (Figure 6.1). It is the most southerly of all mammals,
apart from man himself. Breeding groups occur in the South Orkney
Islands (and there is a very small one in South Georgia), where the association with ice is less marked (or, in the case of the South Georgia colony, absent altogether), but in general this seal is highly adapted to ice.
Alone of the antarctic seals, the Weddell seal maintains breathing holes
in the ice, as does the ringed seal in the north. The holes are first made
in the autumn in leads as they freeze over and are kept open throughout
the winter. The seals abrade the ice with their procumbent upper canines and incisors. The resulting wear on the teeth eventually exposes
the pulp cavity, whereupon necrosis sets in. Tooth wear caused in this
way is an important mortality factor (Stirling, 1969a), since once the
teeth have decayed, the seal cannot keep a breathing hole open. Stirling
(1977) has drawn attention to the different method used by the ringed
seal, which scrapes the ice away with the strong claws on its foreflippers.
The use of claws, which grow throughout the life of the animal, is less
limiting than the use of teeth, whose regrowth is impossible once the
pulp cavity is exposed.

The Weddell seal appears to be largely sedentary (Stirling, 1969b),
though it has been suggested that a northward migration into the pack
ice occurs during the winter (Smith, 1965). There is certainly some
seasonal dispersion and aggregation. The observed aggregations in the
spring might be caused by the scarcity of secure areas with recurring
tidal cracks suitable for breeding sites (Figure 6.1). However, similar
aggregations are seen in the South Orkneys, where the seals are not de-

---

*I should point out that the trivial names of both the Weddell seal and the Ross seal are
correctly spelled with the *-ii* ending, as this was the form used in the original descriptions.
(See Index Animalium, 1801–1850, pp. 7001 and 5553 respectively.)
**Though where krill is very abundant—for example, in Admiralty Bay—leopard seals
may feed extensively on krill.

Figure 6.1. Right: Female Weddell seal and pup on fast ice in McMurdo Sound. Below: Weddell seal pupping colony by Big Razorback Island, McMurdo Sound. This photograph shows the typical distribution around a recurring tide crack. Photos: Ian Stirling.

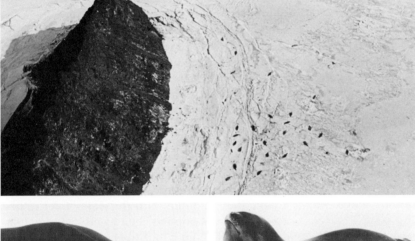

Figure 6.2. Upper left: A female leopard seal and her pup on pack ice near the South Shetland Islands. Photo: R. M. Laws. Upper right: Ross seal showing characteristic posture and patterning. Photo: British Antarctic Survey. Lower right: Crabeater seal family group on pack ice near the South Shetland Islands. The U.S. Research Vessel *Hero* is in the background. Photo: Ian Stirling.

pendent on tide cracks for successful breeding. Weddell seals return at the breeding season to the general area of their birth but not necessarily to the same site (Stirling, 1969b; Smith and Burton, 1970), so the existence of localized populations, as indicated by serum protein polymorphisms, is not surprising (Shaughnessy, 1969; Seal et al., 1971).

The peak of the pupping season occurs around September 23 in the Antarctic Peninsula (Bertram, 1940) but not until the latter part of October in the vicinity of Ross Island (Stirling, 1969b; Siniff et al., 1971). This difference can be related to the seasonal breakup of the sea ice and the consequent destruction of the pupping sites. However, at South Georgia, where the seals pup on the snow-covered beaches, the pups are born in September. Typically, breeding assemblies form along pressure cracks or tide cracks in the ice. Most of the seals to be seen on the ice are pregnant females or females with their pups, as the males spend most of their time in the water. At the periphery of the rookery are found nonbreeding and immature seals of both sexes.

The pup when born is clad in a thick coat of fine grey hair, curly at the base and straight towards the tip, giving an appearance of underfur and guard hair. This natal pelage begins to moult at about two weeks and is completely lost at six weeks (Bonner and Laws, 1964). The newly moulted pup has a silky coat with adult markings. The mother lies near her pup for the first 8–10 days, but thereafter enters the water for short periods. Pups usually follow their mothers into the water for the first time soon after this, but a two-day-old pup has been seen swimming (Siniff et al., 1970). Weaning follows at about 6 or 7 weeks. The time of mating is not certain. Copulation has been observed only once; it occurred under water (Cline et al., 1971) on December 7, 43 days after the birth of a pup, which was still nursing.

Male Weddell seals during the breeding season bear scars, most of them around the hind flippers and genital region, probably the result of intrasexual fighting. However, Kaufman and his co-workers (1975) have observed a nonreceptive female biting a bull about the genital orifice, so such wounds may be the result of rejection by females instead of male/male encounters. Agonistic behavior between males has been observed under water (Ray, 1967; Kooyman, 1968).

It is assumed that these seals are polygynous, though the extent of polygyny and male exclusion has not been determined. Perhaps the degree of polygyny has been insufficient to cause the Weddell seal to embark on the series of changes postulated by the Bartholomew model. There is little difference in size between male and female; indeed the female may be marginally larger than the male—329 cm and 297 cm average length respectively (King, 1964). As Stirling (1975) pointed out, aggregations of Weddell seals are never so dense as they are in the terrestrially breeding dimorphic gregarious pinnipeds, since the females are not very tolerant of each other. This may be a consequence of the limited availability of breathing holes, and perhaps food resources, in any particular region. The three-dimensional nature of the territory must set a narrow limit to the area which can be defended, expressed in terms of the wide spacing of females along the tide crack. This might be expected to result in the inability of the bulls to achieve the degree of polygyny observed in the dimorphic seals. Another possibility is that, in an aquatic territory, speed and agility in the water may be more important than sheer bulk in intrasexual fighting, so that selection has pursued another course. Clearly this represents a field where more research is needed, particularly on the extent of polygyny.

Weddell seals feed mostly on benthic and midwater fish, generally medium-sized nototheniids, though individuals of *Dissostichus mawsoni* up to 54 kg in weight have been taken (Kooyman, 1968). Besides fish, a variety of squids, crustaceans, lamellibranchs, and even holothurians have been recorded in the diet (Dearborn, 1965; Øritsland, 1977). Because of the great depth of the continental shelf around Antarctica, which is depressed by the weight of the ice cap, it has been advantageous for Weddell seals to develop the ability to dive to great depths in their quest for benthic food organisms. Kooyman (1968) and his co-workers (Kooyman et al., 1970) have shown that feeding dives may extend to 300–400 m and commonly last 8–15 minutes. Longer and deeper dives, to 45 minutes and 600 m, occur but do not seem to be associated with feeding. The seals show a nocturnal behavior pattern, being most active in the water from midnight to 1000 hours local time (Siniff et al., 1970), but in high latitudes such a cycle is not closely correlated with daylight.

Crabeater Seal

Crabeater seals are essentially seals of the drifting pack ice. They are rarely seen far from the ice and almost never haul out on shore. They have a circumpolar distribution and no subspecies have been recognized, nor have significant polymorphisms been found in serum protein analysis (Seal et al., 1971). Although the general water circulation in the Southern Ocean is west to east around the continent, local gyres exist, notably in the Weddell Sea. It seems likely that separate stocks of crabeater seals exist, but with a fair degree of genetic exchange between them. Groups of crabeater seals are occasionally seen at sea swimming in a directional manner (Bertram, 1940; Bonner and Laws, 1964; Solianik, 1964), but the extent of these migrations (if they are migrations) has not been determined.

The crabeater seal is moderately gregarious, often forming groups of a dozen or so, though smaller groupings (a group mean of 2.2 seals, according to Siniff et al., 1970) are more usual. Recent research by Siniff and his colleagues (1979) has given us a much fuller, though still incomplete, understanding of the reproductive behavior of this species. During the breeding season the adult males and females form pairs, each pair on a separate floe in the pack ice, where they remain for extended periods, as evidenced by feces, urine, and compacted snow (Figure 6.2). The males are very intolerant of the approach of other seals, and this may explain the large groups of immature crabeaters seen on fast ice at this time.

The pups are born in September and October, with a peak in the early to middle part of October. They are clad in a woolly coat variously described as grey-blue or brown. Circumstantial evidence from the tooth structure suggests that lactation lasts about five weeks (Bonner and Laws, 1964), but Siniff and his colleagues (1979) have suggested a shorter period of around four weeks. Despite the fact that the family groups (or "triads," since the pup of the group may not be the progeny of the male) are widely dispersed in the pack ice, frequent competition for reproductive rights still occurs and the males bear wounds characteristic of intraspecific encounters.

Copulation is presumed to take place on the surface of the ice, since the males seem to make extraordinary efforts to keep the females from leaving the ice. Male and female engage in a great deal of agonistic behavior (perhaps a consequence of the male's testing the female for sexual receptivity) that leaves both of them covered with blood, particularly the female on her back and sides.

Comparison of the crabeater and Weddell seal social systems is instructive since they each represent solutions to problems of breeding in ice habitats—the Weddell seal on fast ice with an absence of predators, and the crabeater in the pack where predators abound. The male Weddell seal maintains its underwater territory along the cracks in the fast ice and mates with (probably) several females within this territory. Crabeaters occupy separate floes in the pack ice and—in contrast to most ice-breeding seals (Stirling, 1975)—mate on the surface, since this removes them from the risks of possible predation by killer whales (*Orcinus orca*) and leopard seals. Crabeater seal pup growth rates are probably faster than those of the Weddell seal, since selection favors a shorter lactation in the less stable pack.

The food of the crabeater seems to consist almost exclusively of krill. It has been suggested, though not confirmed, that in the most southern parts of their range it may be *Euphausia crystallorophias* (Marr, 1962), but for the great majority it is *E. superba*. Squid and fish have also been found in the stomachs of crabeater seals (Perkins, 1945; Øritsland, 1977), but krill forms over 90 percent of the diet.

Leopard Seal

The leopard seal is the largest of the antarctic seals. Adult males may reach 320 cm and adult females 338 cm in length. It is distributed throughout the Antarctic and subantarctic and is regularly seen near coasts, particularly in the vicinity of penguin rookeries. It is a solitary animal, though groups of several tens have been seen in winter (Marr, 1935; Bérchevaise, 1967). In my experience at South Georgia the larger groups have all been formed of juvenile animals. Leopard seals are most abundant in the subantarctic in the winter, and numbers increase near shore in the Antarctic from early December to mid-January (Hofman et al., 1975). However, these sightings probably relate to movements of the pack ice, which forms the main habitat of this species.

Little is known of the breeding behavior of the leopard seal. Pupping occurs in the pack ice some time from October to November (Figure 6.2). A caged female at Heard Island gave birth to a (stillborn) pup on November 14 (Brown, 1952). However, I have seen a pup that did not appear to be more than about three weeks old on shore at South Georgia on September 11. Perhaps there is a wide spread in the breeding season, as in the Weddell seal. Similarly, the time of mating is unknown; Marlow (1967) observed courtship and mating in a captive pair in a zoo in Australia in January and November, but it is difficult to relate this to behavior in the wild.

The leopard seal has a wider diet than other antarctic seals, being the only species that preys regularly on the flesh of warm-blooded animals. There are many observations of leopard seals feeding on penguins of various species. However, this reflects observer-bias. Human observers tend to spend a disproportionate amount of time in the neighborhood of penguin rookeries, and leopard seals when feeding on penguins are conspicuous as they hunt them. The birds are caught under water, usually just seaward of the break of the waves. The seal holds the penguin by the head at the water's surface and tosses it back and forth until it is badly mauled or dead (Penney and Lowry, 1967). The violent head movements of the seal can shake a penguin out of its skin, but this is not invariably done, and the feces of a leopard seal that has been feeding on penguins always contain many feathers. Penguins sometimes escape from leopard seals, and it is possible that on occasions the seals are merely playing with the birds without seriously intending to eat them. They may behave in this way with other prey animals. Leopard seals are also seen feeding on fish near shore. When hunting along a coastline or at a penguin rookery, the seals are solitary, though Penney and Lowry doubted that they have territorial hunting areas. This was not my conclusion at South Georgia.

The reliance of leopard seals on penguins and fish when feeding near the shore conceals their main food habits in the pack ice. Øritsland (1977), who sampled in August and September to the east and northeast of the South Shetland Islands, found that krill made up more than half of the stomach contents, cephalopods and fish together nearly a quarter, and penguins about a sixth. Some leopard seal stomachs contained fragments of crabeater seals. The importance of krill in the diet of leopard seals was noticed also by Hofman and his co-workers (1975) at Palmer Station, on the basis of observed behavior patterns and fecal analyses. Although penguins were abundant in the study area, the leopard seals were feeding almost exclusively on krill and only two penguin kills were seen in 120 hours of observations.

There are many anecdotal accounts of leopard seals feeding on other seals, but the evidence that juvenile crabeater seals form a significant part of their diet was assembled by Laws (1977b). Virtually all crabeater seals more than a year old bear characteristic scars whose spacing corresponds to the intercanine distance of the leopard seal. In samples taken in summer months, 83 percent of fresh scars were found on seals up to 18 months old. The high incidence of scarring on adult crabeaters indicates that few avoid an encounter with a leopard seal, though many escape, perhaps because of agility, or perhaps because the leopard seal was only playing with its prey, as they do with penguins.

There is no doubt that the dentition of the leopard seal is well adapted to eating flesh. The enormous canines and enlarged lateral incisors can grasp a penguin and shake it to pieces, or tear a chunk of blubber from another seal. The postcanine teeth, on the other hand, are not of a pattern that one would associate with a flesh-eating diet. Shearing edges, characteristic of the carnassial teeth of the fissipeds, are totally lacking. Instead, there is an intermeshing array of tricuspid teeth which are very similar to the multilobed teeth of the crabeater seal which, as Barrett-Hamilton (1901) noted, "may form a sieve through which is strained the water taken into the mouth with the *Euphausia*."

Judith King (1961) pointed out that the elongation of the mandibular symphysis creates a scooplike lower jaw, a feature similar to that seen in *Phoca hispida*, another plankton feeder, and some other *Phoca* species. However, she missed the essential similarity of the crabeater's dentition to that of the leopard seal, supposing that the three-pronged cheek teeth would be suitable for eating larger prey such as squid and penguins. Indeed, a look at these teeth with their recurved points shows that this would not be the case. They might function well for retaining fish, but would not serve for cutting flesh. As Øritsland (1977) pointed out, they form a sieve, analogous to the dentition of the crabeater seal.

Racovitza (1900) seems to have been the first to suggest that the crabeater feeds like a baleen whale, swimming along with its mouth open. I think this is unlikely to be true of either the crabeater or the leopard seal. In the baleen whales the filtering device is large in comparison with the rest of the body; this is not so in the case of the seals. If the seal took a mouthful of water without specially orienting on a krill, it is unlikely that more than two or three individuals would be engulfed.

King felt that it would not be economic for the crabeater seal to catch krill one at a time, but I think she was mistaken. I suspect that a crabeater or leopard seal when feeding on krill first locates a dense krill swarm and then orients on an individual krill. Holding the mouth slightly open to make a gap bounded by the incisors above and below and by the canines on either side, it sucks the krill into its mouth by depressing its tongue. The water taken in is expelled through the sieve formed by the cheek teeth and voided to the exterior from the corners of the mouth. Possibly the vibrissae are used as vibration sensors to localize the krill in front of the snout, where it can scarcely be visible. Provided the seal does not have to make major readjustments of its whole body for each successive krill, there seems to me no reason why such a method of feeding should not be "economic," though it would necessarily depend on the presence of krill in swarms.

Ross Seal

The Ross seal (Figure 6.2) is the least well known of all the antarctic seals. It was once considered to be very rare, and up to 1945 there had been fewer than fifty sightings. Man's increased capability of entering the pack ice has revealed, however, that the species is much more abundant than was previously supposed. Recently it has been shown that the Ross seal is especially abundant (for reasons as yet unknown) in the King Haakon VII Sea, between 6°E and 6°W, in pack ice of 6/10–7/10 density and also at a lower density of about 3/10 (Condy, 1976). Ross seals are not found in large groups, but Condy (1979) has demonstrated a clumped distribution, perhaps brought about by social bonds.

Pupping and mating probably occur in November and December. Øritsland (1977) found on the basis of 15 specimens that Ross seals feed predominantly on small (less than 25 cm) squid, though they also take some larger squid and fish. The dentition of the Ross seal is the least well developed of all the lobodontine seals; the five postcanines are basically tricusped, with weak or absent anterior and posterior cusps, the principal cusp being slightly recurved. This accords with the dentition of other squid-eating seals, in which a similar reduction of the postcanine dentition is noted.

Distribution and Food

We can summarize the distributional and feeding ecology of these seals in the form of the diagrams (modified from Laws, 1977b) in Figure 6.3. The pie diagrams show the composition of the food, while the bars indicate the latitudinal distribution (all the species, with the exception of the fur seal, are circumpolarly distributed). The Weddell seal eats mainly fish, together with some crustacea, and its distribution (apart from some minor isolated populations) is neritic around the continent and over the shelf, with a minor extension into the pack ice. The leopard seal, a versatile predator, has the widest range, from the shores of the continent through the pack ice and beyond the Antarctic Convergence to the subantarctic islands. The crabeater seal, with its extreme stenophagy, lives in the pack ice, as does the Ross seal. These avoid competition with each other by taking different food. Beyond the northern limit of pack ice, the Ross seal is replaced by another squid-feeder, the elephant seal, while the antarctic fur seal fills the niche for a krill-feeding seal north of the pack ice.

To understand how the seals fit into the general ecology of the Antarctic, it is necessary to have some information about the size of their populations. The remoteness and inaccessibility of the Antarctic have made such information very hard to come by. Seals by their nature spend a large part of their time in the water, where they are not available for counting. Such quantification as can be done must be performed on seals which have hauled out. For this reason little progress could be made until icebreakers became available that could penetrate the pack and provide opportunities for sighting seals hauled out on the floes.

Much of what we know has been due to the efforts of Erickson and his co-workers (Erickson et al., 1971; Gilbert and Erickson, 1977), who developed a technique for making sample surveys and relating them to total populations. They used counts made directly from icebreakers and helicopters operating from an icebreaker and indirectly from aerial photographs taken from 350 m altitude. Not surprisingly, the helicopter direct counting method proved the most effective for acquiring data. For this technique, sample strips along lines of longitude are selected at random from a population defined at 3-minute intervals. Once a flight path has been determined, surveys are conducted with two helicopters flying in vertical tandem (Figure 6.4). The upper tracking helicopter maintains a sufficient altitude to remain in the ship's radar, allowing the ship's crew to plot its position and relay corrections to keep the helicopter on the flight path. The observation helicopter, from which the counts are made, flies at 152 m (500 feet) altitude and follows the tracking helicopter visually. Seals 450 m on either side of the flight line (as determined by marks on the helicopter's windows and sponsons) are counted, and ice

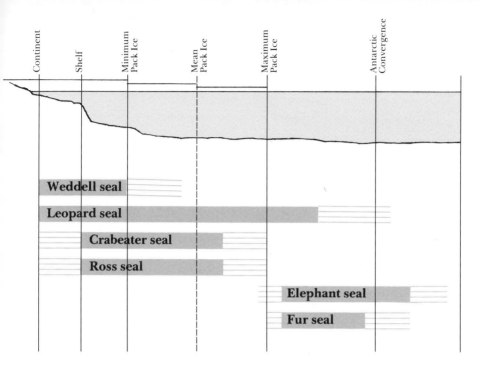

Figure 6.3.   Feeding ecology of antarctic seals. The latitudinal range of the seals is shown as though the Antarctic coast were towards the left of the figure; the composition of the diet is shown in the pie diagrams below. After Laws, 1977b.

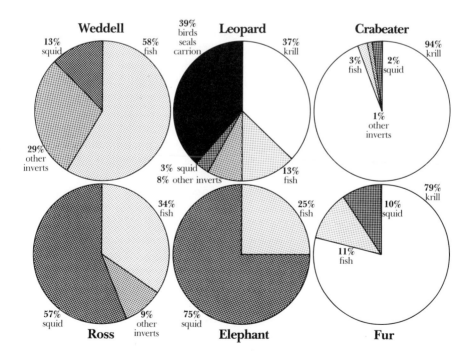

Figure 6.4. Aerial survey technique used for censusing antarctic seals. For further explanation, see text. After Gilbert and Erickson, 1977. By permission of the Smithsonian Institution Press.

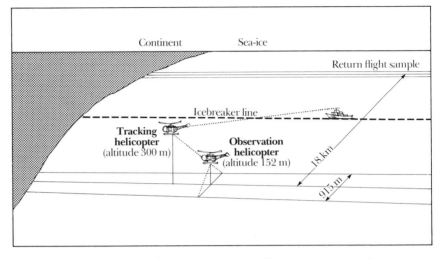

character assessed at 3-minute intervals. All surveys are made between 1100 and 1400 hours local apparent time, when the largest number of crabeater seals are on the ice. Within this period, counts are adjusted to compensate for changes in daily activity pattern.

In this way, 19 strips covering 4,257 square kilometers were sampled from helicopters in the Amundsen and Bellingshausen seas in 1972. The count showed 7,496 seals, or a mean density of 1.76 seals per square kilometer. When adjusted for activity patterns this corresponds to a mean density of 3.66 seals (all species) per square kilometer. Similar observations were made off the Oates and George V coasts.

The use of these figures to provide population estimates of the antarctic seals requires wide extrapolation which needs qualification. However, as Gilbert and Erickson point out, if these data are combined with those of Siniff et al. (1970) and Erickson et al. (1971), then some 72 percent of the residual antarctic pack ice has been sampled. Using estimates of pack ice extent derived from satellite observations, they determined likely population figures to be as follows: crabeater seal, 14,858,000; Weddell seal, 730,000; leopard seal, 222,000; Ross seal, 220,000.

These figures are probably underestimates since they relate only to seals on the ice, and even at the time of maximum haulout it is certain that some seals remain in the water. Furthermore, the estimates take no account of seals in areas of open water away from the pack ice. We should not regard the figures as much more than broad indications, yet it is clear that the crabeater seal is a very abundant mammal, comprising about half of the pinnipeds alive today. Indeed, none of the antarctic seals can be regarded as a rare mammal.

Laws (1977b), using these estimates of Gilbert and Erickson and the findings on food consumption reported by Øritsland (1977), produced

Table 6.1. Crude estimates of antarctic seal populations, biomass, and food consumption (modified from Laws, 1977b)

Species	Stock ($\times 10^3$)	Mean weight (kg)	Population biomass (10^3 tonnes)	Annual food consumption (10^3 tonnes)			
				Total	Krill	Squid	Fish
Crabeater	14,858	193	2,868	67,245	63,210	1,345	2,017
Weddell	732	246	180	4,211	–	463	2,232
Leopard	222	272	60	1,403	519	112	182
Ross	220	173	38	892	80	571	196
Elephant	600	500	300	6,000	–	4,500	1,500
Fur	400	50	20	469	375	47	47

approximate estimates for population biomass and annual food consumption of the various seal species (Table 6.1). The massive yearly consumption of krill by the crabeater seal dominates these figures. This species alone is now the single most important krill predator in the Southern Ocean. The 63 million tons of krill consumed each year by the crabeater seals compares with about 43 million tons consumed by the surviving antarctic baleen whales (Laws, 1977b).

Conservation

I have shown how seal stocks in other parts of the world have been subject to exploitation. The antarctic seals represent a major economic resource to man, but it is one that has been all but untouched. Unquestionably, they owe their immunity to their remoteness. Whereas the fur seals and elephant seals could be reached in the northern island groups, the pack ice provides a haven for the lobodontine seals. Some of the early whaling pioneers in the Antarctic took a few seals (we are not certain which species), and many scientific expeditions to the Antarctic made a practice of cropping seals to feed their sled dogs. Stirling (1971) has discussed the population aspects of harvesting Weddell seals at McMurdo Sound. Most such operations were essentially on a small scale, and though damage may have been done to some local populations of Weddell seals, the impact on the stock as a whole was negligible.

The immunity of the antarctic seals is not, however, inviolable. In the 1960s concern for the future of the harp seal stocks led to a suggestion that sealing boats should be diverted from the north to hunt crabeater seals and other species in the antarctic pack ice in the hope that this would take the pressure off the harp seals. This suggestion, though well meant, was ill advised. Had sealing effort been diverted in this way and the southern sealing been successful, it would probably have resulted in continued hunting of harp seals at a level which would have been otherwise uneconomic without the support of the southern enterprise. In fact, however, the only vessel to investigate the prospects of antarctic sealing was the Norwegian M.V. *Polarhav*, which from August 25 to October 31, 1964, hunted in the pack ice of the Southern Ocean, around the South Shetlands and South Orkneys. The total catch amounted to only 852 seals (Øritsland, 1977), so the expedition was not a commercial success.

The operation of *Polarhav* demonstrated the lack of any form of international fishery agreement to regulate sealing on the high seas in the Antarctic. The nations scientifically active in the Antarctic had earlier agreed on an Antarctic Treaty, signed in Washington in 1959, which when it came into force in 1961 provided for the preservation and conservation of living resources in the Antarctic. The first article of the agreed measures of the treaty prohibits the killing, wounding, or capturing of any native mammal or bird. This prohibition may be relaxed to provide indispensable food for man and dogs in the area, and specimens for scientific study, museums, and zoos. Certain species, designated "specially protected species," can be taken only under permits issued for a compelling scientific purpose. Currently, the Ross seal and fur seals of the genus *Arctocephalus* are so designated.

These provisions might appear to provide for the adequate protection of antarctic seal stocks, yet such was far from being the case. For political reasons the Antarctic Treaty covered only that area of land and fast ice south of 60°S; the rights of signatories on the high seas in that region were specifically reserved. A further international agreement was required to give protection to seals in the sea and on floating ice. This was achieved when the Convention for the Conservation of Antarctic Seals was signed in London in 1972 by the same group of nations as had negotiated the Antarctic Treaty.

The Seals Convention applies to all species of seals found in the seas and floating ice south of 60°S (it was necessary for the same political reasons to restrict its application in this way), but it also has provision for reporting catches of seals to the north of this limit. An annex to the Convention sets out catch limits, which are subject to review (Table 6.2). These catch limits are very conservative, and it is likely that they would be adjusted upwards if an industry developed. The Southern Ocean is divided into six zones, one to be rested from sealing each year in rotation. Three sealing reserves are designated. It is forbidden to kill or capture Ross seals, elephant seals, and fur seals of the genus *Arctocephalus*; and in order to protect the breeding stock it is forbidden to kill or capture Weddell seals one year old or older between September 1 and January 31 in any year.

Table 6.2.   Catch limits for antarctic seals, as specified by the Convention for the Conservation of Antarctic Seals

Species	Permissible catch	Percentage of total stock
Crabeater	175,000	1.2
Leopard	12,000	5.4
Weddell	5,000	0.7

Special permits to take seals for essential food or for study specimens are available as under the agreed measures of the Antarctic Treaty. If an industry began, reports on the numbers of seals killed in each zone and relevant biological information and material would be provided to the Scientific Committee for Antarctic Research (SCAR), which would be invited to suggest amendments to the annex of the Convention and to report on any harmful effects the harvest of seals might have. The Convention provides for a review of its operation at five-year intervals.

The Convention, though untested, would appear to afford an ideal instrument for controlling the possible harvest of seals in the Antarctic. During the drafting of the Convention, it was apparent that some negotiators would have preferred a treaty that banned altogether the development of sealing in the Southern Ocean, and equally apparent that others were determined to keep open their option of hunting seals in that area. It was therefore necessary to reach a compromise lest potential sealing nations, finding the Convention too restrictive, declined to accede to it. The Convention as drafted contains no reference to the international inspection of sealing operations. This was regarded as a serious defect by the U.S. negotiating team, perhaps by analogy with the application of the International Whaling Convention, at whose meetings the issue of international inspection has long been debated. Yet there is no evidence that local infractions of the regulations have been a major cause of the decline of the whale stocks or of the failure of protected stocks to recover. Rather it has been the absence of specific catch limits related to the sustainable yields of the stocks involved which allowed the more economically attractive species to be depleted one by one by an oversized catching fleet. The Seals Convention, with its conservative catch limits, could avoid this trap.

Currently, no nation appears to be interested in undertaking antarctic sealing, and the lobodontine seals find themselves in a unique position for an exploitable resource. Not yet subjected to overharvesting, they are protected by an international agreement which should control any major exploitation and prevent a harvest-induced population crash.

Perhaps it is a simplistic view to assume that the Convention assures the future of the antarctic seals. Increasing interest in the exploitation of krill in the Antarctic, the central component of the region's food web, may mean that the real threat to the seals (and the whales, penguins, and other organisms feeding on krill) is the depletion of their food supply. There is need for another Convention, with a multispecies approach, to regulate harvests with regard to their effect on other components of the ecosystem. This is provided by the Convention on the Conservation of Antarctic Marine Living Resources (CAMLR), which was signed at Canberra in May, 1980. Though, like the Convention for the Conservation of Antarctic Seals, this is as yet untested, it should provide a firm basis for the conservation of the entire antarctic marine ecosystem.

References

Barrett-Hamilton, G.E.H. 1901. Seals. Rés. Voy. S.Y. "Belgica" cn 1897–1899. Rapp. Sci. Zool. 9:1–19.

Bérchevaise, J. 1967. The leopard is not for branding. Vict. Nat. 79:237–243.

Bertram, G.C.L. 1940. The biology of the Weddell and crabeater seals, with a study of the comparative behavior of the Pinnipedia. Brit. Graham Land Exped., 1934–37. Sci. Rep. 1(1):1–139. Brit. Mus. (Nat. Hist.), London.

Bonner, W.N. and Laws, R.M. 1964. Seals and Sealing. Pp. 163–190 *in* Antarctic Research, ed. R. Priestley, R.J. Adie and G. de Q. Robin. Butterworths, London.

Brown, K.G. 1952. Observations on the newly-born leopard seal. Nature, Lond. 170:982–983.

Cline, D.R., Siniff, D.B., and Erickson, A.W. 1971. Underwater copulation of the Weddell seal. J. Mammal. 52:216–218.

Colyer, F. 1936. Variations and Diseases of the Teeth of Animals. John Bale, Sons and Danielsson, London.

Condy, P.R. 1976. Results of the third seal survey in the King Haakon VII Sea, Antarctica. S. Afric. J. Antarct. Res. 6:2–8.

Condy, P.R. 1979. Population biology, population dynamics and feeding ecology of the Ross seal *Ommatophoca rossi* (Gray, 1844). Report on the progress made during the first field season of research, January to March 1979 (mimeo).

Corner, R.W.D. 1971. Observations on a small crabeater seal breeding group. Brit. Antarct. Surv. Bull. 30:104–106.

Dearborn, J.H. 1965. Food of Weddell seal at McMurdo Sound, Antarctica. J. Mammal. 46:37–43.

Erickson, A.W., Siniff, D.B., Cline, D.R. and Hofman, R.J. 1971. Distributional ecology of antarctic seals. Pp. 55–76 *in* Symposium on Antarctic Ice and Water Masses, ed. G. Deacon. SCAR, Cambridge.

Gilbert, J.R. and Erickson, A.W. 1977. Distribution and abundance of seals in the pack ice of the Pacific sector of the Southern Ocean. Pp. 703–740 *in* Adaptations within Antarctic Ecosystems, ed. G.A. Llano. Smithsonian Institution, Washington.

Hofman, R.J., Reichle, R., Siniff, D.B. and Müller-Schwarze, D. 1975. The leopard seal (*Hydrurga leptonyx*) at Palmer Station, Antarctica. Pp. 769–782 *in* Adaptations within Antarctic Ecosystems, ed. G.A. Llano. Smithsonian Institution, Washington.

Kaufman, G., Siniff, D.B. and Reichle, R. 1975. Colony behavior of Weddell seals, *Leptonychotes weddelli*, at Hutton Cliffs, Antarctica. Rapp. P.-v. Réun. Cons. int. Explor. Mer 169:228–246.

King, J.E. 1961. The feeding mechanism and jaws of the crabeater seal (*Lobodon carcinophagus*). Mammalia 25:462–466.

King, J.E. 1964. Seals of the World. Brit. Mus. (Nat. Hist.), London.

King, J.E. 1966. Relationships of the hooded and elephant seals (genera *Cystophora* and *Mirounga*). J. Zool. 148:385–398.

Kooyman, G.L. 1968. An analysis of some behavioural and physiological characteristics related to diving in the Weddell seal. Pp. 227–261 *in* Biology of the Antarctic Seas, 3. Antarct. Res. Ser. Am. Geophy. Union, Washington.

Kooyman, G.L., Kerem, D.H., Campbell, W.B. and Wright, J.J. 1970. Diving behavior and respiration in Weddell seals and emperor penguins. Antarct. J. U.S. 5:132–133.

Laws, R.M. 1953. Seals of the Falkland Islands and Dependencies. Oryx 2:87–97.

Laws, R.M. 1964. Comparative biology of antarctic seals. Pp. 445–454 *in* Biologie Antarctique, ed. R. Carrick, M.W. Holdgate and J. Prévost. Hermann, Paris.

Laws, R.M. 1977a. The significance of vertebrates in the antarctic marine ecosystem. Pp. 411–438 *in* Adaptations within Antarctic Ecosystems, ed. G.A. Llano. Smithsonian Institution, Washington.

Laws, R.M. 1977b. Seals and whales of the Southern Ocean. Phil. Trans. R. Soc. Lond. B 279:81–96.

Marlow, B.J. 1967. Mating behaviour in the leopard seal, *Hydrurga leptonyx* (Mammalia: Phocidae) in captivity. Aust. J. Zool. 15:1–5.

Marr, J.W.S. 1935. The South Orkney Islands. "Discovery" Rept. 10:283–382.

Marr, J. 1962. The natural history and geography of the antarctic krill (*Euphausia superba* Dana). "Discovery" Rept. 32:33–464.

Øritsland, T. 1970. Sealing and seal research in the south-west Atlantic pack ice, Sept.–Oct. 1964. Pp. 367–376 *in* Antarctic Ecology, Vol. 1, ed. M.W. Holdgate. Academic Press, London and New York.

Øritsland, T. 1977. Food consumption of seals in the antarctic pack ice. Pp. 749–768 *in* Adaptations within Antarctic Ecosystems, ed. G.A. Llano. Smithsonian Institution, Washington.

Penney, R.L. and Lowry, G. 1967. Leopard seal predation on Adelie penguins. Ecology 48:878–882.

Perkins, J.E. 1945. Biology at Little America III, the West Base of the United States Antarctic Service Expedition, 1939 1941. Proc. Am Phil. Soc. 89:270–284.

Racovitza, E.G. 1900. La vie des animaux et des plantes dans l'Antarctique. Bull. Soc. Belge Géogr. Brussels 24:177–230.

Ray, G.C. 1967. Social behavior and acoustics of the Weddell seal. Antarct. J. U.S. 2:105–106.

Seal, U.S., Erickson, A.W., Siniff, D.B. and Cline, D.R. 1971. Blood chemistry and protein polymorphisms in three species of antarctic seals (*Lobodon carcinophagus, Leptonychotes weddelli* and *Mirounga leonina*). Pp. 181–192 *in* Antarctic Pinnipedia, ed. W.H. Burt. Vol. 18, Antarct. Res. Ser. Am. Geophys. Un. Washington.

Shaugnessy, P.D. 1969. Transferrin polymorphism and population structure of the Weddell seal *Leptonychotes weddelli* (Lesson). Aust. J. Biol. Sci. 22:1581–1584.

Siniff, D.B., Cline, D.R. and Erickson, A.W. 1970. Population densities of seals in the Weddell Sea, Antarctica, in 1968. Pp. 377–394 *in* Antarctic Ecology, Vol. 1, ed. M.W. Holdgate. Academic Press, London and New York.

Siniff, D.B., Teste, J.R. and Keuchle, V.B. 1971. Some observations on the activity patterns of Weddell seals recorded by telemetry. Pp. 173–180 *in* Antarctic Ecology, Pinnipedia, ed. W.H. Burt. Vol. 18, Antarct. Res. Ser. Am. Geophys. Union, Washington.

Siniff, D.B., Stirling, I., Bengtson, J.L. and Reichle, R.A. 1979. Social and reproductive behaviour of crabeater seals (*Lobodon carcinophagus*) during the austral spring. Can. J. Zool. 57:2243–2255.

Smith, M.S.R. 1965. Seasonal movement of the Weddell seal in McMurdo Sound, Antarctica. J. Wildl. Manage. 29:464–470.

Smith, E.A. and Burton, R.W. 1970. Weddell seals of Signy Island. Pp. 415–428 *in* Antarctic Ecology, ed. M.W. Holdgate. Vol. 1, Academic Press, London and New York.

Solianik, G.A. 1964. Some information on antarctic seals. Eng. trans. in Soviet Antarct. Exped. Inform. Bull. 5:179–182, 1965.

Stirling, I. 1969a. Toothwear as a mortality factor in the Weddell seal, *Leptonychotes weddelli.* J. Mammal. 50:559–565.

Stirling, I. 1969b. Ecology of the Weddell seal in McMurdo Sound, Antarctica. Ecology 50:573–586.

Stirling, I. 1971. Population aspects of Weddell seal harvesting at McMurdo Sound, Antarctica. Polar Rec. 15:653–667.

Stirling, I. 1975. Factors affecting the evolution of social behaviour in the Pinnipedia. Rapp. P.-v. Réun. Cons. int. Explor. Mer 169:205–212.

Stirling, I. 1977. Adaptations of Weddell and ringed seals to exploit the polar fast ice habitat in the absence or presence of surface predators. Pp. 741–748 *in* Adaptations within Antarctic Ecosystems, ed. G.A. Llano. Smithsonian Institution, Washington.

CHAPTER SEVEN

Seals and Fisheries

For the Seal no hooks are fashioned nor any three-pronged spear which could capture it: for exceeding hard is the hide which it has upon its limbs as a mighty hedge. But when the fishermen have unwittingly enclosed a seal among the fishes in their well-woven nets, then there is swift labour and haste to pull the nets ashore. For no nets, even if there are very many at hand, would stay the raging seal, but with its violence and sharp claws it will easily break them and rush away and prove a succour to the pent-up fishes but a great grief to the hearts of the fishermen. But if betimes they bring it near the land, there with trident and mighty clubs and stout spears they smite it on the temples and kill it: since destruction comes most swiftly upon seals when they are smitten on the head.

(Oppion, *Halieutica*, vol. 1, pp. 376–91, translated by A.W. Main, Loeb Library ed., London/New York, 1928)

So far, the only interaction I have discussed between man and seal has been that of hunter and prey. From the hunter's point of view, the more plentiful the seals are, the better it is for him. A sustainable yield from as large a stock of seals as possible is what the prudent hunter aims for, though, as we have seen, this objective has rarely been achieved. However, there is another type of interaction which today is more widely spread than the hunting relationship. This is the interaction between seals as major fish predators and fishermen who see the seals as animals which damage their nets and catches and as competitors for what are nowadays often increasingly scarce stocks of fish. Few fishermen are indifferent to seals where they occur in more than moderate numbers, and a commonly expressed opinion is "the fewer seals the better."

There are three main ways in which seals can be said to damage fisheries. To most fishermen the most conspicuous damage is that which the seals do to the fishing gear and the fish already caught. Second, and often assumed to be more serious, is the toll taken by seals from the general stock of fish in the wild. This is usually inconspicuous, though occasionally a seal may bring a large fish to the surface to eat it in full view of an annoyed fisherman who has been less successful. Calculations, sometimes based on very little firm evidence, of the numbers of seals and the amount of food consumed by them can indicate surprisingly large quantities of fish taken by seals and therefore no longer available to fishermen. A third form of damage to fisheries done by seals is as definitive hosts of parasites which spend their larval stages in food fishes.

Direct Damage

The first two kinds of fisheries damage can be found almost everywhere that seals and fishermen co-exist, but in illustrating them I shall choose my examples mainly from the seals of European waters and particularly the grey seal. Damage to gear and captured fish tends to be most common where set nets or lines are used, though it is not confined to these types of gear. Some of the loudest protests against seals have come from salmon fishermen, probably because of the great intrinsic value of Atlantic salmon, which is now exclusively a luxury food, and perhaps to some extent because seals seem to show a definite liking for salmon. In the United Kingdom much of the work of assembling the evidence linking seals, particularly grey seals, with damage at salmon nets, was done by Bennet Rae and his colleagues at the Marine Laboratory, Aberdeen, and I shall quote extensively from his work.

A common type of fixed net used for taking salmon on the Scottish coast, and elsewhere in Europe, consists of a netting bag, either fixed to poles driven into the sea floor or moored with anchors. The entrance to the bag, the door, faces out to sea and consists of two reflexed walls of netting, the cheeks; usually three doors are arranged in line with successively narrower openings. In front of the outermost door a wall of netting, the leader, extends some hundred or so meters out to sea (Figure 7.1). The net operates on the principle that the salmon, working their way along the coast in search of their spawning river, encounter the leader and turn inshore along it until they come to the bag. Here they can enter quite easily through the door but are unable to find their way out again past the back-directed cheeks. The salmon continue through the narrower doors and accumulate in the final compartment, the inner court.

Seals cause damage to these nets in two principal ways (Rae, 1960). They, like the salmon, can enter the net through the door, but then finding it difficult to escape, they tear the meshes of the net with their teeth or claws and leave the net through the resulting hole, through which any uneaten salmon or other fish subsequently entering the door can escape. The other main form of damage is caused by a seal outside the net which herds a salmon into the angle between the inner mouth of the net and the outer wall and then seizes it through the netting, thus tearing the meshes. Both these types of damage have been observed by watchers on cliffs overlooking the nets. Indeed, it is customary to site these nets, where possible, so that the net skipper (often armed with a rifle) can get

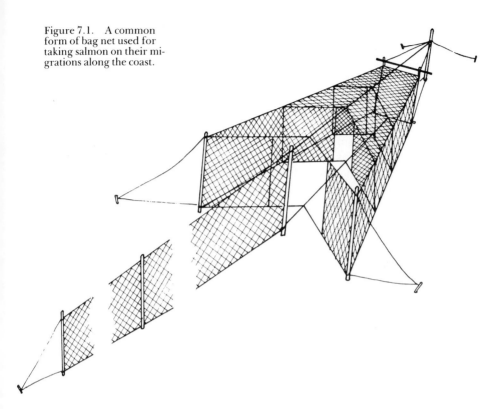

Figure 7.1. A common form of bag net used for taking salmon on their migrations along the coast.

a good view of the bag from the cliffs above. However, the efficacy of shooting at seals in the water as a means of controlling damage is low.

The general introduction of synthetic fibers to replace the tarred cotton twine previously used has greatly reduced seal damage to the netting, but it has not solved all the netters' seal problems. Rae (1960) recorded that at a salmon netting station near Montrose four natural fiber nets and an experimental nylon net were in use. The natural fiber nets were damaged on ten occasions in eight days. Although the synthetic fiber net was not torn, seals entered it through the door on each day in the observation period and not one marketable fish was taken from it. In an attempt to stop this type of depredation, some salmon fishers fitted the doors of their nets with sealproof steel bars 7.5 cm apart (Lockley, 1966). However, it is probable that such narrow doors reduced the efficiency of the nets in catching salmon, since King-Webster (1965) found that salmon tended not to pass through a gap narrower than 15–18 cm.

It is rarer for drift nets set for salmon to be damaged by seals, but seals certainly take gilled fish from these nets and may damage others they do not consume. Rae and Shearer (1965) reported how in one sample of 286 salmon caught in Scottish drift nets, 70 (24.5 percent) had been damaged by seals. It has been estimated that on the northeast coast of England about 5 percent of salmon caught in drift nets had been removed by seals and a further 1.4 percent damaged (Potter and Swain, 1979). Drift nets streamed for herring or mackerel are also liable to seal damage (Bonner, 1972). Fish may be attacked from either side of the net and their head or body bitten off. More headless bodies than separate heads are recovered from nets, but this may be because the severed heads fall away from the nets when the body is devoured. Fish may also be lost if the seal shakes them out of the net as it pulls its own fish free.

Long-lining may be adversely affected by seals that eat the baits from the hooks or take the hooked fish. Rae (1960) gives an account of a seal that had stripped the fish from every hook up to the one on which it was itself caught and drowned.

Besides the immediate damage to captured fish or gear, seal activity can cause consequential damage. A damaged net fishes less effectively— and in the case of a trap net, like a salmon bag, may not fish at all—if the fish swims in through the door and out through the hole made by the seal. On one occasion a grey seal, alarmed in a net by a fisherman, was seen to burst its way out through the netting, to be followed by most of the catch of 20–30 salmon. It may be difficult to recognize that a net has been damaged by a seal if no indication of its visit is left in the form of salmon heads or other remains. In such circumstances, the hole left by the escape of a seal may remain undetected for several days, during which time the net will fail to catch any fish. Many fishermen believe that, even if no damage is done, the visit of a seal to a salmon net may render it less effective in catching fish for several days afterwards, as the scent of the seal scares the fish away. Bearing in mind the refined olfactory sense of fish and the strong smell of seals, this seems not unlikely. Alderdice et al. (1954) found that rinses of mammalian skin, particularly from hair seals and sea lions, produced alarm reactions in Pacific salmon.

The repair of nets damaged by seals may not be expensive in terms of materials, but it can be very time-consuming. In eastern Canada, gill nets set for mackerel, pollock, and cod are often damaged by seals. A seal passing completely through the net makes a large hole about 120 cm in diameter, while numerous small holes 10–15 cm in diameter are caused by the seal's biting or tearing the mesh when removing gilled fish. A net so damaged as to become ineffective is usually brought ashore and stored until the winter when time can be found to repair it (Mansfield and Beck, 1977). In East Anglia the longshore herring season in recent years has been very short, and no time is available for mending nets during it; damaged nets mean a loss of fish for the rest of the season.

The activities of a seal in a fishing net may cause fish to escape. The loss of fish through holes in nets has already been mentioned, but even an undamaged net with a seal in it may lose fish. Seals enter trap nets set for schooling fish such as herring and mackerel in the Maritime Provinces by sliding over the float lines at the top of the nets. The presence of seals inside the net may drive the captive fish back through the mouth of the net and out to sea. Because of this, a net left with fish in it must be guarded by men with guns (Mansfield and Beck, 1977).

Even fishing operations in the open sea are not safe from disturbance caused by seals. Purse seining operations off the coast of South Africa are attended by cape fur seals which cause damage in several ways (Shaughnessy et al., 1981). The main problem is that the seals frighten the fish so that they dive rapidly and escape from the net before pursing is complete, but other more bizarre problems have arisen. Once three seals clambered up a net and boarded a vessel. Another even less fortunate seal was caught in the fish pump, blocked it, and finally died.

The habit some seals have of eating the bait from lobster traps damages the fishery because the seals, in opening the traps to get at the bait, may release lobsters already caught, and a trap without bait, even if its door is still operating properly, will not catch more lobsters. Bait eating by seals is said to be much reduced if the baits are salted for at least a week before use (Mansfield and Beck, 1977).

A form of damage observed in the Scottish salmon fishery is the "marking" of salmon. This damage is inflicted on the fish in the wild, but it is only when the salmon is caught and offered for sale that the harmful effect of marking is felt. The markings consist of tears or scars, mostly single but sometimes multiple, usually from 2.5 cm to 15 cm long and from 2.5 cm to 4 cm deep. They can be found on almost any part of the fish; most are fresh, but some have apparently healed. Marked fish fetch a lower price on the market even if no parts are missing or the wound has left a clean scar.

Although direct evidence is lacking, the marks are believed to be inflicted by the claws of seals. Grey seals and harbor seals both use their foreflippers to manipulate food when feeding, though I do not know if food is ever captured with the flippers. As toothmarks do not invariably accompany the putative claw marks, the manner of inflicting the latter is puzzling. Presumably the marks are made when a salmon seized by a seal is sufficiently agile to escape, though they might also be the result of a seal "playing" with a salmon, with no immediate intention of eating it. The finding that fewer grilse (young salmon on their first return to fresh water) were found to be clawed or bitten than older salmon (Rae and Shearer, 1965) supports the former belief, since the larger fish has a better chance of escaping with only minor injuries; the smaller fish are less likely to survive their first encounter with a seal. Besides claw marks, salmon are often captured with tooth marks or deep bites which correspond to the jaws of a seal.

Depletion of Fish Stocks by Seals

To assess the general damage done to a fishery by seals feeding on the exploited stocks of fish, three sets of data must first be assembled: the size and composition of the stock of seals concerned; the qualitative and quantitative composition of their diet; and their daily food requirement, with appropriate adjustments for age class, season, etc. None of this information is easy to acquire.

Population

The various means of estimating seal abundance have recently been reviewed by Laws (1979). The task is relatively easy only in those species which pup on land in a few large colonies and whose pups remain ashore for a lengthy period. The grey seal along the British coasts fulfills these criteria rather well, and methods have been developed for estimating grey seal population size from pup production data (Boyd and Campbell, 1971; Bonner, 1976). Given an adequate life table (Hewer, 1964; Mansfield and Beck, 1977; Harwood and Prime, 1978), the population can be estimated by using a multiplier with the total pup production. For most grey seal populations a multiplier of 3.5–4.5 is appropriate, depending on whether the population is stable or changing in size. Total pup production is difficult to assess directly unless frequent visits can be made to the breeding rookeries. At the Farne Islands, for example, for many years all pups have been tallied in a sequence of counts in which each pup born since the preceding count is marked with a dye peculiar to its counting period; this tally gives estimates of pup production that are very accurate (Coulson and Hickling, 1964; Bonner and Hickling, 1971).

In many cases it is not practicable to make repeated visits to a seal colony. Radford et al. (1978) devised a statistical procedure for estimating pup production from a single census, despite the variable date at which pupping began. This relied on classifying the count of pups into morphological age classes which enables the form and timing of the birth-rate curve to be determined. They were able to determine the duration of each of the pup classes they used from a series of classified counts taken over one season. This information allows total pup production to be calculated from a single classified count. The precision of the final result naturally depends on the timing of the count in relation to the mean birth date; estimates from the counts made before the mean birth date are inaccurate, but those from counts 10–25 days after the peak of pupping agree with each other to within 8 percent.

If ground counts cannot be made it is sometimes possible to use aerial photography to assess the number of pups present. It has been

Figure 7.2. Recoveries of harbor seals tagged in the Wash, East Anglia. After Bonner and Witthames, 1974.

found that counts of grey seal pups made from stereo pairs of aerial photographs taken under suitable conditions agree to within 5 percent of counts made simultaneously on the ground (Bonner, 1972, 1976; Vaughan, 1971a). It is not possible to make classified counts of grey seal pups from aerial photographs, however, as the imagery is not detailed enough. Hiby and Harwood (1979) showed that population estimates of grey seals based on aerial photographs are liable to be biased upwards, but the amount of this bias is small (less than 2 percent).

In species such as the harbor seal, which are born between tide-marks and can swim within a few minutes of birth, direct counts of the pups cannot be made. Vaughan (1971b) used aerial surveys at low water when seals were hauled out on sandbanks as a means of assessing the number of seals in the Wash, East Anglia. However, he found that the recorded totals were highly variable and did not correlate with season, wind direction, or tide cycle. Population estimates based on mark-recapture experiments (Summers and Mountford, 1975) indicated a consistently higher population than that indicated by aerial photographs. Vaughan (1978) explained this discrepancy by supposing that in a relatively small area such as the Wash, many animals are compelled to seek food outside and travel considerable distances out into the North Sea. From time to time these animals return to the security of the Wash sandbanks to bask, but the whole population is never present at one time. Evidence of tag recoveries of Wash-marked seals 200–300 km from the point of tagging (Bonner and Witthames, 1974) supports this theory (Figure 7.2).

A species like the ringed seal presents the greatest difficulty in making population assessments. This seal is distributed over a wide area, is easily alarmed, and produces its pups in lairs in the snow which are not easily located. Trained dogs can be used to sniff them out (Smith, 1973), but this method is very time consuming. During the moulting season in May and June, ringed seals can be counted on the ice where they haul out to bask. The use of an aircraft flying at 12–30 m at speeds of about 220 km per hour enables large areas to be covered and the seals counted before they have time to react to the aircraft. However, the interpretation of these counts depends on a detailed knowledge of the diurnal and seasonal variation in the haul-out pattern of the seals.

Despite the difficulties involved much effort has gone into estimating the size of seal populations. Special techniques—ultraviolet photography used to reveal white harp seal pups on ice (Lavigne et al., 1977) for example, and the statistical surveys of antarctic seals (Siniff ct al., 1970)—have been developed for this purpose. Not only do seal numbers have relevance to fisheries problems (often the main cause behind government funding of seal research), but population size and changes are of prime interest in management, conservation, and environmental monitoring.

Diet

Most studies on the diet of seals which have any pretensions to a quantitative approach depend on the examination of stomach contents. Unfortunately, it is a common observation that a high proportion of stomachs examined are empty or contain no recent food fragments. Digestion in these carnivores is rapid. Havinga (1933) was unable to determine how long food remains in the stomach but concluded that all traces of a meal will have disappeared in 3 hours. Charcoal in fish fed to harbor seals reappeared in the feces within 6–14 hours. Besides rapid transmission times, other factors may result in empty stomachs. Seals shot in the water often, perhaps usually, vomit food if the stomach is full. Rae (1960) suggested that seals trapped in salmon nets panic and vomit their stomach contents—a conclusion supported by the well-digested food particles found in water taken from oily patches near salmon nets.

When whole fish are found in stomachs there is usually little difficulty in producing quantitative estimates of diet. Of the 175 stomachs of harbor seals from Scottish waters that Rae (1968) examined, 64 contained recognizable food remains. Gadoids (mainly whiting, *Gadus merlangus*, and saith, *G. virens*) were most abundant, appearing in more than 40 percent of the stomachs examined (Figure 7.3). From 322 stomachs of grey seals, of which 176 contained recognizable food, Rae (1968) again found gadoids (particularly cod, *Gadus morhua*) to be most abundant, followed by salmonids, largely salmon, *Salmo salar* (Figure 7.4).

Figure 7.3.   Occurrence of food items in the stomachs of harbor seals taken in Scottish waters. From Rae, 1968.

Figure 7.4.   Occurrence of food items in the stomachs of grey seals taken in Scottish waters. From Rae, 1968.

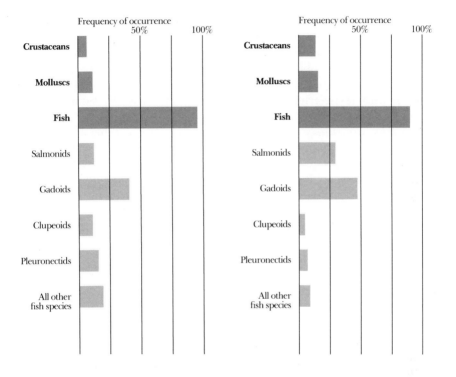

Havinga (1933), after examining 238 stomachs of harbor seals from Dutch coastal waters, determined the most important items of the diet to be flounders, *Pleuronectes flesus*, which made up not less than 30 percent of the food, followed by whiting (17 percent), herring, *Clupea harengus* (17 percent), and two sea scorpions, *Cottus scorpius* and *Agonus cataphractus* (16 percent together). Havinga's determinations were made on otoliths recovered, and he noted that otoliths from some fish might remain longer than those from others in a seal's stomach, thus introducing a source of error into his analyses. Anderson et al. (1974) also used otoliths, recovered from scats, as an indication of species eaten, together with a rough estimate of their size, but this method did not allow a quantitative treatment.

Sergeant (1951) reported on 202 harbor seal stomachs from the Wash. Only 25 of these contained recognizable food (besides milk), and Sergeant concluded that mollusks, mainly the whelk, *Buccinum undatum*, predominated in the diet, forming 92 percent by weight at time of consumption. This weight, however, included the massive shell of the mollusk. It seems likely that whelk opercula (on which Sergeant's determinations had been made) accumulate in the stomach, giving a false impression of the importance of these mollusks in the diet of Wash seals. Stomachs of the same species from the Norfolk coast, 100 km by sea from the Wash, showed an overwhelming preponderance of fish remains, mainly pleuronectids and gobies, *Gobius minutus* (Bonner, 1972).

Even if the data obtained from examining stomach contents are not themselves misleading, the provenance of the sample is unlikely to be random with respect to the feeding range of the seals. Bennet Rae's (1968) finding of the importance of salmon in the diet of Scottish grey seals, for example, may have been influenced by the fact that a large part of his sample was obtained by salmon fishermen in or near their nets.

Most examinations of the diet of seals show them to be highly versatile feeders. At least 29 species of fish, together with some invertebrates, were found to be taken by both grey and harbor seals in the United Kingdom, of which 13 were common to both species. With such a wide spectrum of food, large samples of seals are needed to give precise data, bearing in mind possible variation with time of year, site of feeding, and age class of the seals concerned. Perhaps largely because it is much more difficult to sample phocids pelagically than it is otariids, there are no European studies that compare in extent of coverage with classic works from the North Pacific, such as that of Taylor et al. (1955) on the northern fur seal. We must await an effective means of sampling seals approximately randomly on their feeding grounds before we can claim to have an adequate knowledge of their diet. I do not know of a single example of a European grey seal or harbor seal being collected at sea more than a few tens of meters from land, except in association with fishing nets or lines.

Food Consumption

Even if adequate quantitative data are believed to be available on the composition of the food, it may still be difficult to relate this to the amount of food consumed by a stock of seals in a period of time, say a year. It would be virtually impossible to conduct a comprehensive study of food consumption rates of seals in the wild. Because of this, estimates of food consumption have relied heavily on the feeding rates of seals held in captivity and from general considerations of the energy requirements of marine mammals for metabolism and growth.

Keys (1968) was the first to provide extensive data on captive feeding rates. He concluded that about 6–10 percent of body weight per day is a reasonable estimate for the amount of food eaten daily, the higher rate to apply to the younger animals. Geraci (1975) gave a lower rate of

4–7 percent of body weight per day; this probably refers to adult seals, as Geraci (1972) records that two young harp seals consumed between 6.9 and 8.4 percent of body weight per day.

David Sergeant (1969) calculated the feeding rate of cetaceans by considering the ratio between heart weight and body weight as being 11 percent of the ratio of daily food requirement and body weight. Applied to seals this would indicate a daily food requirement of 5–6 percent of body weight. Christina Lockyer (unpublished) concluded from a consideration of the likely energy expenditure of grey seals and the calorific contents of various possible diets that a food consumption rate of 5–6 percent of body weight per day is probable for adults and a slightly higher rate for juveniles. A very much higher requirement was postulated by Miller (1978), who calculated from metabolic studies that female northern fur seals and males of under four years need 14 percent of body weight of food daily for maintenance alone, and that water temperature is an important factor in determining the requirement.

The highest rates of food consumption have been recorded in captive seals that have ample room in which to exercise and are fed a significant portion of their diet after dark. At the Seattle Aquarium, four-year-old female and five-year-old male northern fur seals were kept in a large tank 4.5 m deep and had been fed up to one-third body weight per day of mixed fish and squid. The seals were fed to just short of satisfaction, and the ration has now settled down to 26–27 percent of body weight per day, which allows normal body growth (John Nightingale, Seattle Aquarium, personal communication).

Captive feeding studies and physiological calculations thus indicate a wide range of food requirements. A seal in the wild will balance its energy budget, eating enough food to provide the energy it expends in activity as well as in growth, either of the body generally or of the blubber layer specifically (and in the case of pregnant females, the fetus). The undeterminable variable in this is the activity of the animal in the wild. We have little direct information on this. The instrumentation of seals in the wild with some form of activity recorder would yield interesting results.

To reach a realistic yearly stock consumption of food it is necessary to divide the stock into juveniles and adults (with their differing food requirements), and the year into periods of feeding and of the fasting associated with breeding and moulting. And even when this has been done, the fishermen are still unlikely to be satisfied with the result, justly claiming that the amount of food consumed may be substantially less than the amount killed. Protectionists might retort that seals feed on predator fish whose removal from the population enhances the survival of other, smaller fish (Council for Nature Seals Group, 1979). Clearly, any attempt to assess damage to fisheries caused by seals eating wild fish is fraught with difficulty. It might be thought self-evident that if seals were eliminated entirely, so that fish stocks increased and fishermen landed more fish, then the fishermen would be better off. But even this simple assumption has been challenged (Williams in Council for Nature Seals Group, 1979). Demand elasticity models for fish indicate that increased landings might in fact result in depressed prices and smaller net revenues to the fishermen.

Seals as Parasite Hosts

The third form of fisheries damage I referred to at the beginning of this chapter relates to the seal's position as a host to parasites. This position is most significant and conspicuous with regard to the codworm.

Infestation of cod with the larvae of an anisakine nematode, *Phocanema* (= *Porrocaecum,* = *Terranova*) *decipiens* or codworm, is a serious problem in Canada, the United Kingdom, and Norway. Although larvae may be abundant in the mesenteries and viscera of an infested fish, these are discarded before the fish is offered for sale, so the worms most troublesome commercially are those found in the musculature, usually in the flaps of muscle surrounding the visceral cavity but also in the axial musculature of the fillet. The presence of codworms in cod flesh obviously poses a marketing problem. Although the worms are killed by freezing or any ordinary method of cooking, so that no health hazard exists, they can be conspicuous and active and are so aesthetically objectionable that they may cause the customer to avoid cod or other fish in the future. Therefore, fillets of cod suspected of being wormy must be examined individually over an illuminated plate and any worms removed by hand. This adds substantially to the processing cost of the fish, especially if the most heavily infested fish must be discarded.

The life cycle of the codworm is still not completely understood (Figure 7.5). Adult and pre-adult worms are found in many marine mammals, but they seem to be particularly abundant in grey seals (Scott and Fisher, 1955; Young, 1972; Mansfield and Beck, 1977). Eggs are shed into the water with the feces of the seal and hatch within 10–60 days, depending on the temperature. The resulting larvae are thought to encyst in the benthic crustaceans that ingest them. When the crustaceans are eaten by demersal fish, the liberated larvae bore their way through the gut wall of the host and encyst on the mesenteries or in the muscles. There they remain until the host fish is eaten by a mammal in whose gut they can mature, to produce the eggs for the next generation (Platt, 1975).

Because grey seals are the major hosts of codworm and both eastern Canada and the United Kingdom have large and increasing populations of these seals, it is not surprising that increases in the infestation rate of

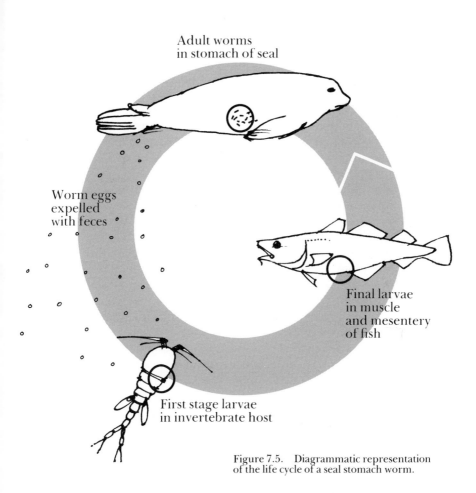

Figure 7.5.   Diagrammatic representation of the life cycle of a seal stomach worm.

cod by codworm have been reported. Rae (1972) noted that the percentage of infested cod in the central northern North Sea increased from 4 percent in 1956–61, to 11 percent in 1962–65, and 47 percent in 1966–70. Other fishing areas showed less definite trends, which Rae supposed might have been due in part to the fishing out of the larger cod, so that the fishery was dependent on the smallest fish, which tend to be less heavily parasitized. Since 1970 there has been no evidence of an increase in the infestation rate around the United Kingdom (Parrish and Shearer, 1977).

Besides *Phocanema*, seals are often hosts to two other anisakine nematodes, *Contracaecum osculatum* and *Anisakis simplex* (and the larvae of several others which, however, do not mature in the seals). *Contracaecum osculatum* develops in cephalopods and has no impact on fisheries. *Anisakis simplex* is the adult stage of the herring worm; however, the principal definitive hosts of this species appear to be small cetaceans.

Control Measures

Faced with fisheries damage caused by seals, the usual response of fishermen is to seek to eliminate the seals. In the case of net damage this may be a relatively simple process. There is evidence that in many cases individual seals are responsible for much of the damage at fixed nets. Salmon fishermen have traditionally dealt with such seals either by shooting them—not an easy task unless there is a convenient cliff above the nets from which a marksman can aim down—or by poisoning. In the Scottish salmon fishery, poisoned baits were prepared by placing a packet of strychnine inside a kelt or a sea trout and hanging the bait in the nets. Poison was said to be very effective, but the use of strychnine has been forbidden for this purpose in the United Kingdom since 1970, and no acceptable substitute has yet been found.

Shooting seals at nets is most effective when the nets are sited in restricted situations such as sea lochs or river mouths. Rae (1960) recounts an episode in which a salmon netsman took over a fishing station which had previously been abandoned because of seal damage. In five seasons the salmon catch rose from 2 to 767, in which time 624 seals, mostly grey seals, had been shot.

Explosives have been used to kill seals. A Canadian halibut fishing boat reportedly spent $4,000 annually on materials to deter sea lions, including large amounts of dynamite (Working Party on Marine Mammals, 1978).

In an attempt to find deterrents less destructive and therefore more acceptable to conservation interests, experiments have been made into the use of sound to keep seals away from nets.

Peter Shaughnessy and his colleagues (Shaughnessy et al., 1981) experimented with various devices to keep Cape fur seals from interfering with purse-seining operations. Weighted firecrackers that exploded underwater after the net had been pursed caused most of the seals to leave the net promptly; but they soon returned, generally within four or five minutes. Seals swimming slowly or lying at the surface of the water responded by diving when a firecracker was exploded; they looked back at the vessel before returning to their previous activities. They reacted similarly, but less promptly, when a second firecracker was exploded. An arc-discharge transducer producing noise levels similar to firecrackers or 0.303-inch bullets hitting the water caused seals to move away from the cod end of a trawl net, but not to leave a purse seine.

In Shaughnessy's experiments the underwater playback of recordings of killer whale (*Orcinus orca*) vocalizations produced observable, though not impressive, changes in seal behavior. Seals which had been swimming slowly or lying at the surface of the water dived, remained submerged for 15–30 seconds, and then raised their heads above the water and looked back toward the vessel with the transducer. None responded by fleeing. Some of the seals in a purse seine also dived and a few moved out of the net over the float line, but others ignored killer whale recordings and continued to feed on fish within the net. The presence of models of killer whale dorsal fins during the playback did not modify the behavior. Shaughnessy and his colleagues concluded that deterrents such as these were ineffective in reducing the disturbance caused by seals at purse seines. They speculated that a method that actually inflicted pain on the seals might be more effective.

Anderson and Hawkins (1978) came to the same conclusion after conducting a series of trials with a young captive harbor seal and seals at a salmon netting station. They used a variety of sounds that spanned the entire hearing range of seals. They found that, as in the South African test, the seals quickly became accustomed to the stimuli and stopped responding to them. It seems almost certain that in the absence of some regular reinforcement, namely the killing or injuring of seals, a sound meant to deter would eventually come to be regarded merely as a dinner gong.

Bounties

More general action against seal populations alleged to be harming fisheries often takes the form of a bounty scheme, whereby hunters killing seals are rewarded on producing proof of the kill. Sometimes such schemes are organized by private fishing interests or fishing associations, but usually they are the responsibility of government or local fishery authorities. Canada instituted a bounty on harbor seals in the Maritimes in 1927 (McLaren, 1977) which locally greatly reduced the seal population (Wiles, 1968). Up until 1949 the bounty was paid for seal snouts, and because of identification difficulties sundry other biological materials (including, it is rumored, the occasional porcupine scrotum) were offered in exchange for bounty. The bounty was thereafter paid for the jaw of the seal, which provided the first firm evidence of the widespread abundance of the grey seal in the Canadian Maritimes. Currently in Canada, the seal bounty is paid for grey seal jaws.

Bounties have been paid for seals in Sweden since 1900 (Söderberg, 1975). Although seals, particularly grey seals, have been greatly reduced in the Baltic since bounties were instigated, this has been more because of the economic value of the carcasses than for the sake of the bounty, which according to Söderberg was not considered high in relation to the trouble involved in claiming it. Since 1974 grey seals have been protected in Sweden, except in the vicinity of salmon nets. Other European countries which have abandoned bounty payments for seals include Denmark, Ireland, and the United Kingdom (where bounties were paid by the Eastern Sea Fisheries Committee for seals, mostly harbor seals, killed in the Wash).

In general, bounty schemes are most effective where there is already some regular hunting effort. Even then the bounty kill often takes many more young animals than breeding stock and is thus less likely to reduce population size, usually the intention of the scheme.

Direct killing of seals by government agencies is another means of reducing seal stocks. In eastern Canada large numbers of grey seals have been killed in the Gulf of St. Lawrence and on the Basque Islands in an attempt to control the population (Mansfield and Beck, 1977). In the United Kingdom the Fisheries Departments organized kills of grey seal pups at the Farne Islands and in Orkney in 1959 and 1960; at the latter location some adults were killed also (Hickling, 1962; Consultative Committee on Grey Seals and Fisheries, 1963). The efficacy of these attempts is doubtful and, unless a valuable product can be obtained, they are very costly.

Harvesting

One means of reducing costs to central funds for controlling the seal population is to promote or encourage commercial harvesting of the seals. The annual harvest of grey seal pups in Orkney (which I shall refer to later) is such an example, as is the harvest of Cape fur seals in southern Africa. The African seals are a substantial problem to purse seiners for pilchard and anchovy and to trawlers for hake. The justification of the annual maximum permitted harvest of 70,000 "yearling" seals (7–10 months old) is based partly on the need to control the fisheries damage (Best, 1973).

Harvests related to fisheries protection offer a potentially effective means of controlling seal populations. Provided the seals afford a sufficiently valuable product, the operation can be self-financing, and if the sealing is adequately monitored, the size of the exploited stock can be reduced and maintained at the desired level by carefully calculated quotas. Although the ultimate effect on the commercial fishery may be hard to predict, as explained earlier, the existence of a controlled sealing operation may serve to restrain fishermen from taking independent action against the seals, which is likely to be uncontrolled and unreported and ultimately more damaging to the seal population (Shaughnessy, 1976).

References

Alderdice, D.F., Brett, J.R., Idler, D.R. and Fagerlund, U. 1954. Further observations on olfactory perception in migrating adult coho and spring salmon—properties of the repellant in mammalian skin. Fish. Res. Bd. Canada, Pacific Coast Station, Prog. Rep. 98:10–12.

Anderson, S.S., Bonner, W.N., Baker, J.R. and Richards, R. 1974. Grey seals, *Halichoerus grypus*, of the Dee Estuary and observations on a characteristic lesion in British seals. J. Zool., Lond. 174:429–440.

Anderson, S.S. and Hawkins, A.D. 1978. Scaring seals by sound. Mammal Rev. 8(1 & 2):19–24.

Best, P.B. 1973. Seals and sealing in South and South-West Africa. South Africa Shipping News and Fishing Industry Rev. 28(12):49–57.

Bonner, W.N. 1972. The grey seal and the common seal in European waters. Oceanogr. Mar. Biol. Ann. Rev. 10:461–507.

Bonner, W.N. 1976. Stocks of grey seals and common seals in Great Britain, NERC Publ. Series C. No. 16. 16pp.

Bonner, W.N. and Hickling, G. 1971. The grey seals of the Farne Islands: report for the period October 1969 to July 1971. Trans. Nat. Hist. Soc. Northumberland, Durham and Newcastle upon Tyne (NS) 17(4):141–162.

Bonner, W.N. and Witthames, S.R. 1974. Dispersal of common seals (*Phoca vitulina*) tagged in the Wash, East Anglia. J. Zool., Lond. 174:528–531.

Boyd, J.M. and Campbell, R.N. 1971. The Grey seal (*Halichoerus grypus*) at North Rona, 1959–1968. J. Zool., Lond. 164:469–512.

Consultative Committee on Grey seals and Fisheries. 1963. Grey Seals and Fisheries: Report of the Consultative Committee on Grey seals and Fisheries. The Nature Conservancy. Her Majesty's Stationery Office, London.

Coulson, J.C. and Hickling, G. 1964. The breeding biology of the grey seal, *Halichoerus grypus* (Fab.) on the Farne Islands, Northumberland. J. Anim. Ecol. 33:485–512.

Council for Nature Seals Group. 1979. A report to the Secretary of State for Scotland. Council for Nature, London. 56pp. (mimeo).

Geraci, J.R. 1972. Experimental thiamine deficiency in captive harp seals, *Phoca groenlandica*, induced by eating herring, *Clupea harengus*, and smelts, *Osmerus mordax*. Can. J. Zool. 50:179–195.

Geraci, J.R. 1975. Pinniped nutrition. Rapp. P.-v. Reun. Cons. int. Explor. Mer 169:312–323.

Harwood, J. and Prime, J.H. 1978. Some factors affecting the size of British grey seal populations. J. appl. Ecol. 15:401–411.

Havinga, B. 1933. Der Seehund (*Phoca vitulina* L.) in den Hollaendischen Gewassern. Ned. Dierkd. Ver. Tijdschr. 3:79–111.

Hewer, H.R. 1964. The determination of age, sexual maturity, longevity and a life table in the grey seal (*Halichoerus grypus*). Proc. zool. Soc. Lond. 142:593–624.

Hiby, A.R. and Harwood, J. 1979. The reliability of population estimates of grey seals based on aerial photographs. ICES, CM 1979/N:12 (mimeo).

Hickling, G. 1962. Grey Seals and the Farne Islands. Routledge and Kegan Paul Ltd., London.

Keys, M.C. 1968. Nutrition of pinnipeds. Pp. 359–395 *in* The Behavior and Physiology of Pinnipeds, ed. R.J. Harrison, R.C. Hubbard, R.S. Peterson, C.E. Rice and R.J. Schusterman. New York, Appleton, Century, Crofts.

King-Webster, W.A. 1965. Just how does a fixed engine work? Salmon Net 1:10–16.

Lavigne, D.M., Øritsland, T. and Falconer, A. 1977. Remote sensing and ecosystem management. Norsk Polarinstitutt, Skr. No. 166:1–51.

Laws, R.M. 1979. Monitoring whale and seal populations. Pp. 115–140 *in* Monitoring the Marine Environment, ed. D. Nichols. London, Institute of Biology.

Lockley, R.M. 1966. Grey Seal, Common Seal. London, Andre Deutsch.

Mansfield, A.W. and Beck, B. 1977. The grey seal in eastern Canada. Fisheries and Marine Services Tech. Rep. No. 704. 81pp.

McLaren, I.A. 1977. The status of seals in Canada. Pp. 71–78 *in* Canada's Threatened Species and Habitats, ed. T. Mosquin and C. Suchal. Can. Nature Federation. Ottawa.

Miller, L.K. 1978. Energetics of the northern fur seal in relation to climate and food resources of Bering Sea. Report to the U.S. Marine Mammal Commission. MMC-75/08 PB-275 296. January.

Parrish, B.B. and Shearer, W.M. 1977. Effects of seals on fisheries. ICES C.M. 1977/M:14. 6pp. (mimeo).

Platt, N.E. 1975. Infestation of cod (*Gadus morhua* L.) with larvae of codworm (*Terranova decipiens* Krabbe) and herringworm, *Anisakis* sp. (Nematoda Ascaridata), in North Atlantic and arctic waters. J. appl. Ecol. 12:437–450.

Potter, E.C.E. and Swain, A. 1979. Seal predation in the North-east England coastal salmon fishery. ICES C.M. 1971/N:9. 4 pp. (mimeo).

Radford, P.J., Summers, C.F. and Young, K.M. 1978. A statistical procedure for estimating grey seal pup production from a single census. Mammal Rev. 8(1 & 2):35–42.

Rae, B.B. 1960. Seals and Scottish fisheries. Mar. Res. 1960, No. 2. 39pp.

Rae, B.B. 1968. The food of seals in Scottish waters. Mar. Res. 1968, No. 2. 23pp.

Rae, B.B. 1972. A review of the codworm problem in the North Sea and in western Scottish waters, 1958–1970. Mar. Res. 1972, No. 2. 22pp.

Rae, B.B. and Shearer, W.M. 1965. Seal damage to salmon fisheries. Mar. Res. 1965, No. 2. 39pp.

Scott, D.M. and Fisher, H.D. 1958. Incidence of the ascarid *Porrocaecum decipiens* in the stomachs of three species of seals along the southern Canadian Atlantic seaboard. J. Fish. Res. Bd. Canada 15(4):495–561.

Sergeant, D.E. 1951. The status of the common seal (*Phoca vitulina* L.) on the East Anglian coast. J. mar. Biol. Assoc. U.K. 29:707–717.

Sergeant, D.E. 1969. Feeding rates of Cetacea. Fisk. Dir. Skr. Ser. Hav Unders. 15:246–258.

Shaughnessy, P.D. 1976. Controversial harvest. African Wildl. 30(6):26–31.

Shaughnessy, P.D. Semmelink, A., Cooper, J. and Forst, P.G.H. 1981. Attempts to develop acoustic methods of keeping cape fur seals *Arctocephalus pusillus* from fishing nets. Biol. Conserv. 21:141–158.

Siniff, D.B., Cline, D.R. and Erickson, A.W. 1970. Population densities of seals in the Weddell Sea, Antarctica, in 1968. Pp. 377–394 *in* Antarctic Ecology, Vol. 1, ed. M.W. Holdgate, Academic Press, London and New York.

Smith, T.G. 1973. Population dynamics of the ringed seal in the Canadian eastern arctic. Fish. Res. Bd. Canada, Bull. 181. 55pp.

Söderberg, S. 1975. Sealhunting in Sweden. Pp. 104–116 *in* Proc. Symp. on the Seal in the Baltic. Nat. Swedish Environment Protection Board. SNV PM 591.

Summers, C.F. and Mountford, M.D. 1975. Counting the common seal. Nature, Lond. 253(5494):670–671.

Taylor, F.H.C., Fujinaga, M. and Wilke, F. 1955. Distribution and food habits of the fur seal of the North Pacific Ocean. U.S. Fish and Wildl. Serv. 86pp. Government Printing Office, Washington.

Vaughan, R.W. 1971a. Aerial photography in seals research. *In* The Application of aerial Photography to the Work of the Nature Conservancy. Proc. Nature Conservancy Staff Seminar, Edinburgh, 1970 (mimeo).

Vaughan, R.W. 1971b. Aerial survey of seals in the Wash. Natural Environment Council: Seals Research Unit Occas. Publ. No. 2.

Vaughan, R.W. 1978. A study of common seals in the Wash. Mammal Rev. 8(1 & 2):25–34.

Wiles, M. 1968. Possible effects of the harbour seal bounty on codworm infestation of Atlantic cod in the Gulf of St. Lawrence, the Strait of Belle Isle, and the Labrador Sea. J. Fish. Res. Bd. Canada 25(12):2749–2753.

Working Party on Marine Mammals. 1978. Mammals in the Sea. FAO Fishery Ser. No. 5, 1. 264pp.

Young, P.C. 1972. The relationship between the presence of larval anisakine nematodes in cod and marine mammals in British home waters. J. appl. Ecol. 9:459–485.

CHAPTER EIGHT

The Grey Seal in the United Kingdom
Abundance as a Conservation Problem

In the autumn of 1978 the Department of Agriculture and Fisheries for Scotland found itself at the center of a controversy which while it lasted attracted national and even international interest. The strength of feeling aroused was intense, though in general few people were aware of the real issues. For the media it was a nine-day wonder, with strong emotional appeals and romantic backgrounds for their location shots. Questions were asked at Westminster, leaders appeared in the London *Times*. There was even a debate in the European parliament at Brussels, while far off in the USSR, the International Union for the Conservation of Nature and Natural Resources (IUCN) passed a resolution condemning the action proposed.

The matter concerned the grey seals of Scotland. The Department of Agriculture and Fisheries believed them to be increasing too fast and creating a threat to the fishing industry, which the Department had a statutory duty to protect. Acting on information on the size and rate of increase of grey seal stocks received from an independent group of scientists, the Sea Mammals Research Unit of the Natural Environment Research Council (a body funded indirectly by the Department of Education and Science and quite unconnected with the fisheries departments), the Department of Agriculture and Fisheries had decided that an active management policy was required to check the increase and reduce the stock of the Scottish grey seals.

As John Lister-Kaye (1979) has pointed out, rows about seal culls are nothing new in the United Kingdom or elsewhere. However, this was the first time in the United Kingdom that a considered piece of official seal policy based on extensive scientific evidence (though its opponents would claim that the evidence was insufficient) was forced to be abandoned as a result of popular pressure. It is right that governments should be responsive to the people they represent and that public opinion should be listened to in the process of government. However, if in these circumstances a sensible course is to be pursued it is essential that the opinions to which government harkens be informed opinions. In the great grey seal controversy this was very far from being the case. Although the problem was primarily a British one, it is of sufficient interest to be worth examining as a case history.

The grey seal is a peculiarly British seal, though it was not until as late as 1825 that it was properly established as being part of the British fauna (Hewer, 1974). Of the world's population of more than 108,000 grey seals (ICES, 1977), roughly two-thirds occur in the British Isles, mostly around the Scottish islands. The late stage at which the grey seal became known to science in the United Kingdom (a situation that was paralleled in Canada, where the second-largest part of the population lives) arose more from a confusion in nomenclature than from ignorance. Of the two breeding species of seal found in Britain, one—currently the less abundant—was known simply as "the seal" or "the common seal." This was *Phoca vitulina,* or the harbor seal as it is known in North America. There was a tendency to assume that if a seal were abundant in an area, it was a "common seal," and in this way some large groups of grey seals were overlooked though their existence as *seals* was well known. (To avoid any confusion, I have referred to *P. vitulina* as the harbor seal throughout.)

Grey seals have a long history in Britain. I have referred earlier to their importance to prehistoric man. Certainly as far as the archeological evidence goes, grey seals were far more important to the early hunters than were harbor seals. Because of the accident of language that deprived us of a term to distinguish the grey seal from other seals (only in Shetland did there seem to be a separate word in common use that served this purpose), it is often only by inference based on geography and, less commonly, biological detail that we can determine whether an early reference is to the grey seal. When we read in the Durham Household Book (Hickling, 1962) that on December 4, 1531, a "seale calff" taken from the Farne Islands was carried to the Prior, we can be sure that it was a grey seal. A graphic description in an early account of the Orkneys (*Descriptio Insulareum Orcadiarum,* 1529) likewise leaves no doubt:

> In that part of the world great monsters peculiar to the country are taken with nets made of hemp and there is a large rock distant from the land half a mile by name Selk Skerry where sea fowl live and build their nests. On that rock the monsters beforementioned when the tide flows ascend to the top but on the ebbing they fall into a well where by no force can they get out, there being no exit. The peasantry, mutually grumbling among themselves at delays coming in the way draw near to the rock with large hazel sticks; but at first the monsters, eying them with dread and gnashing their teeth with rage, strive to get out of the way with wide open mouth, then they attack with all their strength and voluntarily carry on the combat. If the first escape without injury all the others attack the men with their teeth, but if the first shall fall and die all the others take to flight, and I have seen sixty taken at one time.

The skerry off North Ronaldsay, to this day called Seal Skerry, is still an important hauling-out place for grey seals. There are similar records of sealing in the autumn (and therefore for grey seals, which uniquely pup at that season) at Haskeir in the Hebrides, dating back to 1549.

It is with the seals at Haskeir that this account might well start, since it was this particular seal hunt that led to the legislation that first protected grey seals in Great Britain. Haskeir is a tiny islet some 13 km off the coast of North Uist in the Outer Hebrides (Figure 8.1). To this island, and to several similar ones in the same general area, the crofters from the islands of North Uist, Harris, and Lewis had repaired each autumn to kill the seals on them. It was a tradition that went back many years, indeed centuries. In 1913 a gentleman named Hesketh Prichard described the islanders' clubbing of the seals as "slowly but surely advancing them along the road to extinction" (Prichard, 1913). Since the cropping of the seals at Haskeir had been going on for at least three and a half centuries (and probably many more), the progress along this sad road was certainly slow, though some might doubt if it were really sure.

Nevertheless, Prichard's account, which Rae (1960) caustically remarked "set a standard in emotional appeal, in scientific inaccuracy and in illogical reasoning which appears to have been followed, doubtless under misapprehension, in subsequent press articles and statements on the grey seal," prompted a member of Parliament, Charles Lyle, to introduce a bill to confer protection on the seals. Lyle's bill was drafted without any apparent consideration at the time of the status of the grey seal in the British Isles, or of the effect the legislation might have on fisheries. The supporters of the bill believed that the British stock of grey seals comprised about 500 animals, though there is no evidence to show how this figure was arrived at. While it is certain that the grey seal was much less abundant at the beginning of this century than it is today, there is no doubt that this was a considerable underestimate. However, responding to the sentiments aroused by Prichard's account of the brutality of the slaughter of young and old alike of this the largest of the wild animals that breed in Britain, Parliament passed Lyle's bill, which became the Grey Seal Protection Act of 1914. This act established a closed season from October 1 to December 15 each year in which it was unlawful to kill or take grey seals, and prohibited altogether the killing of grey seals at Haskeir. It was originally intended to provide protection for five years, but was thereafter extended from year to year under the Expiring Laws Continuation Acts.

By the 1920s complaints were becoming numerous of the damage done by grey seals to fisheries, particularly salmon fisheries, and shooting grey seals in the vicinity of salmon nets (as noted earlier) became a common practice. At the same time, conservationists were concerned that many grey seal pups were at risk at both ends of the closed season. Further, it was clear that even the existence of the legislation was widely unknown in the remote places where the seals it was supposed to protect were most abundant.

In an attempt to meet the wishes of the opposing parties, Parliament passed another act to protect grey seals in 1932. The new act extended the closed season from September 1 to December 31, but it contained the important proviso that orders could be made suspending or altering the closed season in specified areas so that control measures could be carried out to protect fisheries. Orders to suspend the closed season would contain regulations prohibiting the killing of grey seals except by persons holding permits and would specify the weapons that were to be used. Perhaps as a sentimental acknowledgment of its role in grey seal protection, Haskeir was singled out as a place where the only order that could be made was one to extend the closed season. No adequate attempt had been made to establish the abundance of grey seals around Scotland generally, but a new population estimate of 8,000 was put forward.

Under the Grey Seal Protection Acts the seals continued to increase in most of their haunts. It is not certain to what extent this was due to the lessening of hunting pressures when the closed season protected the seals in the period they were most easily killed. Probably the most effective factor was the change in economic circumstances which reduced the human population of areas frequented by the seals. The general depopulation of the Highlands and the abandonment of islands such as the Monachs in the Hebrides and North Fara in Orkney afforded new secure breeding places for the seals. The almost total disappearance of the crofter-fisher way of life which regarded seals as a valuable casual asset meant that the seals were able to exploit their new breeding places in comparative safety.

Fisheries interests were well aware of this increase of the seal population and urged action on both the local sea-fisheries boards and the central fisheries departments. The South-western Sea-fisheries Board in 1934 organized a seal control operation on the Cornish coast in which 177 seals were shot. Most of these were probably grey seals, and it was claimed that a number of them were shot illegally in the closed season—another example, perhaps, of the general ignorance of the state of the law in the remotest parts of the kingdom.

As mentioned earlier, individual fishing concerns often organized seal control operations in the vicinity of their nets, but there was agitation for a centralized operation against the seals at their breeding places. A particularly effective lobby for this was made up by the salmon netsmen of the east coast of Scotland. In 1959 the Nature Conservancy, as the principal advisor to the government on wildlife matters, set up a Consultative Committee on Grey Seals and Fisheries to coordinate research on the grey seal in relation to fisheries. After considering the evidence that it gathered from its own research staff, and which was presented to it by the fisheries departments and fishermen, the Consultative

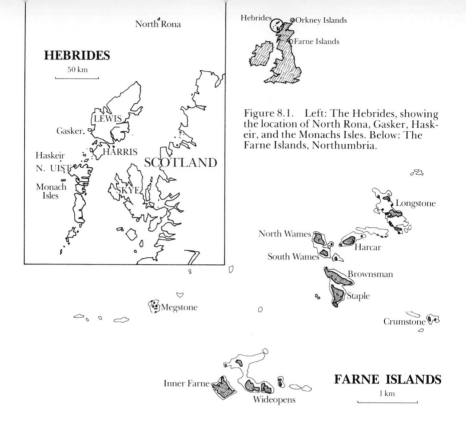

North Rona

HEBRIDES

50 km

Hebrides ● Orkney Islands
Farne Islands

LEWIS
Gasker.
Haskeir · HARRIS
N. UIST
SCOTLAND
Monach
Isles
SKYE

Figure 8.1.   Left: The Hebrides, showing the location of North Rona, Gasker, Haskeir, and the Monachs Isles. Below: The Farne Islands, Northumbria.

Longstone

North Wames
Harcar
South Wames
Brownsman
Megstone
Staple
Crumstone

Inner Farne
Wideopens

FARNE ISLANDS

1 km

Figure 8.2.   Grey seal pup production for three major stocks in the U.K. For the Hebrides (including North Rona) the exponential $N_t = N_0 e^{0.065}$ ($r^2 = 0.86$) is fitted. For Orkney the exponential $N_t = N_0 e^{0.061}$ ($r^2 = 0.99$) is fitted up to 1968. For the Farne Islands the exponential $N_t = N_0 e^{0.07}$ ($r^2 = 0.98$) is fitted up to 1971. It can be seen that in undisturbed populations there has been an exponential increase of 6–7 percent annually. From Summers, 1978.

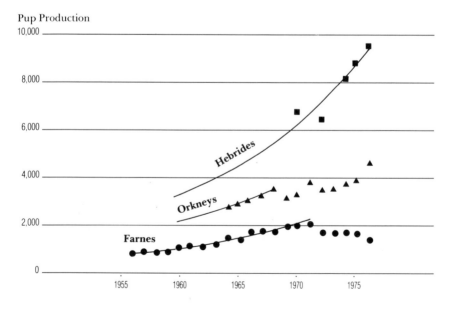

Pup Production

10,000

8,000

6,000

Hebrides

4,000

Orkneys

2,000

Farnes

0

1955   1960   1965   1970   1975

Committee in 1962 issued its report. Among other things the report recommended that the grey seal stocks at two localities, the Orkneys and the Farne Islands, should be reduced by 25 percent to alleviate damage to fisheries.

In Orkney it was decided that the reduction should be achieved by an annual quota of 750 seal pups, taken after they had been weaned. These would be taken by private hunters on licenses issued under an order suspending the closed season of the 1932 Grey Seals Protection Act. This policy, with some changes in the quota (which was increased to 1,000 pups in 1971), has been maintained to the present day; but so far from achieving the desired 25 percent reduction in stock size, the number of seals in Orkney has in fact increased substantially (Summers, 1978) (Figure 8.2). Indeed, when the Consultative Committee set the quota at its original level, it was done in the knowledge that it would be insufficient to effect the desired reduction, but it was felt it would be easy to step it up in the light of the experience of the first year's operation. This experience, however, included a good deal of public hostility, and the quota increase had to wait until the seals themselves had increased very substantially.

At the Farne Islands, which produced a crop of about a thousand pups per year at the time the Consultative Committee was considering its recommendations, the report called for a cull composed partly of adult females and partly of female pups. The recommendation for a cull at the Farne Islands had, in fact, been anticipated by the Nature Conservancy in 1957, and the first fisheries-related cull of grey seals at the Farnes was carried out in the breeding season of 1958, though it extended into January 1959. In the course of this cull only the negligible number of ten pups was killed, but the special position of the Farne Islands as a nature reserve (the United Kingdom equivalent of a national park) owned by the National Trust, a charitable body concerned with maintaining the nation's heritage, caused a great deal of public concern, and further operations were put off until after the Consultative Committee had reported.

After the report appeared, further culls were carried out at the Farne Islands under the auspices of the Ministry of Agriculture, Fisheries and Food between 1963 and 1965, in the course of which 996 seals were killed. After 1965, however, the National Trust declined to allow any more seal culling there on the grounds of fisheries protection, claiming that the fisheries case, as it related to the Farne Islands seals, was insufficiently proven.

Meanwhile the new regular harvesting of grey seal pups in Orkney under the fisheries-related culls stimulated a more general interest in sealing in the United Kingdom. Some of the grey seal hunters turned to taking the young of harbor seals (which produced a much more valuable pelt) in the summer, particularly on the west coast of Scotland and in the Wash.

Although the operations on the west coast of Scotland were conducted discreetly and attracted little public attention, the same was not true of the Wash sealing. Returning sealing boats were met by contingents of journalists and cameramen at their base on one of the rivers that drain into the Wash, and the press regularly featured highly emotional accounts of the hunting. One of the animal protection societies carried out some very simplistic population estimations and concluded that the Wash seals were endangered. This was probably not the case in the Wash, where the annual kill of pups averaged 607 in 1962–70 and never rose above 870 (Vaughan, 1978), representing only 38 percent of the calculated production (Bonner, 1976). There was more cause for concern in some localities in Scotland, particularly in Shetland (Bonner et al., 1973), where extensive boat ownership made intensive hunting easy at the breeding season.

Public realization that extensive hunting was going on led to demands for further legislation that would embrace the hitherto unprotected harbor seal. This resulted in the Conservation of Seals Act, which reached the statute book in 1970 and is the current legislation affecting seals in the United Kingdom. The change in the title from "protection" to "conservation" was significant. The act maintained the existing closed season for grey seals and provided a closed season for harbor seals (June 1 to August 31). It prohibited the taking of seals of either species in the closed season except under a license, which could be granted for the prevention of damage to fisheries, the reduction of a population surplus of seals for management purposes, or the use of a population surplus of seals as a resource. Additionally, the act allowed government representatives to enter private land to kill seals (or collect information about seals) to prevent damage to fisheries—an important provision in line with legislation affecting some agricultural pests, such as deer, and which was designed to prevent landowners from frustrating seal control measures by denying access to their lands.

The new act thus provided a framework within which a rational harvesting policy on the basis of maximum sustainable yield exploitation could be carried out; it provided the legal means, by compulsion if necessary, to reduce seals which were shown to be damaging fisheries; and it recognized that in an environment where the natural predators of seals had ceased to be effective, intervention by man to reduce seal numbers for reasons unconnected with exploitation or fisheries protection might be required to restore the balance of a natural community.

In Scotland the existing pattern of seal control continued (except that hunting of harbor seal pups in Shetland was banned). The harvesting of grey seal pups in Orkney was done under permits which could be

issued either to protect fisheries or to use a population surplus as a resource. However, it was at the Farne Islands that the new concept in the
act—that of reducing the numbers of seals for management purposes—
was first employed.

Although the National Trust had forbidden further killing of seals
at the Farnes on the grounds of fisheries protection, they were aware of
the explosive increase of the grey seal population that had occurred
there (Figure 8.3). Very accurate figures were available for pup production at the Farnes, and this had risen from 751 in 1956 to 2,010 in 1971
(Bonner, 1975), a rate of increase between 1956 and 1966 of almost 9
percent a year.

Only four of the eighteen small islands that make up the Farnes are
used regularly by the main body of breeding seals (Figure 8.1), and
hence the population increase led to a great increase in seal density on
the occupied islands, with substantial crowding and density-dependent
mortality. The relation of pup mortality to the extent of accessible shoreline (a good measure of density) was first shown by Coulson and Hickling (1964), and these data were extended by Bonner and Hickling
(1971a) (Figure 8.4).

Figure 8.3.   Increase of grey seal births at the Farne Islands.

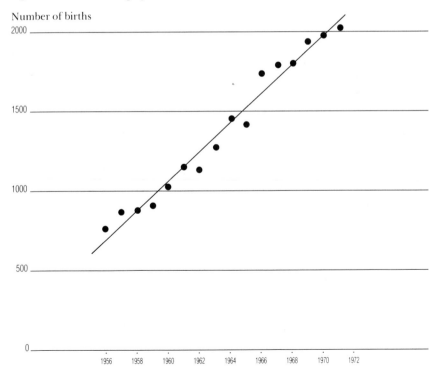

133

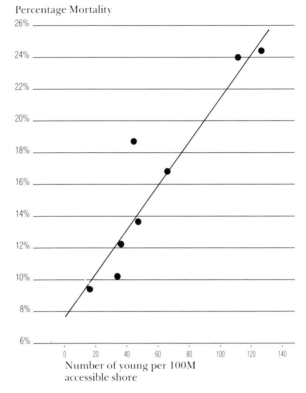

Percentage Mortality

Figure 8.4.   Relation of pup mortality to extent of accessible shoreline for grey seals at the Farne Islands. From Bonner and Hickling, 1971a.

Number of young per 100M accessible shore

Figure 8.5.   Starving pups of grey seals at the Farne Islands. Staple Island, November 1970. In the center of the group a starving pup is trying to suck from another starveling which has started to moult but which is unlikely to survive.

According to their observations, most of the pup deaths were caused by a rupture of the bond that is established at birth between mother and pup. Seals locate their young by a combination of topographic, visual, and olfactory clues (Fogden, 1971). If a disturbance forces a young animal to stray far from its mother, its chances of being found again are greatly diminished. Disturbance arises endogenously in the seal colony when seals on their journeys to and from the sea during the lactation period have to pass through territory occupied by other seals. The farther the breeding areas extend from the shore, the greater the opportunity for aggressive interactions. The failure of the mothers subsequently to locate their strayed pups means that the pups inevitably starve to death. A high level of adoptive suckling (i.e., suckling of a pup by a cow which is not its mother) was noted by Fogden (1971) in crowded and confused situations, but even those pups that sucked from the greatest number of cows.failed to thrive and it is unlikely that this aberrant behavior contributes significantly to survival. Indeed, soliciting feeding from strange cows often results in severe wounds for the hungry pup. Most pups which have lost their mothers succumb to nonspecific infections, often their eyes becoming inflamed and purulent as they gradually starve to death.

The consequence of these interactions was that towards the end of a breeding season on the Farnes in the late 1960s, the islands were littered with starving pups, often with septic wounds and great numbers of carcasses (Bonner and Hickling, 1971a, 1971b) (Figure 8.5). Mortality rates of more than 20 percent of all pups born were a regular feature at the Farnes, though as we have seen (page 15), even with high mortalities, the feedback loops of the Bartholomew model still explain why the seals "choose" to breed in crowded situations.

Another result of increased density of seals at the Farnes was the effect on the soil and vegetation of the breeding grounds (Bonner and Hickling, 1971b). In the 1950s, the seal population—about a quarter of the size it attained in the 1970s—seemed to have very little effect on the vegetation. With increasing seal numbers, however, there was progressive destruction of vegetation with concommitant erosion of the fragile soil cap. Much of the original damage was caused by the burrowing of puffins (*Fratercula arctica*) and the pulling up of plant material by gulls (*Larus* spp.), but the presence of large numbers of seals ashore in the autumn prevented or destroyed regrowth and left the soil exposed to the erosive effects of the wind and rain in the winter. Perennial plants such as sea campion (*Silene maritima*), scurvy grass (*Cochlearia officinalis*), and various grasses tended to be replaced by annuals, notably common orache, *Atriplex hastata*. These die off in the autumn and offer little or no protection to the soil. In some parts of the islands soil losses amounted to as much as 2.5 cm per year.

The effects of increasing numbers on the seal population itself and on the environment of the Farne Islands (which are the only islands on the east coast of England) led the National Trust to plan for active management of the seals, as they were entitled to do under the new legislation. In 1971 a management plan was prepared which recommended that the population be reduced—by shooting cows and their pups, together with some of the bulls—so as to bring it to the level of 1960 (approximately a thousand breeding cows, or half that of 1970), at which time the adverse effects noted in 1970 had not been observed. The operation was to be spread over three years (Bonner and Hickling, 1971b).

In 1972 a control operation was carried out with a chartered Norwegian sealer at the Farnes, in which 132 bulls, 603 cows, and 573 pups were killed. This was not as many as had been planned, owing to the difficulty of shooting large numbers of seals before the herd escaped into the sea, and also to the fact that the hunters' activities deterred many of the seals from coming ashore to pup. Additionally, the work of removing the carcasses (a necessary activity in an area much frequented by tourists in the spring and summer) was hampered by weather which was even worse than usual for the region at that time of year. Despite these difficulties, the cull accounted for approximately 30 percent of the breeding females, calculated on the 1971 stock (Bonner and Hickling, 1974).

In 1975 another control operation was carried out in which 158 bulls, 486 cows, and 804 pups were killed. However, despite the effects of these operations, the resilience of the seal stock was such that it was reduced only to about 70 percent of its 1971 level (Summers, 1978a).

A disappointing feature was that, despite the great reduction in numbers, the remaining seals still crowded densely on the most favored sites and pup mortality remained very high. In 1976 the average pup mortality was 27 percent and reached 35 percent in the most crowded island (Hickling et al., 1977). It was clear that a reduction in numbers, even if substantial, did not result in a proportionate drop in mortality. Although this management objective was not achieved, an important ancillary product of the cull was the scientific data that accrued. These allowed accurate assessments to be made of the population structure of the stock, so that future trends could be predicted with much greater confidence (Harwood and Prime, 1978).

Since 1975, management culls at the Farne Islands have been on a smaller scale and have been confined to the removal of animals from sensitive areas. Stock size has declined so that in 1978 only 1,162 pups were born. This was about the same total as in 1962 and is 58 percent of the maximum of 1971. A consequence of the culls has been the much wider distribution of the seals, with about 44 percent of the pups being born on islands other than the four in use in the 1960s (Hickling and

Table 8.1. Distribution of grey seal pups at the Farne Islands, 1969 and 1978.*
Figures in parentheses are percentages of the total born.

Year	Total born	Brownsman	Staple	North Wames	South Wames	Other islands
1969	1,929	703	637	365	212	12
		(36.44)	(33.02)	(18.92)	(10.99)	(0.62)
1978	1,162	5	85	499	66	507
		(0.43)	(7.31)	(42.94)	(5.68)	(43.63)

*In 1978 artificial measures were employed to keep the breeding seals off
Brownsman and Staple islands. Data from Bonner and Hickling, 1971a, and
Hickling and Hawkey, 1979.

Hawkey, 1979) (Table 8.1). Pup mortality remains high, at 17 percent
for the colony as a whole and 23 percent on the main breeding island.
Further reduction of seal density is still indicated (particularly on one
island) if pup mortality is to be reduced still further, and this will be difficult to achieve. The habitat conservation objective, on the other hand,
has been adequately achieved, with insignificant numbers of seals breeding on the two main soil-covered islands, where the vegetation is regen-
erating.

There was strong public opposition to the Farne Island culls, but in
general it was not too difficult for the National Trust management to
convince its membership and those government officials responsible for
granting licenses under which the culls were conducted, of the need for
positive management at the Farnes.

Meanwhile, further evidence on the status of the grey seal in the
United Kingdom had been collected by the group of scientists working
for the Natural Environment Research Council (which had assumed the
responsibility for seal research that was previously the Nature Conservancy's). This group, the Sea Mammal Research Unit, had shown that
in Scottish waters grey seals had increased from about 35,000 in the
mid-1960s to about 60,000 in 1978 (Summers, 1978a). This increase
amounted over the years to about 7 percent, though of course different
groups of seals were increasing at different rates.

The Department of Agriculture and Fisheries for Scotland estimated the annual fish consumption by the grey seal stocks in the British
Isles to be 168,000, of which it was supposed that 112,000 would consist
of commercially exploitable fish (Parrish and Shearer, 1977). Using a
value of 0.5 for the average rate of exploitation by fisheries operating in
waters adjacent to the British Isles, this consumption was assumed to
represent a total loss to the potential annual fishery of 65,000 tons,
which was claimed to have an estimated market value of £15–20 million
(using the average market price of cod landed in Scotland in 1974 as an

index). The tonnage involved was equivalent to 1–2 percent of the total fish catch taken by all countries in the waters surrounding the British Isles in 1975, and to 5–10 percent of the total catch within the United Kingdom's extended fishery limits, which is probably the area within which the seals feed.

Such a loss was regarded by the Scottish Office as an intolerable threat to fisheries (which would, of course, increase with the expected increase of seal stocks), and the decision was made to reduce the seal stocks to the level they had attained in the mid-1960s, or approximately half the number then existing. The Scottish Office sought the advice of the Seals Advisory Committee of the Natural Environmental Research Council (the successor to the Grey Seals Consultative Committee), which informed them that the best way of achieving this reduction would be to cull 900 breeding cows and their pups, together with 4,000 moulted pups, in each of the six years 1977–82. This was to take place at the three main breeding places—the Hebrides, the isolated island of North Rona, and the Orkneys. Pup culling alone (the method of control then in use in Scotland) was rejected, since it had been shown (Harwood, 1978) that the population equilibrium established by continual pup culling was unstable and that the six-year lag between control operations and their observed effects could leave the stock vulnerable to unforeseen environmental hazards as well as to the control. The killing of adult seals would have an effect that would be observable the following season, but culls of adults were logistically very difficult and expensive. A combination of taking both adults and pups and spreading the cull over several years was the best compromise; since the reduction would be in small steps, the population would never be put at risk, while the method would be flexible and could be continuously monitored. Once the desired reduction had been achieved it would be necessary to stabilize the population by small culls of adults, which could be made proportional to the preceding year's pup production.

The action of the Scottish Office was a response to the assertion that the grey seals were causing insupportable damage to fisheries, which would increase with the seals. This relied on three assumptions: (1) that the population of seals had been accurately assessed; (2) that the food consumption of the seals was known; and (3) that this could be related to the impact on commercial fish landings.

The population assessment was the soundest of these assumptions. Regular censusing and modeling of the population (using data derived from, among other sources, the large samples killed at the Farne Islands) by the Sea Mammals Research Unit had shown that stocks not subject to control increased annually by approximately 7 percent, and would double in about 11 years (Summers, 1978a). Natural regulation by pup mortality on the breeding beaches, the only density-dependent mechanism known (Harwood and Prime, 1978), was unlikely to be significant until all the available breeding sites were in use or until food supplies became limiting, which would almost certainly occur first.

Although population figures were well founded on observation and theory, the same was not true of the other two assumptions made by the Scottish Office. I have noted previously the difficulty in determining the amount of food eaten by seals and still more so the effect that this has on fisheries. Much opposition to the Scottish Office's plan centered on the claim that the grey seals were eating 65,000 tons of fish a year that would have otherwise been landed by fishermen for human consumption. The consumption figures as calculated by Parrish and Shearer (1977) indeed appear to be conservative. They rely on an average consumption of 15 pounds of food per seal per day throughout the year. Using an average population body weight of 120 kg (a very conservative estimate, based on a population consisting of 60 percent immatures at 100 kg and 40 percent adults, with females at 150 kg and males at 200 kg) and applying Keys's (p. 116) feeding rate of 6–10 percent body weight per day, this would give daily rations of between 15.8 and 26.4 pounds. Although this assumes year-round feeding at the same rate, it is still probably a conservative figure; Summers et al. (1978) used a daily feeding rate of 10 kg for a total feeding period of 300 days in the year, equivalent to 18 pounds per day throughout the year. Not only was the daily feeding rate conservatively estimated, but the amount of fish in the diet was set very low, at only two-thirds of the total food intake, though it was assumed that this would consist entirely of commercially exploitable fishes.

Conversion of the amount of fish consumed by seals to impact on fisheries is much more speculative. Although the exploitation rate (0.5) used by Parrish and Shearer (1977) is probably low for the fish stocks concerned, it is simplistic to assume that no other predator would benefit from the reduction of the seals, or that other mortality factors might not increase. The possibility has already been mentioned that an increase in fish landings might result in a fall in fishermen's incomes.

Despite this, the Scottish Office decided to press on with the reduction operation and engaged a Norwegian company (the same one used at the Farne Islands) to perform the cull at a cost calculated to be between £10,000 and £20,000, depending on the number of seals taken (Lister-Kaye, 1979). In 1977 the proposed six-year plan was initiated. *Kvitungen,* the Norwegian sealing vessel, arrived in the Hebrides and started work at the Monach Islands, which like the Farne Islands were a nature reserve, though the work was being done with the approval of the Nature Conservancy, the body responsible for the reserve. As at the Farne Islands, bad weather hampered the cull and the final total was only about 600 seals, so the control measure could scarcely be considered effective.

In July of the following year (1978) the Scottish Office issued a statement that it intended to continue with the plan and cull seals in Orkney and North Rona. The Secretary of State for Scotland, Mr. Bruce Millan, in announcing this, acknowledged that there were many people throughout the country who held strong views on the subject of seal culling, but hoped that they would recognize the need for the action proposed.

It is possible that some people responded to this optimistic appeal, but most did not. In Orkney a group of protesters contacted the Greenpeace Foundation, well known for their work in opposing whaling and sealing in other areas, and at the beginning of October the Greenpeace trawler *Rainbow Warrior* arrived at Kirkwall, the principal harbor of Orkney. The following week a petition with 42,000 signatures against the cull was presented at the Scottish Office; and two days after this, during a debate in the European Parliament, the Commissioner for Agriculture promised a neutral study on seals and their effects on fish stocks. Two days later an emergency motion was passed in the European Parliament calling on the European Economic Community Commission to halt the culling of seals until a scientific investigation had been carried out. Apparently few members of the European Parliament were aware of the extensive research program extending over two decades that had preceded the management plan!

On October 16, the International Union for the Conservation of Nature and Natural Resources, at its conference at Ashkhabad in the USSR, passed a resolution urging the government of the United Kingdom to suspend the cull until adequate data on the impact of grey seals on fish stocks and the role of grey seals in their ecosystems were available. By this time the pressure was too great for the Scottish Office, and it issued a statement saying that the Secretary of State had decided to reduce the cull (this meant abandoning the plan to take adults and restricting the cull to the normal pup hunt) "so that everyone will have the opportunity to study the scientific evidence." Significantly, the statement reaffirmed the government's long-term policy regarding the culling of grey seals in the Orkneys and Hebrides. Nevertheless, the protesters had won, and every national newspaper featured the cancellation of the cull in their headlines the following day.

There are a number of interesting points that arise from this story. As Summers (1978b) has pointed out, the proposed cull was a subject which lent itself perfectly to the kind of emotional treatment that is designed to escalate events from obscurity to the headlines. Perhaps the most regrettable feature was the attitude of apparently reputable national and international conservation and animal welfare organizations, who chose to ignore or obscure the scientific research on which the policy had been based. In the aftermath of the Secretary of State's decision to abandon the policy (for that was what his "reduction" amounted to) no significant new evidence was produced to show that grey seals were not in fact increasing at the rates claimed. Considerable effort went into a detailed analysis of the evidence relating to the feeding habits of seals and the impact that these might have on fisheries (Council for Nature, 1979), but the fact that substantial quantities of fish were eaten by grey seals was not seriously challenged.

Perhaps the most important aspect was that the increase of the grey seals, and hence the increase of any impact they might have on fisheries, is likely to continue. The fact that overfishing, defective fisheries legislation, or the activities of foreign trawlers have a greater impact than seals on fish stocks, or that sea birds and porpoises also eat fish, does not make the uncontrolled expansion of grey seal stocks more acceptable to fishermen. In the virtual absence of natural predators or of hunting activity by man (who for several millenia has probably been the chief predator on grey seals in the British Isles), some form of management is required to regulate grey seal populations if they are to stay in balance with the rest of the ecosystem, which for better or for worse now contains man as a main predator on fish.

Pup hunting remains in Scotland as the sole means of controlling the seals. As noted earlier, this is undesirable as a control method since it puts the population as a whole at risk; moreover, it may well be less humane than a properly organized cull of adults and pups which can be adequately supervised. It will be unfortunate for the cause of conservation as a whole, and not just for seals, if, as Summers put it, "trial of wildlife management by public opinion" becomes standard practice. This could only be acceptable if the public were prepared to become as well informed as the scientists, and this seems an unlikely condition. More than anything else, the episode of the aborted Orkney cull demonstrates that scientists must be aware of the need to present their work to the public in an acceptable form. Publication in the scientific literature and academic discussion will never be sufficient where public interests are involved.

Another important point to note is that the decision to cull was an administrative one, not a scientific one. All conservation or wildlife management decisions involve value judgments on what constitutes the system which it is desired to maintain or achieve. The role of science and scientists in these matters is to provide data and models which will tell the administrators what the current situation is and how it may be modified by selected activities. It is clear in the case of the Scottish grey seals that the scientists need to provide much more hard information on the impact of seals on commercial fisheries. This will not make a decision to reduce the seals any more scientific, but it will make clearer the existing effects of large seal populations on the fishing industry and the consequences of a further increase in seal populations.

References

Bonner, W.N. 1975. Population increase of grey seals at the Farne Islands. Rapp. P.-v. Réun. Cons. int. Explor. Mer 169:366–370.

Bonner, W.N. 1976. The stocks of grey seals (*Halichoerus grypus*) and common seals (*Phoca vitulina*) in Great Britain. Natural Environment Research Council Publ. Ser. C, No. 16. 16pp.

Bonner, W.N. and Hickling, G. 1971a. The grey seals of the Farne Islands: report for the period October 1969 to July 1971. Nat. Hist. Soc. Northumberland, Durham and Newcastle upon Tyne, Trans. 17:141–162.

Bonner, W.N. and Hickling, G. 1971b. Grey Seals at the Farne Islands: a Management Plan. Report submitted to the National Trust. 21pp.

Bonner, W.N. and Hickling, G. 1974. The grey seals of the Farne Islands: 1971 to 1973. Nat. Hist. Soc. Northumbria, Trans. 42(2):65–84.

Bonner, W.N., Vaughan, R.W. and Johnston, L. 1973. The status of common seals in Shetland. Biol. Conserv. 5:185–190.

Coulson, J.C. and Hickling, G. 1964. The breeding biology of the grey seal, *Halichoerus grypus* (Fab.), on the Farne Islands, Northumberland, J. anim. Ecol. 33:485–512.

Council for Nature. 1979. A Report to the Secretary of State for Scotland from the Council for Nature Grey Seals Group. London, 56pp. (mimeo).

Fogden, S.C.L. 1971. Mother-young behaviour at grey seal breeding beaches. J. Zool. Lond. 164:61–92.

Harwood, J. 1978. The effect of management policies on the stability and resilience of British grey seal populations. J. appl. Ecol. 15:413–421.

Harwood, J. and Prime, J.H. 1978. Some factors affecting the size of British grey seal populations. J. Appl. Ecol. 15:401–411.

Hewer, H.R. 1974. British Seals. Collins New Naturalist, London.

Hickling, G. 1962. Grey Seals and the Farne Islands. Routledge and Kegan Paul, London.

Hickling, G. and Hawkey, P. 1979. The grey seals of the Farne Islands: the 1978 breeding season. Nat. Hist. Soc. Northumbria, Trans. 43(3):35–44.

Hickling, G., Hawkey, P. and Harwood, J. 1977. The grey seals of the Farne Islands: the 1976 breeding season. Nat. Hist. Soc. Northumbria, Trans. 42(6):119–126.

ICES. 1977. ICES Working Group on Grey Seals: Report of the First Meeting. 16–20 May 1977, Cambridge, U.K. C.M. 1977/N: (mimeo).

Lister-Kaye, J. 1979. Seal Cull: the Grey Seal Controversy. Penguin Books Ltd., Harmondsworth.

Martin, M. 1703. Description of the Western Islands of Scotland. London: A Beel.

Parrish, B.B. and Shearer, W.M. 1977. Effects of the seals on fisheries. ICES C.M. 1977/M:14. 4pp. (mimeo).

Prichard, H.H. 1913. The grey seals of Haskeir. Cornhill Magazine, 35.

Rae, B.B. 1960. Seals and Scottish fisheries. Mar. Res. 1960, No. 2. 39 p.

Summers, C.F. 1978a. Trends in the size of the British grey seal populations. J. Appl. Ecol. 15:395–400.

Summers, C.F. 1978b. Grey seals: the "con" in conservation. New Scientist 30 Nov. 1978:694–695.

Summers, C.F., Bonner, W.N., and Van Haaften, J. 1978. Changes in the seal populations of the North Sea. Rapp. P.-v. Réun. Cons. int. Explor. Mer. 172:278–285.

Vaughan, R.W. 1978. A study of common seals in the Wash. Mammal Rev. 8(1 & 2):25–34.

CHAPTER NINE

Indirect Human Impacts on Seals

So far the impacts of man on seals that I have discussed have been direct ones—man has set out to kill seals for the sake of their products, or to eliminate them as undesirable competitors in his fishing activities. However, these are only some of the ways in which human populations and activities affect seals. Other interactions may be unintentional, but no less potent for that.

Fishing Nets

The fishing industry has a large and generally unquantified impact on seals in the form of incidental kills in the course of fishing activities. I have mentioned already how seals have been found drowned in salmon nets, caught on hooks set for cod, or even jammed in a fish pump. Fukuhara (in Lander, 1976) reported that about 3,500 northern fur seals were taken annually by Japanese salmon gillnetters on the high seas; the real total may perhaps be nearer 7,000 (Lander, 1976; ACMRR, 1978). In more general terms, estimates of marine mammal mortality due to fishing vessels in the Bering Sea to Aleutian Islands area in 1978 amounted to 8.57 animals (believed to be mostly Steller sea lions) per 10,000 tonnes of groundfish and would total 1,237 animals for a fishery yield of 1,443,500 tonnes (Harry, in North Pacific Fishery Management Council, 1979). Shaughnessy and Payne (1979), in studies of the mortality of South African fur seals during trawl fishing, calculated that 0.023 percent of the population became entrapped in trawl nets each year, and 0.013 percent were killed. They considered that this was similar to the proportion of Steller sea lions entrapped in Alaskan waters. Deaths of South African fur seals occur also in purse-seining operations, but no quantitative data have been collected.

Although most other species of seals (except perhaps the Lobodontine seals in the Antarctic) from time to time may get entangled in fishing nets, I do not know of any other quantified data. Fishermen may be unaware of incidental kills or reluctant to report those they know of. However, even if the data are incomplete, it would seem that incidental kill is not a serious cause of mortality, on a species basis, for any seals.

Not all seals that come in contact with fishing nets drown in them, of course. Probably most can successfully escape. However, another danger is entanglement with scraps of netting. When a fishing net is damaged, it is usual practice to cut out the damaged area and replace it with a patch. The discarded piece of netting, in common with all other unwanted rubbish on a fishing boat, is simply dumped over the side. In the days when nets were made from natural fiber, such discards had a short life. Now, however, with synthetic fibers which are buoyant and virtually indestructible, the fragments may float about for long periods. Seals at sea seem to be attracted by floating objects. Fur seals in particular are often seen in or near beds of floating kelp (Fiscus and Kozloff, 1971), which may conceal concentrations of fish. Before 1960 there were few records of fur seals becoming entangled in netting scraps, but since the introduction of synthetic fibers these have become relatively commonplace. Some 211 net-entangled seals were found in the commercial harvest of Pribilof fur seals in 1975, or about 0.72 percent of the total. The number and rate have fallen since then, being 110 and 0.43 percent in 1979 (Engel et al., 1980). Observations of net-entangled seals ashore probably represent only a small portion of the casualties that occur on the high seas.

The situation is not confined to the northern fur seal; in South Georgia, at the other end of the world, antarctic fur seals have been found with rope or netting collars around their necks (Figure 9.1). Though it has been assumed by some that the rope collars have been deliberately tied around the seals, it seems more likely that the seals have swum into a floating loop of cord on the surface of the sea and been unable to remove it. Karl Kenyon (1980) has drawn attention to the habit of Hawaiian monk seals of apparently purposely entangling themselves in netting scraps washed ashore on beaches. They seem able subsequently to free themselves, but why they entangle themselves in the first place remains a mystery.

Figure 9.1. Juvenile male antarctic fur seal with collar of fish netting. Bird Island, South Georgia, December 1971.

The problem of net entanglements has seemed sufficiently serious for government agencies to issue warning pamphlets to fishermen of the danger caused to seals by these discards. This may be a naive approach since many fishermen strongly disapprove of seals and may discard the netting deliberately once the danger has been publicized (ACMRR, 1978).

Roger Gentry (personal communication) has pointed out one problem associated with net discards that has not yet been addressed. This is the disruption caused to other seals on the breeding grounds by animals with net fragments attached. If the net fragments are big enough to alter the seal's gait on land, the appearance of such an animal may panic the other seals. Although the effects of such disruption are probably slight, the problem deserves attention.

Another risk to seals arising from commercial fisheries is the swallowing of fish hooks. Sea lions, both *Zalophus* and *Eumetopias,* have been observed on several occasions with metal lures, or "herring flashers," protruding from their mouths (Gentry, personal communication; Bruce Mate, personal communication). If the flasher gets snagged on rocks the sea lion may panic at being caught and forcibly pull the hook from its stomach, possibly inflicting a fatal wound. Bruce Mate further tells of seals on the northwest American coast dying from gut obstructions caused by such objects as small buoy markers and styrofoam cups. These are not necessarily associated with fishermen, of course, but they emphasize the danger of the increasing amount of semipermanent waste that now litters the ocean.

Competition for Food

Possibly the major impact the fishing operations have on seals—and on other animals of the sea—is the alteration of the ecosystem of which they form a part, by the removal of very large quantities of fish. There is no direct evidence that any commercial fisheries have adversely affected seal stocks; indeed, the only example of such an interaction is the decline in numbers of the guanay birds as a consequence of the anchoveta fishery off the west coast of South America (ACMRR, 1978). Yet it is hard to believe that fisheries on the scale at which they now operate in the North Pacific and North Atlantic can fail ultimately to affect the seal stocks there.

I have referred already (page 46) to the observations that nursing female harp seals taken in 1978, after the failure of the North Atlantic capelin fishery, had lower energy stores than those taken in 1976 (Innes et al., 1978). The situation is more complicated with the fur seals in the eastern Bering Sea. Sanger (1974) estimated that the northern fur seals from the Pribilof Islands ate the equivalent of about 15 percent of the

Figure 9.2. Landings of ground fish in the eastern Bering Sea by vessels from Japan, the USSR and the Republic of Korea. From North Pacific Fishery Management Council, 1979.

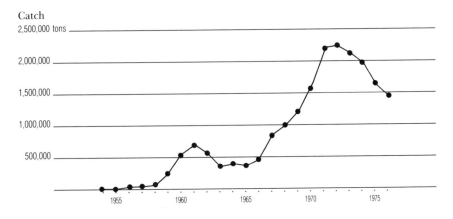

commercial walleye pollock catch, which amounted to 1.8 million tonnes in 1972. Like most seals, the northern fur seal eats a wide range of species. Pollock has varied from 9.7 percent of stomach contents by volume in 1958 to 73.5 percent in 1974 (Lander and Kajimura, 1976), so the significance of exploitation of one component should not be overstressed.

While it is clear that total fish landings in the North Pacific have increased greatly in recent years (Figure 9.2) and cover a range of species, it is not universally accepted that this has led to decreased standing stocks of fish. The DYNUMES III model used to depict the Bering Sea ecosystem indicates that the intensive fishing for pollock is beneficial to the production of fish biomass. Adult pollock are cannibalistic on the smaller fish. By removing the older pollock, the fishery reduces the grazing pressure on the juveniles, whose growth rate is relatively high, and thereby enhances the productivity of the pollock biomass at large (North Pacific Fishery Management Council, 1979). The model does not indicate, however, whether the presumed increased number of younger fish are present in a location, or in a form of association, in which they are available to the fur seals. Furthermore, there are indications that the food requirements of the seals are substantially greater than those used in the model.

The fact that the reduction of the female stock at the Pribilofs in 1956–68 did not result in the expected increase in juvenile survival, despite the fact that the relation of pup mortality to population size was well documented, suggests that the seals were unable to take advantage of the reduced intraspecific competition, perhaps because of increased competition with fishing boats.

The limiting factor in both fur seals and harp seals may be the time spent by females in searching for food to pass on to their young in the form of milk. In the case of the harp seal, reserves for the entire lactation period have to be laid down in the feeding period immediately before parturition. Female fur seals, with their much longer lactation, take food during the nursing period, but their feeding range is limited by the time during which they can leave their pups. If sufficient food is not available within this range, the nutrition of the pups, and their subsequent survival, may be affected.

As man becomes more efficient in cropping the fish stocks in the sea, the situation is likely to deteriorate for the seals and other marine predators. In the past, fisheries tended to be highly selective, taking smaller catches and totally ignoring many of the abundant species. Today, fisheries are much less selective, and any species which can be caught in sufficient quantity will probably be exploited. Seals might be left with few alternative food species to turn to, and the fish population level at which a fishing area is abandoned by man might be too low to support the number of seals that it supported before the start of the fishing (ACMRR, 1978).

Pollution

Increasing industrialization in the Northern Hemisphere and the general tendency to use the ocean as the ultimate dumping ground for unwanted wastes have led to the accumulation of substances—some of them manmade, some occurring naturally, but present in unusually high concentrations—that may have adverse effects on living organisms. Since many of these substances are capable of being concentrated biologically as they pass along the food chain, seals (and odontocete cetaceans) are likely to accumulate high concentrations.

Two groups of substances are of particular concern in marine organisms. The first is organochlorine compounds, such as the insecticides DDT and dieldrin, and the polychlorinated biphenyls (PCBs) which are used for a variety of industrial processes. The second category comprise the "heavy metals," notably mercury and cadmium. A vast literature on the occurrence of these pollutants in seals has accumulated since Koeman and van Genderen (1966) in the Netherlands first drew attention to the presence of organochlorine residues in the blubber of seals and Helminen and his colleagues (Helminen et al., 1968) found mercury in the liver and kidneys of ringed seals from Lake Saimaa in Finland.

It is not easy to summarize these data. In a recent review Holden (1978) pointed out that concentrations of DDT and its degradation products DDE and TDE (commonly referred to as total DDT) and of PCBs in the blubber of seals from areas associated with high industrial or agricultural effort (such as the southern North Sea, the Gulf of St. Lawrence, the California coast, and the Baltic) can reach several hundred parts per million wet weight, though the concentrations found in the fish or plankton on which the seals feed is commonly much less than one part per million. Conversely, very low values for these substances are found in the blubber of seals from remote areas such as the Beaufort and Bering seas (Table 9.1).

Because organochlorines have a high affinity for lipids, they are found in highest concentrations in the blubber, though measurable amounts may be present in other tissues, particularly the liver, kidney, and brain. Frank et al. (1973) found evidence of a blood/brain barrier to

Table 9.1. Mean concentrations of organochlorines in blubber of adult seals ($mg\ kg^{-1}$ fresh weight) (From Holden, 1978)

Area	Species	No.	Dieldrin	Σ D.D.T.	P.C.B.
Arctic					
Canada	Ringed	3	0.13	2.7	3
Norway	Ringed	2	0.18	2.4	1.5
Canada	Ringed	15	—	1.3	4.1
W. Greenland	Ringed	5	—	0.2(D.D.E.)	0.9
	Bearded	5	—	0.5(D.D.E.)	1.8
	Hood	5	—	0.3(D.D.E.)	2.7
Europe					
N. Baltic	Ringed	1	0.14	23.8	22
N. Baltic	Grey	18	—	420	140
S. Baltic	Grey	15	—	210	100
S. Baltic	Ringed	33	—	200	110
Netherlands		5	0.05	9.5	1470
Germany (N. Sea)		4	0.15	6.3	165
E. England	Grey	4	0.46	15.5	152
E. Scotland	Grey	20	0.24	12.4	35
Orkney Is.	Grey	7	0.14	8.3	26.6
Shetland Is.	Grey	8	0.14	8.9	11.1
N.W. Scotland	Grey	6	0.16	7.4	14.4
W. Scotland		8	0.37	22.3	65.8
N. America					
Gulf of St. Lawrence	Grey	5	0.25	45.4	27
	Hood	1	0.09	10.3	3
	Harp	11	0.08	9.0	5.3
N. Brunswick	Harbor	1	0.04	8.6	7.1
Maine, U.S.A.	Harbor	6	0.19	65.4	92.5
California	Sea lion	5	—	906	—
	Sea lion	6	—	824	112

— Denotes not determined.

Table 9.2.   Organochlorine residues in tissues of grey seals (Holden, 1978)

Residue	Seal no.	Blubber	Liver	Muscle	Heart	Kidney	Spleen	Brain
		Concentrations in mg/kg tissue						
Dieldrin	250/1	0.36	0.074	0.016	0.005	0.055	0.004	0.018
	250/2	0.83	0.19	0.033	0.053	0.070	0.022	0.057
	250/3	0.29	0.067	0.003	0.017	0.036	0.012	0.009
Total D.D.T.	250/1	26.6	1.49	0.66	0.12	0.78	0.09	0.20
	250/2	13.8	2.36	0.36	0.70	0.67	0.24	0.34
	250/3	15.2	2.40	0.25	0.53	0.53	0.38	0.28
P.C.B.	250/1	390	10.3	5.0	1.1	6.6	0.7	1.8
	250/2	77	9.7	2.4	4.2	4.2	1.6	3.0
	250/3	118	10.0	1.6	3.3	3.3	2.6	1.7
		Concentrations in mg/kg extractable lipid						
Dieldrin	250/1	0.45	0.87	0.57	0.38	1.2	0.50	0.16
	250/2	0.93	2.9	3.3	2.1	1.8	1.00	0.42
	250/3	0.36	1.24	0.75	0.50	1.2	0.54	0.05
Total D.D.T.	250/1	33.9	17.5	23.6	9.2	17.0	11.5	1.77
	250/2	15.5	35.8	36.0	28.0	16.8	11.5	2.48
	250/3	18.9	44.4	62.5	14.7	17.1	17.3	1.47
P.C.B.	250/1	500	121	179	85	143	88	16
	250/2	86	147	240	168	105	76	22
	250/3	147	180	400	97	106	118	9

organochlorines in harp seals, as the total DDT and PCB concentrations calculated on an extractable fat basis for brain tissue was from one-fifth to one-ninth of that in blubber, liver, or muscle. Holden (1975) found that concentrations of organochlorines in brain lipid were consistently lower than those from other organs (Table 9.2), indicating either the presence of a blood/brain barrier or the possibility that the brain lipids differ in composition from those of other organs. As brain lipids are known to contain large quantities of phosphatides, the latter explanation seems a likely one.

Despite the massive concentrations of organochlorines found in the tissues of seals from certain localities, it has been difficult to identify with certainty any pathological changes associated with the contamination. Many of the highest concentrations noted have been found in seals that were either dead or dying when collected. In these circumstances it is often the case that most of the fat reserves in the blubber (and elsewhere) have been used up, leaving the remaining fat with the whole burden of the pollutant load, which cannot be metabolized, resulting in the high concentrations of the pollutant observed (Bonner, 1970; Holden, 1972). Koeman and his colleagues (1972) suggested that PCB concentrations of 13–89 mg kg^{-1} in the brain of harbor seals in the Netherlands might have been responsible for their deaths, though high concentrations of other pollutants were also found. Brain concentrations are probably good indicators of the seriousness of contamination, but when blubber concentrations are used, it would seem better to express the contamination as total dose of contaminant, for the reason noted above.

In California, Le Boeuf and Bonnell (1971) examined the possibility that an increase of abortions in California sea lions was caused by high concentrations of DDT in blubber lipid, but could not come to definite conclusions. However, PCB concentrations of up to 145 mg kg^{-1} were present also, and these may have been an effective factor (Delong et al., 1973). Subsequent investigations (Gilmartin et al., 1976) showed that the sea lions which gave birth prematurely did have DDT levels much higher than those carrying fetuses to full term; but they also had tissue imbalances of mercury, selenium, cadmium, and bromine, some carried a virus similar to vesicular exanthema virus of swine, and others suffered from leptospirosis. Gilmartin et al. concluded that there was an interrelationship of disease agents and environmental contaminants which resulted in premature parturition.

Perhaps the most convincing evidence of a direct link between pollution and pathological effects on seal populations has come from the Bothnian Bay (the extreme northern part of the Baltic Sea in the wide sense). Here the population of ringed seals has declined abruptly in recent years and the incidence of pregnancy of mature females has been only 27 percent. Scientists from Finland and Sweden working together (Helle et al., 1976) found that about 40 percent of a sample of ringed seal females collected by netting showed pathological changes of the uterus. The lumen of the uterine horn was restricted by stenosis or blocked off by occlusion, thus interrupting the passage from the ovary to the body of the uterus. When DDT and PCB concentrations in the sample were compared, it was found that the females showing stenosis of the uterus had significantly higher concentrations of both total DDT and PCB than normal pregnant females, though there was no significant difference between nonpregnant females without stenosis or occlusion and the pregnant females (Table 9.3).

Because DDT concentrations in California sea lions breeding normally (Delong et al., 1973) were as high as in the nonpregnant pathological group of Bothnian Bay ringed seals, Helle and his colleagues concluded that the PCB concentration was responsible for the pathology. They supported their conclusion with comparisons of laboratory observations on PCB-fed mink which produced fewer pups than those fed a like dose of DDT. The PCB concentrations associated with resorption of

Table 9.3.   Levels of DDT and PCB (mg/kg) in extractable fat from ringed seals in Bothnian Bay (Helle et al., 1976)

Sample		n	Total DDT	PCB
1	Pregnant	24	88 ± 9.7	73 ± 6.6
11	Non-pregnant with stenosis	29	130 ± 10	110 ± 7.8
111	Non-pregnant normal	8	100 ± 15	89 ± 11
	1 vs 11		$p < 0.01$	$p < 0.01$
	1 vs 111		$p < 0.05$	$p < 0.05$

embryos in mink were about the same as in the Bothnian Bay seals, and thus they concluded that it was the PCB contamination that was responsible for the falling reproductive rate of the ringed seals in the Baltic.

Nevertheless, the picture is not a clear one. Apparently healthy seals have been sampled carrying high concentrations of organochlorines. Holden (1978) felt a more detailed study of seals might lead to an understanding of the mechanism that gives a seal some degree of protection from the unusually high concentrations of DDT and PCB often found in its tissues.

Interest in heavy metals in marine organisms was stimulated around 1970 by the discovery of high concentrations of mercury in tuna and swordfish. It is now believed that these for the most part represent natural levels, but this by no means precludes the possibility that unnatural and pathological levels do occur in some marine animals. Mercury in fish is found in the highly toxic alkyl mercury form, but the proportion of methyl mercury (the most abundant alkyl compound) found in seal livers is usually small. Koeman et al. (1973) reported only 2–14 percent of mercury present as methyl mercury in Netherlands Wadden Sea seals, and similar findings have been made in other species and localities.

This suggests that seals possess a mechanism for demethylating mercury ingested with fish. Koeman and his colleagues (1973) found also that there is a one-to-one relationship on a molecular basis between mercury and selenium in seals, dolphins, and porpoises. Selenium has been shown to have a protective effect against the toxicity of mercury in experiments with rats and quail. In general, even high concentrations of mercury do not seem to result in symptoms of toxicity in seals, though many of the specimens analyzed were obtained from seals found dead. Ronald and Tessaro (1976) suggested that harp seals could tolerate levels of 42.9 mg kg^{-1} total mercury in the brain. Many other potentially toxic metals have been detected in seal tissues, such as zinc, copper, lead, and cadmium, but none of these has been shown to be associated with pathological effects or even to occur at abnormal concentrations (Holden, 1978).

Awareness of the problem of pollution in most industrialized countries has resulted in controls on the use of many persistent pollutants and even some voluntary restriction on output by manufacturers, but it is likely that the problem will be with us (and the seals) for many years to come.

Certainly some of the most conspicuous pollution affecting seals is that caused by petroleum, either as crude oil or as marine bunker oil. The first widely publicized incident involving pollution on a massive scale occurred when the supertanker *Torrey Canyon* went aground on the Seven Stones Reef between Land's End and the Scilly Isles off the southwest British coast in March 1967, spilling her cargo of 119,000 tonnes of crude oil into the sea and causing massive contamination of the shore. In many localities attempts were made to clean up with emulsifying detergents. Although about 200–250 grey seals inhabited the area affected by the spill, there were few accounts of seals contaminated with the oil. Gill et al. (1967) reported three oiled seals washed up on beaches, two of which were alive when found but died later. A possibility exists that the seals had been affected by the highly toxic detergents rather than by the oil. Another possibility, perhaps even more likely, is that the death of the seals was not connected in any way with the oil spill, and that the specimens recorded represented normal casualties which were reported because of the increased vigilance on the shore.

When crude oil from the Santa Barbara Channel oil spill washed up on the beaches of San Miguel Island in 1969, more than one hundred elephant seal pups were coated with oil, sand, and detritus, but Le Boeuf (1971) was unable to find evidence of significant or long-term (1–15 months after contamination) deleterious effects on their health. However, had the spill occurred when the females were feeding their pups, so that the latter ingested the oil, he felt the results might have been more serious.

Davis and Anderson (1976) examined a number of oiled grey seal pups on the coast of Wales, but could not detect any effect on behavior or mortality, though the peak weight of oiled pups was less than that of pups not affected by oil. Although this would almost certainly have affected survival, it is possible that the lower weights of the oiled pups resulted from disturbance associated with attempts at cleaning, veterinary inspection, and visiting observers. They concluded that attempts to clean oiled pups were probably not justified unless recontamination could be ruled out.

Geraci and Smith (1976) carried out experiments on the effect of crude oil on ringed seals and harp seals. The seals were either placed in crude oil-covered water, had oil painted on them with a brush, or were given oil by mouth. Geraci and Smith found that 24-hour exposure to light crude oil damaged the eyes of healthy ringed seals and there were minor kidney and possibly liver lesions; the seals recovered rapidly when placed in clean water and no permanent damage was observed. On the other hand, captive seals already suffering from stress died within 71 minutes after oil was introduced into their pool. When 3- to 4-week-old whitecoat harp seal pups were coated with oil no significant differences in core body temperature were noted and no other deleterious effects were observed. No significant lesions or behavioral changes were noted in ringed or harp seals fed oil with their food or dosed with oil with as much as 75 ml of crude oil (Norman Wells) in a single dose. From these observations it can be concluded that oil contamination or ingestion in quantities that might reasonably be expected in the course of a spill is unlikely to be irreversibly harmful to a healthy seal population.

Oil pollution would thus seem to be of minor direct significance to phocid seals. With fur seals, the loss of thermal insulation associated with matting of the fur by oil would be expected to have much more serious consequences. The general effect of oil pollution on the productivity of the marine ecosystem would of course have a secondary effect on seals, but this appears to be unquantified and currently of negligible significance.

Manmade Disturbance

Marine mammals are less affected by habitat destruction than their terrestrial cousins, though they are not totally exempt. To the extent that pollution destroys habitat, they are affected, though, as we have seen, pollution is a minor factor for most seal populations. Actual destruction of habitat may occur with coastal and estuarine species (perhaps only the harbor seal?) when land is reclaimed for agriculture or other purposes. This has happened on a large scale only in the Netherlands, where polderization over several centuries has removed vast areas of shallow sea and sandbanks that once formed ideal habitat for harbor seals. Harbor seals are not confined to this habitat, however; most of them are found in areas that are quite unaffected by this type of activity.

Anthropogenic disturbance is another factor which adversely affects seals. Most seals (other than the antarctic species) are timid animals, and close approach by man, however benign in intent, disturbs them. Disturbance inevitably results from the growth and development of towns and harbors in localities used by seals. This is a process that has been going on for a very long time. A much more recent factor has been the greatly increased mobility of human populations and individuals. A tourist industry has built up which specializes in taking visitors into previously remote areas to view the wildlife. Tourists can now, if they can afford it, travel in luxury to the haunts of the once inexpressibly remote antarctic seals. The intention of this type of penetration is rarely, if ever, to harm the wildlife, but even benign interference may have serious consequences for breeding seals, particularly when groups with newborn young are disturbed (Bonner, 1975). Drescher (1978, 1979) has drawn attention to the need of harbor seals for an undisturbed nursing period. Disturbance by passing sailboats or power craft can seriously reduce the survival of the pups.

This kind of disturbance has increased greatly in recent years in the Wadden Sea of the Netherlands and Germany. New leisure activities, such as sailing, wadloping (a strange sort of cross-country racing across the sandbanks with the incoming tide as a competitor), and powerboating, coupled with other stresses of civilization—low-flying military aircraft (estuaries are often chosen for this type of training), oil and natural gas exploitation, and land reclamation—all add to the disturbance of harbor seals in the Wadden Sea, where the total population has fallen from about 1,500 in 1968 to 485 in 1977 (Summers et al., 1978; Drescher, 1978, 1979).

Drescher (1978) noticed that many of the harbor seals he examined from the Schleswig-Holstein Wadden Sea showed pathological changes in the skin, often a large ulcerative lesion on the belly around the umbilicus. He considered that these sores arose as umbilical infections in pups a few days old. From such an infection septicemia could spread to cause secondary infections elsewhere. Healing, followed by fresh infection, could occur, and the lesions might persist for many years. Drescher associated these lesions with the seals' habit of hauling out on sandbanks. Disturbance, usually resulting from human activity, forces the seals to move over the sand off the banks, and pups following in the tracks of other seals with open ulcers might pick up the infection. Drescher considered that protecting haul-out sites from disturbance would lessen the risk of infection, as well as give the unweaned pups greater opportunity to obtain milk from their mothers (which will feed them only on the sandbanks), thus establishing a better nutritional status and resistance to disease.

The harbor seal is a highly resilient species, with a large and widely distributed population. It may disappear locally, but it is certainly capable in many parts of its range (parts of the west coast of Scotland, for example) of adapting to tourists. Boats regularly set out from Oban in Argyllshire to view the "seal islands" and the harbor seals basking on the skerries permit close approach by the boats without entering the water. Grey seals also submit to close inspection by tripper boats on parts of the

English coast, such as the Farne Islands and near St. Ives in Cornwall. The seals obviously come to recognize the regular tourist boats and remain on the rocks, but take to the water on the approach of a strange craft. My belief is that they recognize the engine note.

Monk seals, on the other hand, seem much less able to tolerate disturbance. Karl Kenyon (personal communication) has suggested to me that they are a species highly specialized for isolation. Sergeant and his co-workers (1978) believe that disturbance of reproductive sites at all seasons is seriously reducing the reproductive rate of the Mediterranean monk seal. They believe that effective reproduction probably requires the use of open beaches, rather than the caves mostly used at present, and that the decline in numbers could be attributed to direct human interference (not all of it benign, in the case of this seal), without postulating any possible effect of pollution on reproductive performance.

Kenyon (1972) has similarly drawn attention to the disturbance caused to the Hawaiian monk seal on Midway Island by persons walking the beaches, sometimes accompanied by dogs which worried the seals. Mothers with pups were particularly subject to disturbance, as many people wanted to be photographed holding a pup and the mother seals were upset when their pups were handled.

A very indirect effect of human activities may have been the disease which was a serious mortality factor for Hawaiian monk seals on Laysan Island from December 1977 to July 1978. Seals suffering from this condition appeared comatose or nearly paralyzed, and lay about on the beaches for several days or even weeks before they died. Necropsies indicated that the seals were suffering from "fish poisoning," or ciguatera. The poison responsible for this condition, ciguatoxin, is produced by a group of dinoflagellates, minute phytoplanktonic organisms. When a bloom of these dinoflagellates occurs, the ciguatoxin may be concentrated in the food chain so that the flesh of fish becomes toxic to men and, presumably, seals. Kenyon (1980) suggests that the prime source of the ciguatera observed in the seals is the coral reefs that were dredged at Midway Atoll to enlarge the harbor there. Ciguatera outbreaks have been observed in other areas after coral reefs have been disturbed, and fish at Midway have become toxic to man in recent years (though no sick seals had been reported from Midway).

This depressing catalog of adverse indirect impacts of man on seals is by no means complete. A subject scarcely investigated so far is the effect of sound pollution on seals. Seals within the range of underwater detonations used in seismic surveys must suffer acute discomfort, if not physical damage. Recent geophysical investigations and oil exploration in polar regions must have affected many thousands of seals in this way, but there is no evidence of long-term effects. Terhune et al. (1979) have shown that there is a marked decrease in harp seal underwater vocalizations after a vessel with engines running arrives in the vicinity. We do not know the significance of these vocalizations in the social organization of harp seals, but we now know that they are affected (inadvertently) by sound-generating activity, and the result may be an adverse one.

Probably there are other impacts as yet unsuspected. What is certain is that increasing human populations of increasing sophistication will continue to increase their impact on all wildlife, and marine mammals cannot be excluded from this. Protection can be provided—the U.S. marine mammal legislation gave a good lead in this direction—but I feel we must face the prospect ultimately of planned exploitation of all available resources. In this planning, the resources that seals can provide may be considered, but we must hope that adequate provision will be made for their trophic and environmental needs. However, it is inevitable that seals will have a much lower priority than man's own requirements, particularly with regard to the allocation of food resources.

Manmade Benefits

If this sounds a gloomy forecast, is there a brighter prospect anywhere for seals? In some respects this may indeed be the case. There are even some, though not many, beneficial impacts of man's activities to be considered.

Chief among these have been the shifts of human populations and culture changes which have acted to the benefit of seals. The largest single colony of grey seals in the world is found at North Rona, an isolated island about 45 miles northwest of the extreme northwestern tip of the British mainland. North Rona is uninhabited and has been so for more than a century, yet up to the beginning of the nineteenth century it was occupied by a small community of about thirty people. It once formed part of the parish of Barvas on the Isle of Lewis, where records were kept of the exports and imports of Rona. They make no mention of seal oil or seal skins, nor do seals figure in the early accounts of the island (Hewer, 1974), so it is reasonable to assume that there was no permanent seal colony of any size there up to the time the island was last permanently inhabited, in 1844. The first record of grey seals breeding at North Rona was in 1883, when 107 were killed there. Today the grey seal population at North Rona numbers around eight or nine thousand, with some 2,200–2,500 pups born yearly (Summers et al., 1978).

Another very large grey seal breeding colony in the Hebrides is found at the Monach Isles, off North Uist (Figure 8.1). The last permanent inhabitants of the Monachs left in 1942. By 1961 a grey seal colony producing perhaps fifty pups a year had been established; by 1975 pup production had risen to about 2,350 (Anderson and Curry, 1976). Increases of this magnitude cannot be due to the natural increase of a few colonizing seals; immigration on a major scale from other colonies—in this case probably from Gasker, a large colony a few kilometers to the northeast—must have played a large part, while the sighting at the Monachs of two branded animals from North Rona confirms immigration from this source (Anderson and Curry, 1976).

In general, much of the population increase of European grey seals can be attributed to the withdrawal of human settlement from small offshore islands which, once vacant, offer ideal breeding sites for the seals. This has been coupled with a change in culture. The crofters who remain in mainland settlements near seal islands are now much less likely to hunt the seals as part of their livelihood, and boat ownership (an essential for seal hunting) is declining. In the Baltic there are now no longer any people who are solely, or even mainly, dependent on seal hunting as a source of income (Bonner, 1975). Even amongst Inuit or Greenlandic peoples, where seal skins are still an important article of trade, there is a general turning away from a dispersed way of life, which facilitated hunting, to more centralized societies.

Recreational hunting, which in civilized societies replaces the subsistence hunting of their forebears, used to attract considerable numbers of sportsmen in Europe to shoot seals (though the effect on seal stocks was probably slight), but many countries have now banned the hunting of seals, except by *bona fide* fishermen (e.g., Sweden), or absolutely (e.g., Netherlands), and in many societies the ethics of sport-hunting are questioned.

Before turning to the broader question of changes of ethics and the consequences these may have for seals, I should like to consider one area where it seems that man's activities may have *increased*, rather than diminished, the food supplies available to seals. This has occurred in the Southern Ocean. The development of the antarctic whaling industry, from its inception in 1904, through its expansion in the 1920s, to its present decline on account of the lack of whales to hunt, has wrought great changes on the antarctic marine ecosystem. Laws (1977) calculated that the biomass of baleen whales in the Antarctic had been reduced from an initial 43 million tonnes before the arrival of the whalers to a current 7 million tonnes. The majority of the food eaten by these whales is krill, *Euphausia superba*, so consumption by whales of krill has declined in the same period from about 190 million tonnes to about 43 million tonnes per year. This means that there is a greater food resource available to other consumers of krill. Two species of seal, the crabeater and the antarctic fur seal, are exclusively or predominantly krill eaters, and for both of them there is evidence to suggest that they have benefited from the enhanced food availability.

The cementum layers on the roots of the crabeater seal's teeth that are laid down in the immature years are usually broader and more ir-

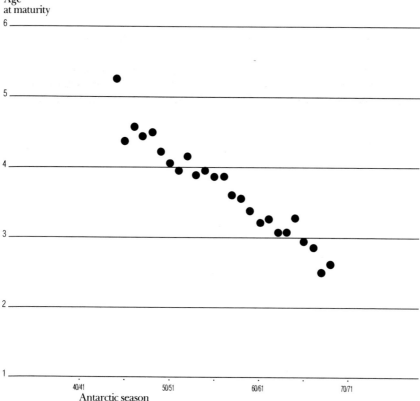

Figure 9.3.   Age of sexual maturity of year classes of crabeater seals from the Bellingshausen Sea. From Laws, 1977.

Age at maturity

Antarctic season

regular than those laid down in adult years. Using this character, Laws (1977) was able to show that the mean age of puberty of crabeater seals taken to the west of the Antarctic Peninsula was about 4 years in 1955, but fell to about 2.5 years in 1970 after this area had been extensively whaled (Figure 9.3). Because crabeater seals are not hunted in significant numbers this suggests that stocks have increased substantially over recent decades.

Definite evidence for such an increase is available for the antarctic fur seal, as mentioned earlier (page 64 *et seq.*), and the rate at which this has taken place is greater than that recorded for other fur seals—or indeed, for any other pinniped. The fur seals at South Georgia have increased at a rate of about 16.8 percent per year over the last thirty years, while at Marion Island an allied species, *Arctocephalus tropicalis,* has increased only 10.5 percent per year, though protection of the seals there has probably been as effective as at South Georgia.

It is possible that other forms of selective harvesting besides whaling have left more food available at lower trophic levels. Selective removal of large cod by fishermen, for example, may have resulted in larger biomass of smaller species, such as sand eels, on which the large cod feed. Since grey seals also feed on sand eels, this may have contributed to the spectacular increase of grey seals around the North Sea (Bonner, 1978). However, in this case the relationship is less clear than in the baleen whale-krill-crabeater seal (or Antarctic fur seal) example, and we can note it only as a possibility. The fishing of pollock in the Bering Sea, resulting in increased biomass for the benefit of pollock consumers, among them fur seals, has already been mentioned.

Perhaps ultimately the most important development in recent years to affect seals is the reappraisal of attitudes toward wildlife and the increasing awareness that natural resources may have values other than those associated only with the commercial products they can yield (Bonner, 1978). A growing body of influential opinion in the western world favors the ethic of conservation and opposes uncontrolled (or even, in some cases, regulated) exploitation. The killing of the white-coated pups of harp seals on the ice has in particular excited strong feelings, not necessarily rational, and may have contributed more than any other single factor to the present attitudes toward animal protection. The apparent trust of the helpless white-coated pup, with its rounded form and flattened face framing large dark eyes from which tears trickle, evokes powerful feelings of sympathy in many people, and the white-coat, along with the giant panda, has become a symbol of concern for wildlife.

A willingness to consider resource allocation based on improved multispecies models may do much to ensure the survival of seal stocks. There is real concern today that the ultimate threat to seals is the indirect impact of excessive human exploitation of their food supply. Existing controls are not adequate to protect and conserve all seals; nevertheless, many influential nations are now aware of the problems and are willing to attempt their solution. These attitudes provide the intentions which may make the continued survival of seal stocks in the wild more assured now than it has been at any time in the last two hundred and fifty years. As one who feels honored to have been bitten and spat upon (and at times, even worse) by seals in both hemispheres, I devoutly hope that man can control his demands upon the environment so that the world can find a place for seals through the continuing future.

References

ACMRR. 1978. Mammals in the Seas. Rep. of the Advisory Committee on Marine Resources Research; Working Party on Marine Mammals, Vol. 1. F.A.O. Rome.

Anderson, S.S. and Curry, M.G. 1976. Grey seals at the Monach Isles, Outer Hebrides, 1975. ICES C.M. 1976/N:9. 4pp. (mimeo).

Bonner, W.N. 1970. Seal deaths in Cornwall, Autumn 1969. Nat. Envir. Res. Council. Publ. Ser. C. No. 1. 20pp.

Bonner, W.N. 1975. International legislation and the protection of seals. Pp. 12–29 *in* Proc. from the Symposium on the Seal in the Baltic, June 4–6, 1974. Lidingö, Sweden. Nat. Swedish Envir. Protection Bd. SNV PM 591.

Bonner, W.N. 1976. The stocks of grey seals (*Halichoerus grypus*) and common seals (*Phoca vitulina*) in Great Britain. Nat. Envir. Res. Council. Publ. Ser. C. No. 16. 16pp.

Bonner, W.N. 1978. Man's impact on seals. Mammal Rev. 8(1 & 2):3–13.

Condy, P.R. 1978. Distribution, abundance, and annual cycle of fur seals (*Arctocephalus* spp.) on the Prince Edward Islands. S. Afr. J. Wildlife Res. 8:159–168.

Davis, J.E. and Anderson, S.S. 1976. Effects of oil pollution on breeding grey seals. Mar. Pollution Bull. 7(6):115–118.

DeLong, R.L., Gilmartin, W.G. and Simpson, J.G. 1973. Premature births in California sea lions: association with high organochlorine pollutant residue levels. Science, N.Y. 181:1168–1169.

Drescher, H.E. 1978. Hautkrankheiten beim Seehund, *Phoca vitulina* Linne, 1758, in der Nordsee. Säugetierkd. Mitt. 26(1):50–59.

Drescher, H.E. 1978/79. Present status of the harbor seal, *Phoca vitulina,* in the German Bight (North Sea). Meeresforschung 27:27–34.

Drescher, H.E. 1979. Biologie, Ökologie und Schutz der Seehund in schleswig-holsteinischen Wattenmeer. Beiträge zur Wildbiologie Heft 1. Meldorf. 73pp.

Engel, R.M., Lander, R.H., Roppel, A.Y., Kozloff, P., Hartley, J.R. and Keyes, M.C. 1980. Population data, collection procedures and management of the northern fur seal, *Callorhinus ursinus,* of the Pribilof Islands, Alaska. NWAFC Processed Rep. 80–11. Northwest and Alaska Fisheries Center, National Marine Fisheries Service. Seattle, Washington.

Fiscus, C.H. and Kozloff, P. 1971. Appendix E. Fur seals and fish netting. Fur Seal Invest. 1971. U.S. Dept. of Commerce, National Marine Fisheries Serv. Northwest Fisheries Center.

Frank, R., Ronald, K. and Braun, H.E. 1973. Organochlorine residues in harp seals (*Pagophilus groenlandicus*) caught in eastern Canadian waters. J. Fish. Res. Bd. Can. 30:1053–1063.

Geraci, J.R. and Smith, T.G. 1976. Direct and indirect effects of oil on ringed seals (*Phoca hispida*) of the Beaufort Sea. J. Fish. Res. Bd. Canada 33(9):1976–1984.

Gill, C., Booker, S. and Soper, A. 1967. The Wreck of the "Torrey Canyon." David and Charles, Newton Abbott. 28pp.

Gilmartin, W.G., DeLong, R.L., Smith, A.W., Sweeny, J.C., Lappe, B.W., Risebrough, R.W., Griner, L.A., Dailey, M.D. and Peakall, D.B. 1976. Premature parturition in the California sea lion. J. Wildl. Diseases 12:104–115.

Helle, E., Olsson, M. and Jensen, S. 1976. PCB levels correlated with pathological changes in seal uteri. Ambio 5(5 & 6):261–263.

Helminen, M., Karppanen, E. and Kovisto, J.I. 1968. Saimaan norpan elohopeopitoisuudesta 1967. (Mercury content of the Lake Saimaa ringed seal.) Finsk Vet. Tidskr. 74:87–89.

Hewer, H.R. 1974. British seals. Collins New Naturalist. London.

Holden, A.V. 1972. Monitoring organochlorine contamination in the marine environment by the analysis of residues in seals. Pp. 266–272 in "Marine Pollution and Sea Life" ed. M. Ruivo. Fishing News (Books) Ltd. London.

Holden, A.V. 1975. The accumulation of oceanic contaminants in marine mammals. Rapp. P.-v. Réun. Cons. int. Explor. Mer 169:353–361.

Holden, A.V. 1978. Pollutants and seals—a review. Mammal Rev. 8(1 & 2):53–66.

Innes, S.R., Stewart, E.A. and Lavigne, D.M. 1978. Growth in northwest Atlantic harp seals, *Pagophilus groenlandicus*: density-dependence and recent changes in energy availability. Can. Atl. Fish. Sci. Advisory Comm. Working paper 78/46.

Kenyon, K.W. 1972. Man versus the monk seal. J. Mammal. 53(4):687–696.

Kenyon, K.W. 1980. No man is benign: the endangered monk seal. Oceans 13(3):48–54 (May 1980).

Koeman, J.H., Peeters, W.H.M., Smit, C.J., Tjioe, P.S. and De Goeij, J.J.M. 1972. Persistent chemicals in marine mammals. TNO-Nieuws 27:570–578.

Koeman, J.H., Peeters, W.H.M., Koudstaal-Hol, C.H.M., Tjioe, P.S. and De Goeij, J.J.M. 1973. Mercury-selenium correlation in marine mammals. Nature, Lond. 245:385–386.

Koeman, J.H. and Van Genderen, H. 1966. Some preliminary notes on residues of chlorinated hydrocarbon insecticides in birds and mammals in the Netherlands. J. Appl. Ecol. 3(Suppl.):99–106.

Lander, R.H. 1976. Alaskan or northern fur seal. ACMRR Scientific Consultation on the Conservation and Management of Marine Mammals, Bergen, 1976. Pinniped Species Summaries, WP 14. 8pp. (mimeo).

Lander, R.H. and Kajimura, H. 1976. Status of northern fur seal. ACMRR Scientific Consultation on the Conservation and Management of Marine Mammals, Bergen, 1976. ACMRR/MM/SC/34. 50pp. (mimeo).

Laws, R.M. 1977. Seals and whales of the Southern Ocean. Phil. Trans. R. Soc. Lond. B. 279:81–96.

Le Boeuf, B.J. 1971. Oil contamination and elephant seal mortality: a "negative" finding. Pp. 277–285 *in* Biological and Oceanographical Survey of the Santa Barbara Channel Oil Spill, 1969–1970, ed. D. Straughan. 1. Biology and Bacteriology. Spec. Publ. Alan Hancock Foundation. University of Southern California (Sea Grant Publ. No. 2).

Le Boeuf, B.J. and Bonnell, M.L. 1971. DDT in California sea lions. Nature, Lond. 234:108–109.

North Pacific Fishery Management Council. 1979. Fishery Management Plan for the Groundfish Fishery in the Bering Sea–Aleutian Islands area. Anchorage, Alaska. November 1979.

Payne, M.R. 1977. Growth of a fur seal population. Phil. Trans. R. Soc. Lond. B 279:67–79.

Ronald, K. and Tessaro, S.V. 1976. Methyl mercury poisoning in the harp seal (*Pagophilus groenlandicus*). ICES C.M. 1976/N:8 (quoted in Holden, 1978).

Sanger, G.A. 1974. A Preliminary Look at Marine Mammal-Food Chain Relationships in Alaskan Waters. NOAA, Nat. Mar. Fish. Serv., Marine Mammal Div. Seattle, Wash. 29pp. (mimeo).

Sergeant, D.E., Ronald, K., Boulva, J. and Berkes, F. 1978. The recent status of *Monachus monachus*, the Mediterranean monk seal. Biol. Conserv. 14:259–287.

Shaughnessy, P.D. and Payne, A.I.L. 1979. Incidental mortality of cape fur seals during trawl fishing activities in South African waters. Fish. Bull. S. Afr. 12:20–25.

Summers, C.F., Bonner, W.N. and Van Haaften, J. 1978. Changes in the seal population of the North Sea. Rapp. P.-v. Réun. Cons. int. Explor. Mer 172:278–285.

Terhune, J.M., Stewart, R.E.A. and Ronald, K. 1979. Influence of vessel noise on underwater vocal activity of harp seals. Can. J. Zool. 57:1337–1338.

Index

Italic page numbers denote illustrations

Age determination, using teeth,
  antarctic fur seal, 66
  crabeater seal, 94, 157-158
  northern fur seal, 50
  southern elephant seal, 83, *83*
Aircraft
  for counting seals, 113-114
  for sealing, 43
  see also Helicopters
Alaska Commercial Company, 48-49
Alaskan Eskimo sealing, 24, *24*, 28, 33
Allodesmus, 11, *11*
Allu, see Breathing hole
Altherarn, Captain George F., 61
American sealing,
  northern fur seals, 48-50, *51*
  southern fur seals, 59, 61-64
  southern elephant seals, 77
Amsterdam Island fur seal (*Arctocephalus tropicalis*)
  distribution, *56*, 57-58
  hybrids with *A. gazella*, 57
  population increase, 69, 158
  sealing, 61
Angiut, 22, *23*
Anguvigang, 27
Anholt sealing, *20*, 30-32
Anisakis simplex (Nematoda), 119
"Ann," 62
Antarctic (Kerguelen) fur seal
  (*Arctocephalus gazella*)
  breeding, 66, *68*, 69
  conservation, 62-63
  distribution, *56*, 57-58, *68*
  food, 69, 90, 98, *99*, 101, 157-158
  hybrids with *A. tropicalis*, 57
  injuries from netting scraps, 144, *144*
  population studies, 64-69
  pup mortality, 66
  sealing, 59, 61-64
  white-coated, 67-69, *68*
Antarctic (Lobodontine) seals, 89-106
  conservation, 101-104
  population studies, 98-101, *100*, 114
  sealing, 101-103
Antarctic Treaty, 102, 103
Aquatic environment, 4,

  adaptation to, 4-8
Arctocephalus fur seals, 56-71
  conservation, 102
  distribution, *56*, 57-58
  fur, 6
  sealing, 58-64, 75
Arctocephalus
  australis, see Southern fur seal
  doriferus, see Australian fur seal
  forsteri, see New Zealand fur seal
  galapagoensis, see Galapagos fur seal
  gazella, see Antarctic fur seal
  philippii, see Juan Fernandez fur seal;
  pusillus doriferus, see Australian fur seal;
    A. pusillus pusillus, see Cape fur seal
  townsendi, see Guadalupe fur seal
  tropicalis, see Amsterdam Island fur seal
Arteriovenous anastomoses (AVA's), 8
"Aspasia," 62
Australian fur seal (*Arctocephalus pusillus doriferus*), *56*, 57-58
AVA's, 8
Avautang, *26*, 27

Baffin Island, 22-24
Baltic Sea, 21, 28-29, *29*, 121, 148, 150, 151
Barents Sea, 37
Bartholomew model, 11-16, *13*, 92, 135
Bass Strait, 58, 59
Bearded seal (*Erignathus barbatus*)
  food, 4
  sealing, 25
Beaters, 37
Beddington and Williams model, 45
Bering Island (Commander Islands), 46
Bering Sea, 49, 52, 146
"Betsy," 60
Blanket pieces, see Horse pieces
Blastocyst, 14
Blubber
  as food reserve, 8, 14, 46, 74, 145
  as insulation, 7-8
  pollutants in, 147-150
  processing, 75, 77, 80-82
  of southern elephant seals, 74, 75, 77, 80-82
  uses for man, 19, 27, 37, 77

Bird Island (South Georgia), 64-67, *65, 68*
Boas, Franz, 22, 25
Bothnian Bay, 28, *29,* 150, 151
Bounty Islands, *56,* 61
Bounty payments, 32, 121-122
Bouvetøya, *56,* 58, 63, 67
Breathing hole
  of ringed seal (allu), 24
  of Weddell seal, 90, 93
Breeding, 9-16
  antarctic fur seal, 66, *68,* 69
  crabeater seal, *91,* 93-94, *158*
  elephant seal, 11, 14, 15
  grey seal, 10, 129, 135, 156-157
  harbor seal, 9-10, *9,* 153-154
  harp seal, 10, 35-37, *38,* 46, 146-147
  Kuril Islands seal, 10
  leopard seal, 9, *91,* 95
  northern fur seal, 11-12, *47, 51,* 66, 146
  Otariidae, 11, 15
  ringed seal, 24, *24*
  Ross seal, 97
  southern elephant seal, 11, 14, 15, *72,* 73-74, 76
  Weddell seal, 90-93, *91,* 94
British Antarctic Survey, 64

California sea lion (*Zalophus californianus*), *opp p.1*
  diseases, 150
  pollutants in, 150
  swallowed fish hooks, 145
Callorhinus ursinus, see Northern fur seal
Canada
  fishing and seals, 110-111, 120-122
  sealing, 39, *40,* 41-43, 46, 49, *51,* 121-122
Cape (South African) fur seal (*Arctocephalus pusillus pusillus*)
  distribution, *56,* 57-58
  in fishing nets, 143
  scaring from nets, 120-121
  sealing, 59, 122
Capelin (*Mallotus villosus*), 37, *45,* 46, 145
Carribean monk seal (*Monachus tropicalis*), 89
Carvings
  Eskimo, 22, *23,* 33
  Stone Age, 20, *20,* 22, *23*
Cetacea, see Whales
China trade, 59
Ciguatera, 155
Cleveland, Captain Benjamin, 63
Clubs, sealing
  Canadian, 42
  Norwegian, 42
  Stone Age, 21
Cod (*Gadus morhua*), *3*
  food of, 159
  parasites in, 118-119, *119*

Cod, polar (*Boreogadus saida*), 37
Codworm (*Phocanema decipiens*), 118-119, *119*
Commander Islands 46, 47, *47,* 49
Common seal, see Harbor seal
Committee on Seals and Sealing (COSS), 43
Conservation
  Anholt, 30-32
  antarctic fur seal, 62-63
  antarctic seals, 101-104
  Arctocephalus seals, 102
  crabeater seal, 101-104
  grey seal, 30-31, 128-132, 140-142
  harp seal, 39, 41, 43-46, 159
  leopard seal, 101-104
  northern fur seal, 48-53
  Ross seal, 101-104
  southern elephant seal, 78-79, 83-84, 87, 102
  Weddell seal, 102-103
  see also Management
Conservation of Seals Act (UK), 132
Consultative Committee on Grey Seals and Fisheries (UK), 129, 131, 138
Contracaecum osculatum (Nematoda), 119
Convention for the Conservation of Antarctic Marine Living Resources (CAMLR), 104
Convention for the Conservation of Antarctic Seals, 102, 103
Cook, Captain James, 61
Crabeater seal (*Lobodon carcinophagus*)
  breeding, *91,* 93-94, *158*
  conservation, 101-104
  food and feeding, 3, *3,* 89-90, 94, 96-97, 98, *99,* 101, 157
  migration, 93
  population studies, 98-101, 157-158, *158*
  predation by leopard seals, 94, 96
  sealing, 101-102
  teeth, 96-97
  length of lactation determined from, 94
Crozet Islands, *56,* 58, 61

"Daisy," 63
Dampier, W, 60
DDT, 147-151
Delayed implantation, 14
Department of Agriculture and Fisheries for Scotland, 126, 137-138
Detergents, effects on seals, 152
Dieldrin, 147-151
Dinoflagellates, 155
Distribution
  harp seal, 35-36, *38*
  monk seals, 89
  northern elephant seal, 89
  northern fur seal, 46-48, *47*
  southern fur seal, *56,* 57-58

Disturbance
 by man, 153-155
 by seals entangled in netting scraps, 145
Diving, 7, 93
DYNUMES III model, 146

Eared seals, see Otariidae
Eastern Sea Fisheries Committee (UK), 122
Elephant seals (*Mirounga* spp)
 breeding, 11, 14, 15
 food reserves, 14
 hair, 6
 moult, 8, *8*, 75
 size, 15
 see also Northern elephant seal,
  Southern elephant seal
"Emelia," 60
Energy budgets, 117
Energy store (blubber), 8, 14, 46, 74, 145
Engravings, see Carvings
Epigamic characters, 13
"Era," 63
Erignathus barbatus, see Bearded seal
Eskimo
 carvings, 22, *23*, 33
 boats, kayak, 25, *26;*
  umiak, 25
 guns, 28
 harpoons, Alaskan, 24, *24;* kayak, 25-27,
  26; unang, 24-25
 sealing, 22-28, 33, 157
 trophy hunting, 33
"Esprito Santo," 62
Estrus, 14
Eumetopias jubatus, see Steller sea lion
Euphasia superba, see Krill
European Parliament, 126, 140
Evolution, 1-17, *2*, 89

Falkland Islands, *56*, 58, 59, 62, *68, 72*, 73,
 78
Fanning, Captain Edmund, 60, 61
Farne Islands (UK), *130*
 disturbance of seals, 155
 management of seals, for fisheries, 131;
  for habitat, 133-137
 population studies of seals at, 138-139
 pup mortality at, 16, 133-135, 137
 sealing at, 122, 127, 131, 136
 trading at, 32
Fasting, 14, 74
Feeding rates, 116-117
Firearms, in Eskimo families, 28
Fish as food of seals, 3, *3*, 85, 93, 94, 95-96,
 97, *99*, 114-116, *115*, 137, 139, 141,
 145-146, see also Capelin, Cod and
 Salmon

Fisheries and seals, *45*, 107-125, 143-147,
 146
 Cape fur seal, 120-122, 143
 grey seal, 108, 110-112, 128-131, 137-
  141
 harbor seal, 111, 114-115, 121-122
 harp seal, 37, 45-46, 145
 northern fur seal, 143, 145-146
Flensing (southern elephant seal), 75, 80-
 82, *81*
"Flying Fish," 62
Food and feeding, 3-4, *3*
 antarctic fur seal, 60, 90, 98, *99*, 101,
  157-158
 bearded seal, 4
 cod, 159
 crabeater seal, 3, *3*, 89-90, 94, 96-97, 98,
  99, 101, 157
 grey seal, 116, 137-138, 139, 141, *151*,
  159
 harbor seal, 3, *3*, 114-115, *115*
 harp seal, 37, 46
 king penguin, 87
 leopard seal, 3, *3*, 89-90, 95-97, 98, *99*,
  101
 northern elephant seal, 89
 northern fur seal, 3, *3*, 116, 117, 145-147
 ringed seal, 96
 Ross seal, 90, 97, 98, *99*, 101
 southern elephant seal, 86, 90, 98, *99*,
  101
 Steller sea lion, 3, *3*
 walrus, 3, 4
 Weddell seal, 89-90, 93, 98, *99*, 101
 whales, 96-97, 101, 117, 157
 see also Capelin, Cod, Fish, Krill,
  Penguin, Squid
Food reserves (blubber), 8, 14, 46, 74, 145
"Franklin," 63
Front (Labrador), 36, *38*, 43
Fur, see Hair and Skins
Fur seals, see Amsterdam Island fur seal,
 Antarctic fur seal, *Arctocephalus* fur seals,
 Australian fur seal, Cape fur seal,
 Galapagos fur seal, Guadalupe fur seal,
 Juan Fernandez fur seal, New Zealand
 fur seal, Northern fur seal, South
 American fur seal

Galapagos fur seal (*Arctocephalus
 galapagoensis*), *56*, 58
Gough Island, *56*, 58
Green, Captain Daniel, 62
Greenland, 22, *38*, 46, 157
Greenland Sea, 37
Greenpeace Foundation, 140

Grey seal (*Halichoerus grypus*), 126-142
  adoptive suckling, 135
  breeding, 10, 129, 135, 156-157
  bounty payments, 32, 121-122
  conservation, 30-31, 128-132, 140-142
  detergents, effects of, 152
  disturbance of, 154-155
  and fisheries, 108, 110-112, 128-131,
    137, 139, 141
  food and feeding, *115*, 116, 137-138,
    139, 141, 159
  management for fisheries, 120-121, 131-
    132; for habitat, 132-137
  oil contamination, 152
  parasites, 118-119, *119*
  population studies, 112-113, 129, *130*,
    132, *133*, *134*, 136-139
  pup mortality, 16, 133-135, *134*, 137
  sealing, Anholt, *20*, 30-32
    Baltic, 28-29, *29*
    Cornwall, 129
    Farne Islands, 122, 127, 131, 136
    Haskeir, 127-128
    Hebrides, 28, 127-128, *130*, 138-139
    Hesselø, 21
    Orkneys, 122, 127, 131-132, 138, 140
Grey Seal Protection Acts 1914, 1932 (UK),
  128, 129, 131
Guadalupe fur seal (*Arctocephalus townsendi*)
  distribution, *56*, 57
  sealing, 58
Gulf of St. Lawrence (The Gulf), 36, *38*, 43,
  122, 147

Hair, 6, 7, 13, see also Moulting, Skins
Hakapik, 42
Halichoerus grypus, see Grey seal
"Hancock," 60
Harbor (Common) seal (*Phoca vitulina*), opp.
    p.1, *23*, 127
  breeding, 9-10, *9*, 153-154
  bounty payments for, 121-122
  disturbance to, 153-154
  and fisheries, 111, 114-115, 121-122
  food and feeding, 3, *3*, 114-116, *115*
  population studies, 113, *113*
  sound, reaction to, 121
  sealing, trophy hunting, 33; in the Wash,
    131-132
Harpoon
  Eskimo, Alaskan, 24, *24*; kayak, 25-27,
    26; unang, 24-25
  Stone Age, 21-22, *21*
Harp seal (*Phoca groenlandica*), 35-46
  beaters, 37
  breeding, 10, 35-37, *38*, 46, 146-147
  conservation, 39, 41, 43-46, 159
  distribution, 35-36, *38*

  energy store, 46, 145
  and fisheries, 37, 45-46, 145
  food and feeding, 37, 46
  migration 37
  oil, effects on, 153
  pollutants, 148-149, 151-152
  population studies, 37, 43-46
  products from, 37
  ragged jackets, 36, 41
  sealing, 21, 35, 37-46; Baltic, 21; Jan
    Mayen, 38-39; Northwest Atlantic, 41-
    46; White Sea, 39-41
  vocalizations, 155-156
Haskeir (Hebrides), 127-128, *130*
Hawaiian monk seal (*Monachus
    schauinslandi*)
  distribution, 89
  entangled in netting, 144
  "fish poisoning" (ciguatera), 155
Heard Island, *56*, 58, 67, 69, *72*, 73, 77, 95
Heavy metal pollution, 147, 150, 151-152
Hebrides, 28, 127-129, *130*, 138-140, 156
Helicopters, 42, 43, 98-100, *100*, see also
  Aircraft
"Hersilia," 62
Hesselø, *20*, 21, 22, 30
Horse pieces, 75
Hybrids, 57
Hunting,
  walrus, 33, 35
  trophy, 32-33, 157
  see also Sealing
Hydrurga leptonyx, see Leopard seal

International Commission on Northwest
    Atlantic Fisheries (ICNAF), 43, 44
International Union for the Conservation
    of Nature and Natural Resources
    (IUCN), 126-140
Inuit, see Eskimo
Iparang, 24

Jan Mayen, 35, 36, 38-39, *40*
Japanese sealing, 49-50, *51*
Juan Fernandez fur seal (*Arctocephalus
    philippii*)
  distribution, *56*, 57-58
  sealing, 59, 60

Kayak, 25, *26*
  harpoon, 25-27, *26*
Kerguelen fur seal, see Antarctic fur seal
Kerguelen Islands, *56*, 58, 59, *72*, 73
Krill (*Euphausia superba*), 3, *3*, 69, 86, 94, 98,
  99, 101, 104, 157
Kuril Islands, 10, 11, 46-47, *47*
Kuril Islands seal (*Phoca vitulina kurilensis*),
  breeding, 10
  evolution, 11

Landsman, 42-43
Lanugo, see White coats
Laysan Islands, 155
Leopard seal (*Hydrurga leptonyx*), 95-97
  breeding, 9, *91*, 95
  conservation, 101-104
  food and feeding, 3, *3*, 89-90, 95-97, 98,
    99, 101
  population studies, 98-101
  predation on crabeater seals, 94, 96
  sealing, 78-79, 101-102
  teeth, 96-97
Leptonychotes weddellii, see Weddell seal
Littorina Sea, 21
Lobodon carcinophagus, see Crabeater seal
Lobodontine seals, see Antarctic seals,
  Crabeater seal, Leopard seal, Ross seal,
  Weddell seal

Macquarie Island, *56*, 57, 58, 73, 86
Mallotus villosus, see Capelin
Management
  grey seals at Farne Islands, 132-137; for
  fisheries, 120-121, 129-132
  fur seals on Pribilofs, 49-53
Marine Mammal Protection Act (USA), 33,
  156
Marion Island (Prince Edward Islands), 57,
  58, 158
Mediterranean monk seal (*Monachus
  monachus*), 89
Mercury pollution, 147, 150, 151-152
Migration
  crabeater seal, 93
  harp seal, 37
  northern fur seal, 48
  Weddell seal, 90
Ministry of Agriculture, Fisheries and Food
  (MAFF), 131
Mirounga, see Elephant seals
Monach Isles (Hebrides), 129, *130*, 139,
  156-157
Monachus
  monachus, see Mediterranean monk seal
  schauinslandi, see Hawaiian monk seal
  tropicalis, see Carribean monk seal
Monk seals (*Monachus* spp), 89, see also
  Hawaiian monk seal
Moulting, in southern elephant seal, 8, *8*,
  75

National Trust (UK), 131, 133, 136-137
Natural Environment Research Council
  (UK), 126, 137
Nature Conservancy (UK), 129, 131, 137,
  139
Naulang, 24
Nematodes, 118-119
Neolithic, see Stone Age

Nets, drift, 109
  fixed, 108-109
  gill, 110
  lying, 29
  purse seine, 111, 120-121
  repairing, 110
  salmon, 108-109, *109*, 120, 128
  seals caught in, accidentally, 143-145;
    intentionally, 22, 29, 35, 41
  causing damage to, 108-111
  entangled in fragments, 144-145, *144*
  poisoning at, 120
  scaring from, 120-121
  shooting at, 120, 128
  standing, 29
  trap, 111
New Zealand fur seal (*Arctocephalus forsteri*)
  distribution, *56*, 57-58
  sealing, 58, 59, 61
Newfoundland, 35, 36, *38*, *40*, 41-42
North American Commercial Company, 49
North Fara (Orkney), 129
North Pacific Fur Seal Commission, 50
North Pacific Fur Seal Convention, 49, 50
North Rona (Hebrides), 10, *130*, 138, 140,
  156, 157
Northeast Atlantic Sealing Commission, 39
Northern elephant seal (*Mirounga
  angustirostris*),
  distribution, 89
  feeding grounds, 89
  pollution, effects on, 152
Northern fur seal (*Callorhinus ursinus*), 46-
  53
  breeding, 11, 12, *47*, *51*, 66, 146
  conservation, 48-53
  distribution , 46-48, *47*
  and fisheries, 143, 145-146
  food and feeding, 3, *3*, 116, 117, 145-147
  fur, 6
  management, 49-53
  migration, 48
  nets, entangled in, 143-144
  population studies, 48, 50-52
  products, 53
  pup mortality, 16, 146
  sealing, 35, 46-53, *51*
Norwegian sealing
  grey seals, 136, 139-140
  harp seals, 38-40, *40*, 42

Odobenidae (walruses), *opp p.1*, 1
Odobenus rosmarus, see Walrus
Oil from blubber
  grey seal, 32
  harp seal, 37
  Juan Fernandez fur seal, 60
  southern elephant seal, 75, 77, 82
Oil, petroleum, as pollutant, 152-153

Ommatophoca rossii, see Ross seal
Oppian, 107
Organochlorine compounds, 147-151
Orkney Islands, 122, 127, 129, *130,* 131-132, 138, 140
Otariidae (eared seals), *opp p.1,* 1
  breeding, 11,15
  dimorphism, 11
Otoliths, 115

Pandalus borealis, see Shrimp
Parasites, 118-119, *119*
Paris Tribunal of Arbitration, 49
Pathology, 135, 149-151, 154
Penguins, as food of seals, 95-96
Phoca groenlandica, see Harp seal
  hispida, see Ringed seal
  vitulina, see Harbor seal
  kurilensis, see Kuril Islands seal
Phocanema decipiens, see Codworm
Phocidae (true seals), *opp. p.1,* 1
Pilosebaceous units, 6, 7, see also Hair
Pitman, Captain, 62
Plants, see Vegetation
Poisoning
  Hawaiian monk seal, 155
  grey seals at salmon nets, 120
"Polarhav," 102
Pollution and seals, 147-153
  heavy metals, 147, 150, 151-152
  oil, 152-153
  organochlorine compounds, 147-151
  PCB's, 147-151
  sound, 155-156
Polychlorinated biphenyls (PCB's), 147-151
Polygyny, 10-12, 14, 87, 92-93
Population studies
  Amsterdam Island fur seal, 69, 158
  antarctic fur seal, 64-69, *65*
  antarctic seals, 98-101, *100,* 114
  crabeater seal, 98-101, 157-158, *158*
  grey seal, 112-113, 129, *130,* 132, *133, 134,* 136-139
  harbor seal, 113, *113*
  harp seal, 37, 43-46
  leopard seal, 98-101
  northern fur seal, 48, 50-52
  ringed seal, 114
  Ross seal, 98-101
  southern elephant seal, 82-86, *85*
  Weddell seal, 98-101
Porrocaecum decipiens, see Codworm
Pribilof Islands, 46-53, *47, 51,* 144, 146
Prince Edward Islands, *56,* 57, 61
Products, seal
  blubber, 19, 27, 37, 75, 77, 80-82
  felt, 59
  ivory, 24, 27, 33

oil, 32, 37, 60, 75, 77, 82
meat, 32, 43
skins, 19, 24, 25, 27, 37, 43, 53, 59, 60, 75, 80-82
Protection, see Conservation
Puffins (*Fratercula arctica*), 135
Pup mortality, 15-16
  antarctic fur seal, 66
  grey seal, 16, 133-135, *134,* 137
  northern fur seal, 16, 146

Qatirn, 25, *26,* 27

Ragged jackets, 36, 41
Ringed seal (*Phoca hispida*), *23*
  breathing hold (allu), 24
  breeding lair, 24, *24*
  food and feeding, 96
  pathology, 150
  pollutants in blubber, 147-148, 150
  population studies, 114
  as prey of walrus, 3
  size, 6
  sealing, 22, 24-25
Robben Island (Sea of Okhotsk), 46, 47, *47,* 48, 49, *51*
Ross seal (*Ommatophoca rossii*), *91*
  breeding, 97
  conservation, 101-104
  food and feeding, 90, 97, 98, *99,* 101
  population studies, 98-101
Russian-American Company, 48
Russian (Soviet) sealing
  harp, 39-42, *40*
  northern fur seal, 46, 48, 49, 50, *51*

St. George Island (Pribilof Islands), 46, 52
Salmon
  damaged by grey seals, 110-111, 120; by harbor seals, 111
  fisheries, grey seal effect on, 108-111, 128
  food of grey seals, 116; of harbor seals, 114-116
  nets, 108-109, *109;* control of grey seals at, 108, 120-121, 128
Stone Age engravings of, 20, *20*
"San Juan Nepomuceno," 62
San Miguel Island, *47,* 48, 152
Scientific Committee for Antarctic Research (SCAR), 103
Scottish Office, 138-140
Sea Mammals Research Unit (UK), 126, 137, 138
Sea otter (*Enhydra lutris*), 46
Seal Fisheries Ordinance (Falkland Islands), 78

Sealing
  localities
    Alaska, 24, *24*, 28, 33
    Anholt, *20*, 30-32
    Baffin Island, 22-24
    Baltic, 21, 28-29, *29*
    Bass Strait, 58, 59
    Bering Sea, 49
    Bothnian Bay, 28, *29*
    Bounty Islands, 61
    Commander Islands, 49
    Cornwall, 129
    Crozet Islands, 61
    Falkland Islands, 59, 62, 72
    Farne Islands, 122, 127, 131, 136
    The Front, 43
    Greenland, 157
    The Gulf, 43, 122
    Haskeir, 127-128,
    Hebrides, 28, 127-128, 138-139
    Hesselø, 21, 30
    Jan Mayen, 38-39, *40*
    Juan Fernandez, 59-60
    Kerguelen Islands, 59, 73
    Macquarie Island, 86
    Monach Isles, 139
    New Zealand, 58, 59
    Newfoundland, 35, *40*, 41-42
    North Rona, 138, 140
    Northwest Atlantic, 41-46
    Orkney Islands, 122, 127, 129, 131-
      132, 138, 140
    Pribilof Islands, 48-53, *51*, 144
    Robben Island, 49, *51*
    Shetland, 132
    South Georgia, 59, 61-62, 63, 72, 77,
      78-84
    South Orkney Islands, 63, 102
    South Shetland Islands, 62, 63, 64,
    Strait of Belle Isle, 35
    The Wash, 122, 131-132
    Wattenmeer, 33
    White Sea, 39-41, *40*
  for management
    bounties, 32, 121-122
    for fisheries, 120-121, 131-132
    for habitat, 136-137
  sealers
    American, 48-50, *51*, 59, 61-64, 77
    Canadian, 39, *40*, 41-43, 46, 49, 51,
      121-122
    Eskimo, 22-28, *24*, *26*, 33, 157
    Japanese, 49-50, *51*
    Landsmen, 42-43
    Norwegian, 38-40, *40*, 42
    Russian, 39, *40*, 42, 46-50, *51*
    South American Indian, 58

Stone Age, 19-22, 28, 30, 32
seals
  Amsterdam Island fur seal, 61
  antarctic fur seal, 59, 61-64
  antarctic seals, 101-103
  Arctocephalus fur seals, 58-64, 75
  bearded seal, 25
  Cape fur seal, 59, 122
  crabeater seal, 101-102
  grey seal, 21, *20*, 28-29, *29*, 30-32, 121-
    122, 127-132, 136, 138-140
  Guadalupe fur seal, 58
  harbor seal, 33, 121-122, 131-132
  Juan Fernandez fur seal, 59-60
  leopard seal, 78-79, 101-102
  New Zealand fur seal, 58, 59, 61
  northern fur seal, 35, 46-53, *51*
  ringed seal, 22, 24-25
  South American fur seal, 58, 59
  southern elephant seal, 75-83, *81*, *85*,
    87
  walrus, 33, 35
  Weddell seal, 78-79, 101-102
  subsistence, 19-32, 35, 58
Seals Advisory Committee (UK), 138
Shetland Islands, 127, 132
Shrimp (*Pandalus borealis*), 37, *45*, 46
Skins, 19, 27
  Arctocephalus fur seals, 59, 60, 75
  harp seal, 37, 43
  northern fur seal, 53
  ringed seal, 24, 25
  southern elephant seal, 80-82
Slagkrok, 42
Smith, Captain William, 62
South African fur seal, see Cape fur seal
South American fur seal (*Arctocephalus
    australis*)
  distribution, *56*, 57, 58
  sealing, 58, 59
South Georgia, *56*, 58, 59, 61-62, 63, 64-67,
    68, 69, *72*, 73, 74, 77, 78-84, 87, 90, 92,
    95, 144, 158
South Orkney Islands, *56*, 58, 63, 67, *68*,
    69, 82, 90, 102
South Sandwich Islands, *56*, 58, 63, 67, *68*
South Shetland Islands, *56*, 58, 62, 63, 64,
    67, *68*, 69, 96, 102
Southern elephant seal (*Mirounga leonina*),
    72-88, *72*, 89
  age determination, 83, *83*
  biomass, 84, *85*
  blubber, 74, 75, 77, 80-82
  breeding, 11, 14, 15, *72*, 73-74, 76
  conservation, 78-79, 83-84, 87, 102
  distribution, *72*, 73
  fasting, 74

food and feeding, 86, 90, 98, *99*, 101
moulting, 8, *8*, 75
oil, 75, 77, 82
population studies, 82-86, *85*
sealing, 75-83, *81*, *85*, 87
sexual dimorphism, 11, 14
size, 73
Squid, 3, *3*, 86, 93, 98, *99*, 101
"States," 59
Steller, Georg Wilhelm, 46
Steller sea lion (*Eumetopias jubatus*)
  and fisheries, 143, 145
  food, 3, *3*
Stone Age
  clubs, 21
  engravings, 20, *20*, 22, *23*
  harpoons, 21-22, *21*
  sealing, 19-23, *23*, 27, 32,
  sites, 20-22, *20*
Strait of Belle Isle, 35
Surface/volume relationship, 5, *5*
Swimming, 5, 6

Tasmanian fur seal, see Australian fur seal
Teeth
  age determination from
    anarctic fur seal, 66
    crabeater seal, 94, 157-158
    northern fur seal, 50
    southern elephant seal, 83, *83*
  crabeater seal, 96-97
  leopard seal, 96-97
  Weddell seal, wear causing death, 90
Terranova decipiens, see Codworm
Thermoregulation, 5-8, *7*, *8*
Tokang, *26*, 27
"Torrey Canyon" oil spillage, 152
Traps
  gin, 30
  floating, 30, *30*
  lobster, seal damage to, 111
  pitfall, 22
  snag-hooks, 30
Trophy hunting, 32-33, 157
True seals, see Phocidae
Tryworks, 75, 77

Umiak, 25
Unang, 24, 25

Väkare, 28-29
Vegetation, damage to at Farne Islands,
  135

Wadden Sea, 151, 154
Walrus (*Odobenus rosmarus*), *opp p.1*
  food, 3, 4
  hair, lack of, 6
  hunting, 33, 35
  ivory, 24, 27, 33
The Wash (UK), 113, *113*, 115-116, 122,
  131-132
Water, properties of, 4
Wattenmeer, 33
Webster, W.H.B., 63
Weddell, Captain James, 62, 63
Weddell seal (*Leptonychotes weddellii*), 90-93
  breathing holes, 90, 93
  breeding, 90-93, *91*, 94
  conservation, 102-103
  food and feeding, 89-90, 93, 98, *99*, 101
  migration, 90
  population studies, 98-101
  scars, 92
  sealing, 78-79, 101-102
  tooth wear, 90
Whalers and whaling, 38, 41, 59-60, 64, 75,
  77, 78, 79, 87, 157
Whales (Cetacea)
  biomass, 157
  bowhead baleen, 24
  food and feeding, 96-97, 101, 117, 157
  killer whales, 94
  narwhale ivory, 27
Whelping, 10, 36
White coats (harp seals), 36
White Sea, 35, 36, *38*, 39-41, *40*
"Williams," 62
Williams, C.A., 63-64
Willis Islands (South Georgia), 64, *68*
Woodward, Captain Roswell, 62

Zalophus californianus, see California sea
  lion